Macroeconomic Policy, Credibility and Politics

FUNDAMENTALS OF PURE AND APPLIED ECONOMICS

EDITORS IN CHIEF

J. LESOURNE, Conservatoire National des Arts et Métiers,
Paris, France
H. SONNENSCHEIN, University of Pennsylvania,
Philadelphia, PA, USA

ADVISORY BOARD

K. ARROW, Stanford, CA, USA
W. BAUMOL, Princeton, NJ, USA
W. A. LEWIS, Princeton, NJ, USA
S. TSURU, Tokyo, Japan

Fundamentals of Pure and Applied Economics is an international series of titles divided by discipline into sections. A list of sections and their editors and of published titles may be found at the back of this volume.

Macroeconomic Policy, Credibility and Politics

Torsten Persson

Torsten Persson
Institute for International Economic Studies, Stockholm, Sweden

and

Guido Tabellini
Department of Economics, University of California, Los Angeles, USA

A volume in the Macroeconomic Theory section
edited by
Jean-Michel Grandmont
CEPREMAP, Paris, France

 harwood academic publishers
Australia • Canada • China • France • Germany • India • Japan
Luxembourg • Malaysia • The Netherlands • Russia • Singapore
Switzerland • Thailand • United Kingdom

Copyright © 1990 Harwood Academic Publishers.

First published 1990
Third printing 1996

Amsteldijk 166
1st Floor
1079 LH Amsterdam
The Netherlands

Library of Congress Cataloging-in-Publication Data

Persson, Torsten.
    Macroeconomic policy, credibility and politics/Torsten Persson and Guido Tabellini
    p.   cm.—(Fundamentals of pure and applied economics, ISSN 0191-1708; v. 38.
Macroeconomic theory section)
    Includes bibliographical references.
    ISBN 3-7186-5029-0
    1. Monetary policy—Mathematical models.   2. Macroeconomics—Mathematical models. I. Tabellini, Guido Enrico, 1956– . II. Title III. Series: Fundamentals of pure and applied economics; v. 38   IV. Series: Fundamentals of pure and applied economics. Macroeconomic theory section.
HG230.3.P48   1990
339.5—dc 20   90-4380
                                                   CIP

Contents

Introduction to the Series

Drawing on a personal network, an economist can still relatively easily stay well informed in the narrow field in which he works, but to keep up with the development of economics as a whole is a much more formidable challenge. Economists are confronted with difficulties associated with the rapid development of their discipline. There is a risk of "balkanization" in economics, which may not be favorable to its development.

Fundamentals of Pure and Applied Economics has been created to meet this problem. The discipline of economics has been subdivided into sections (listed at the back of this volume). These sections comprise short books, each surveying the state of the art in a given area.

Each book starts with the basic elements and goes as far as the most advanced results. Each should be useful to professors needing material for lectures, to graduate students looking for a global view of a particular subject, to professional economists wishing to keep up with the development of their science, and to researchers seeking convenient information on questions that incidentally appear in their work.

Each book is thus a presentation of the state of the art in a particular field rather than a step-by-step analysis of the development of the literature. Each is a high-level presentation but accessible to anyone with a solid background in economics, whether engaged in business, government, international organizations, teaching, or research in related fields.

Three aspects of *Fundamentals of Pure and Applied Economics* should be emphasized:

—First, the project covers the whole field of economics, not only theoretical or mathematical economics.

—Second, the project is open-ended and the number of books is not predetermined. If new and interesting areas appear, they will generate additional books.

—Last, all the books making up each section will later be grouped to constitute one or several volumes of an Encyclopedia of Economics.

The editors of the sections are outstanding economists who have selected as authors for the series some of the finest specialists in the world.

J. Lesourne   *H. Sonnenschein*

Preface

The theory of economic policy has recently taken a new course. In contrast to most earlier work, the new work treats the government as responding to incentives, not to orders. At a general level, the new work adopts a traditional neoclassical approach: It specifies a government objective and views equilibrium policy as the optimal choice given the objective and the relevant constraints. This approach leads to positive models of economic policy in alternative institutional environments. It also leads to normative prescriptions, not about specific policies, but rather about institutional reforms. For without a change in government incentives there will be no change in equilibrium policy.

Our goal in this monograph is to present a survey of this recent development in the theory of economic policy. We focus on two traditional areas of macroeconomics, namely monetary policy—which is covered in Part I—and fiscal policy—which is covered in Part II. Throughout we give particular attention to the incentive constraints that the policymaker faces.

Our target group is graduate students, as well as economists who have not followed this particular strand of the literature too closely. The monograph should be useful for teaching, since we aim at integrating seemingly disparate contributions in a common framework. However, we not only integrate old results, but also present some new results. Part II, in particular, contains material that may be new to many macroeconomists. 'Notes on the Literature' at the end of each section give broad but selective hints on the relevant background literature.

The presentation is as nontechnical as possible, but we do not shy away from difficult issues. The goal is not to prove general theorems. Rather, we try to make our points with the aid of simple, although reasonably complete, examples. Following the presentation should require no special background beyond standard first-year graduate micro and macro courses. However, the understanding may be facilitated by some familiarity with game theory, at the level of Tirole [133] (Chapter

11), and public finance, at the level of Atkinson and Stiglitz [14] (Chapters 12–14). Many of our colleagues have provided useful feedback.

Without implicating them, we would particularly like to thank: Alberto Alesina, Charlie Bean, Alex Cukierman, Nils Gottfries, Henrik Horn, John van Huyck, Assar Lindbeck, Ken Rogoff and Lars Svensson. We also thank: Matt Canzoneri, Ishaac Diwan, Allan Drazen, Herschel Grossman, Pablo Guidotti, David Levine, Peter Isard, Richard Portes, Shegowan Oh, Maury Obstfeld, Ole Risager, Carol Rogers, Marco Terrones, Eric van Damme and Jörgen Weibull. We would also like to thank Cindy Miller and Kerstin Blomqvist for expert secretarial and editorial assistance. Finally, we thankfully acknowledge financial support from the Bank of Sweden Tercentenary Foundation.

Torsten Persson
Guido Tabellini

Macroeconomic Policy, Credibility and Politics

TORSTEN PERSSON

Institute for International Economic Studies, Stockholm, Sweden

GUIDO TABELLINI

Department of Economics, University of California, Los Angeles, USA

1. ECONOMIC POLICY AS A GAME

1.1. Introduction

Until very recently, the theory of macroeconomic policy dealt with the economic consequences of given policy rules. Knowing these consequences and the policy objectives, one would then select the optimal policy rule. Implicit in this approach to policy design is a particular view of the policymaker, namely that he is a passive agent that can be programmed like a machine. Once the optimal rule is identified, the policymaker implements it and the private sector adapts to it.

This approach to the analysis of economic policy contrasts sharply with the way in which policy is carried out in practice. The policymaker is typically a rational and maximizing agent, or collection of agents, who respond to incentives and constraints just like the rest of the economy. A theory of economic policy that neglects these incentives in policy formation is incomplete and is bound to yield misleading prescriptions. For this reason, the recent literature on the theory of economic policy has changed focus. At the core of the research program—together with the study of the consequences of alternative policy rules—is now the analysis of the policy formation process.

At an abstract level, the new approach can be described as the analysis of a principal-agent problem, with many principals and possibly more than one agent. The individual citizens are the principals. They operate as political as well as economic actors. In their

1

political role, they delegate the formulation of economic policy to an agent (or to several agents), the policymakers(s). The agent in turn selects a policy that maximizes his objectives, subject to the relevant constraints. These constraints include the private economic responses to the policy that the principals choose in their role as economic actors. The normative problem is how to design such incentives that the agent implements a policy that maximizes the collective interests of the principals. Thus, this theory incorporates both positive and normative elements. From a positive point of view, the theory describes the policymaker's behavior under alternative incentive constraints. From a normative point of view, it suggests how to embed desirable incentive constraints in the existing political and economic institutions, through appropriate institutional reform.

In this section we do three things. First we introduce intuitively some of the important concepts upon which we will heavily rely in the following arguments. In the later sections, these concepts will be defined more precisely and will be related to notions familiar from game theory. Second, we introduce two economic models that will form the basis for much of the analysis in the monograph and use the models to illustrate the discussion about equilibrium policy. Third, with these two models as stepping stones, we outline the contents of the remaining sections.

1.2. Credibility and Politics

We can distinguish between two types of incentive constraints on the policymaker's optimization problem. First, those relating to a possible conflict of interest between the agent (the policymaker) and his principals *in their political role*. We call these the political constraints on economic policy. Second, those incentive constraints that correspond to a conflict of interest between the policymaker and the principals *in their economic role*. Since these constraints are related to the expectations of the economic actors, we call them credibility constraints.

In macroeconomics, the analysis of the policymakers' incentives originated with the pioneering work of Kydland and Prescott and Calvo on credibility. We also start from there.

1.2.1. *Credibility Constraints*

Let us suppose for now that there is no conflict of interest between the political actors and the policymaker. Thus, we neglect all political constraints: the policymaker has objectives which coincide with the collective interests of society as a whole. Kydland and Prescott and Calvo were the first to point out that, even in this case, the policymaker may be subject to a binding incentive constraint. Following earlier work on consumer theory by Strotz, they defined a policy plan to be time inconsistent if—given that it is expected by the private sector—the optimal plan made for period t + j at time *t* is different from the optimal plan made for that period at time t + j. Hence, if a policy is time inconsistent, the government would like to deviate from it during its implementation. Time inconsistency may thus imply lack of credibility.

Clearly, an equilibrium policy must be optimal for the government as well as credible to the private sector. For the private sector would not expect a policy which leaves incentives for policy surprises to be carried out. To determine what we should require from an equilibrium policy, we have to discuss two questions. First, does the policymaker possess the *technical possibility* of generating policy surprises? Second, does he have an *incentive* to generate policy surprises? The answers to these questions decide whether credibility imposes a binding constraint on policy.

Timing When does the policymaker have the possibility of generating policy surprises? Clearly, the answer depends on the timing of policy relative to private actions. Specifically, we can think of two different rules for playing the policy game. These rules correspond to alternative institutional environments.

In the first policy environment, policy is chosen once-and-for-all before any private sector decision, and the private sector chooses having observed policy. For example, we can think of the decision of joining a fixed exchange rate system (such as the EMS or Bretton Woods) as being taken in this way: once the decision is made, it is costly to reverse it because of political or economic sanctions that would be imposed by the international community. These costs of reneging then provide a commitment technology. The timing assumption can thus be thought of as capturing the costs of changing a given policy decision.

Even if incentives to surprise exist, no policy surprises are carried out in this setup, by virtue of the commitment technology in the economico-political decision process. Therefore, credibility is not a binding constraint in this case and the equilibrium policy rule maximizes the policymaker's objective at an initial point in time. This setup was in fact implicit in the analysis of policy rules in the early rational expectations literature. In the second policy environment, the timing is reversed. Or, put differently, the immediate costs of deviating from a preannounced policy are relatively small. At least some policy instruments can therefore be chosen after (or at the same time as) private economic decisions and after earlier policy decisions. In the terminology used in the literature, policy is chosen under discretion. Here, the capacity to surprise exists, since the private sector has to make some economic decisions before observing policy, and hence on the basis of expectations about what policy is going to be. Whether these private expectations impose a binding credibility constraint on the policymaker, depends on the incentives for policy surprise.

Incentives to Surprise   Under what general circumstances does the policymaker have an incentive to surprise the private sector by deviating from a preannounced policy rule? Clearly, this incentive arises only if there is some conflict of interests between the policymaker and the rest of the economy. If there was no conflict of interests, the policymaker and the private individuals in the economy would form a team: They would choose their actions to achieve a common goal, and nobody would have anything to gain by surprising the rest of the team.[1]

Since we are assuming no political disagreement, a conflict of interests between the policymaker and the private citizens can only arise if there are economic externalities: It is individually rational for an atomistic representative consumer to ignore the externalities, whereas it is rational for the policymaker to internalize them. The next subsection discusses other possible sources of conflict between the policymaker and the rest of the economy, due to political disagreement over the ultimate goals of policy.

But even in the presence of conflict, the policymaker has no

---

[1] This intuitive point is proved formally by Chari, Kehoe and Prescott [37].

incentive to surprise if he has enough policy instruments. With enough instruments, the policymaker can achieve a first-best situation relative to his preferences. That is, he is only bound by the aggregate resource constraint. And therefore, policy surprises cannot bring about any gains at all. But if there is a lack of policy instruments, the policymaker finds himself in a second-best (or worse) situation. Then, policy surprises can be viewed as providing additional policy instruments, and hence there may be an incentive to use them.

To summarize, an incentive to surprise exists in second-best situations, which arise when: (i) there is some conflict of interest between the policymaker and the rest of the economy, and (ii) the policymaker lacks some policy instrument. While it may be a useful analytical abstraction to assume that policy can move the economy to a first-best allocation, that is very unrealistic. In most actual policy situations the policymaker has discretion over some or all of his policy instruments and the first best is unreachable. Therefore the credibility requirement will generally impose a binding constraint on equilibrium policy. Since adding a binding constraint normally leads to a worse outcome, we realize that equilibrium policy in a discretionary regime will typically yield a worse outcome to the government than equilibrium policy in a commitment regime. In line with the argument we have just made, we shall focus mostly on discretionary policy environments throughout the monograph. Regimes with commitments will be analyzed as a benchmark for welfare comparisons.

1.2.2. *Political Constraints*
Next, suppose there are no credibility constraints, but instead there is a conflict of interests between the policymaker and the citizens because of disagreement over the final goals of policy. Ultimately, the source of this disagreement must derive from heterogeneity among the citizens that leads them to evaluate differently the effects of particular policies. The role of political institutions is to, somehow, aggregate these conflicting interests into actual policy decisions. Typically, different political institutions are not neutral in that they induce different equilibrium policy choices. That is to say, different institutions impose different incentive constraints on policymakers. We call these incentive constraints *political constraints*. Analyzing the political constraints becomes essential for a positive understanding of policymaker

behavior as well as for making normative prescriptions about institutional reforms.

An example of political institutions that modify the policymaker's incentives is the appointment of government through democratic elections. Elections matter for at least two reasons. First, they may induce policymakers to pay more attention to how the policy appears to the voters than to the policy itself. If the voters are not perfectly informed, this incentive may give rise to electoral policy cycles. Second, elections may create alternation of policymakers with different goals. This 'political instability'—that is, instability in the policymakers preferences—may affect the intertemporal policy choices.

Several other examples can be provided, and will be provided in the subsequent sections. We will not attempt, however, to summarize these political constraints in a general and unified framework, like we did with the credibility constraints. The details of the political constraints depend on the details of the political institution. And there is a variety of such institutions. Hence, it is best to discuss the political constraints with reference to specific examples rather than in the abstract.

All the examples that we will study, however, have two things in common. First, they are choice theoretic. Second, voting—either on candidates or on policies—is the only form of political participation. Even though other forms of political involvement, such as lobbying or protesting, are important, they are perhaps less important for macroeconomic policy than for, say, trade policy or regulatory policy. Almost by definition, macroeconomic policy concerns society at large, and is perhaps more distant from the interests of well-identified constituencies.

1.2.3. *Static and Dynamic Models of Policy*

Following the literature, we will study policy in two different types of models. In Part I we study static models of monetary policy in which there is no economic link between one period and the next (other than possibly the private expectation formation process). We consider first the credibility constraints. In this static context, discretion means that private decisions are made without observing policy; that is, policy is chosen after (or simultaneously with) private sector decisions in any given period. The policymaker's discretion may then capture the fact that private individuals lock themselves into contracts for wages and prices that are hard to change in the short run, while monetary policy can be easily changed at short notice. Then we turn to the political constraints. Here discretion may capture the fact that political candidates are unable to enter into binding commitments about the policies that they will pursue once in office. In both cases, the policymaker's *ex ante* and *ex post constraints* are different. (The *ex ante–ex post* distinction refers to the situation before and after the formation of private contracts and elections, respectively.) It is this difference that creates a temptation for policy surprises and imposes an incentive constraint on policy.

In Part II we study dynamic models of fiscal policy in which state variables—such as capital or debt—provide intertemporal links between periods. The timing issue then comes up in a second way. Consider first the credibility constraint. Typically, the private sector decisions in the current period depend on the expectation of policy in all future periods. Hence, even if the government decides before the private sector in the current period, it can still surprise the private sector in the future, by implementing future policies that differ from those currently expected. Discretion, in this dynamic context, means that the government reoptimizes *ex novo* at the beginning of each period, without being committed to a full sequence of (possibly contingent) actions from the beginning of time onwards. The policymaker now has discretion because private individuals lock themselves into irreversible decisions such as capital accumulation. As in the static models, such decisions may lead to a difference between *ex ante* and *ex post* constraints and an associated credibility problem.

With heterogeneity and political conflict, discretion also means that current policymakers cannot commit the policies of future policymakers with potentially very different political objectives. In this case, there is also an inconsistency of the policymaker's *ex ante* and *ex post preferences*, which results in an additional incentive constraint, besides the credibility constraint discussed above. When the current policymaker sets policy, he takes into account that future policymakers will pursue different goals. This political constraint turns out to distort his intertemporal preferences.

These two Parts can largely be read independently of each other. Whereas Part I is more concerned with presenting the relevant solution concepts and illustrating a method of analysis, Part II is more concerned with specific economic applications and contains material that is more likely to be novel for the reader.

We now turn to a brief description of two basic models that will be used throughout the monograph: A static model of monetary policy that underlies most of Part I; and a dynamic model of fiscal policy that will be used extensively in Part II.

1.3. Monetary policy and the Phillips curve

We now present a simple model of monetary policy. This model provides perhaps the simplest example of credibility problems in economic policy, and for this reason it has been extensively studied.[2]

1.3.1. The Model

The private sector is described by a simple model of the labor market. Competitive firms hire labor up to the point where the real wage equals the marginal product of labor, according to the following labor demand function:

$$x = \alpha - (w - p), \tag{1.1}$$

where x is employment, and w and p are the logs of the nominal wage and the price level, respectively. Each representative wage setter—a firm-specific union, say—sets the nominal wage so as to maximize the expected wage bill, where the wage bill is given by:

$$\exp (w - p)x, \tag{1.2}$$

where exp $(\cdot)$ denotes the exponential operator. The optimization problem is thus to maximize the expectation of (1.2) subject to (1.1). It is straightforward to see that the nominal wage that solves this problem varies one for one with the expected price level, p^e. After some simplifications, we can hence summarize the private sector behavior by means of an expectations-augmented Phillips curve:

$$x = \bar{x} + (p - p^e). \tag{1.3}$$

In this setup, employment varies with the difference between the expected and the realized real wage, or with the difference between

---

[2] A similar model was first suggested by Kydland and Prescott [85] and subsequently popularized and further developed by Barro and Gordon [22].

expected and realized prices, as in equation (1.3).[3] From now on, we will simply describe the private sector by means of (1.3), but the reader should remember that expected prices really stand for nominal wages. The government sets prices directly. Again, this is shorthand for a more complete model in which the government sets the money supply (in a closed economy) or the exchange rate (in an open economy) so as to achieve the desired price level. There is no political disagreement: everybody agrees that the targets are zero inflation, π, and high employment. Thus, the government minimizes a loss function of the following form:

$$L(\pi, x), \qquad (1.4)$$

where $\pi = p - p_{-1}$ (p_{-1} denotes the log of the price level in the previous period). L is assumed to reach a minimum with respect to π at $\pi = 0$ and is increasing in π for $\pi > 0$; moreover, L is deceasing in x for $x \geqslant \bar{x}$ (at least over some range). Even though this loss function is somewhat arbitrary, its specific functional form is generally of no importance. What matters is that positive inflation is costly for the government, whereas employment above the natural level is welfare improving.[4]

The natural level of employment is too low because the labor market equilibrium reflects some distortions or externalities. One example is that unions have a real wage target that is too high (see Footnote 3), another is distortionary labor taxation. Hence the first best cannot be achieved. In this example, it is precisely because desired employment is higher than the natural rate that a conflict of interest arises between the government and the private sector. For simplicity, we disregard political conflicts, even though they can be easily added to the model.

1.3.2. Commitments: The Second Best

Consider an environment in which the authorities can enter into a binding policy commitment before nominal wages are set. That is, suppose that the timing is such that the government first chooses the price level, p. Then, observing p, wage setters choose nominal wages. Finally, employment is determined. What is the optimal monetary

---

[3] Employment is thus always determined by labor demand. This presumes that unions drive up the wage high enough that individual workers are to the left of their supply curve of labor. Thus, the labor market equilibrium has 'union-voluntary,' but 'individual-involuntary,' employment.

policy rule to which the authorities would like to commit? In this environment, monetary policy is neutral: Since inflation is fully incorporated into nominal wages, $p^e = p$ and employment is at the natural level: $x = \bar{x}$. By assumption, inflation is costly for the authorities. Hence, the optimal monetary policy rule is to have zero inflation and accept that employment remains at the natural level. Since commitments can be made this policy is also credible. Equilibrium policy is therefore $\pi = 0$, which together with $\pi^e = 0$ yields $x = \bar{x}$. Clearly this outcome is only a second best, since the labor market distortion remains.

1.3.3. Discretion: The Third Best

Absent a binding commitment, a policy of zero inflation is not credible and therefore not an equilibrium. Surprise inflation provides an additional valuable instrument; by generating a price level higher than expected, the government can reduce real wages and increase labor demand and employment above the natural level. At zero expected inflation, the government has an incentive to surprise with a positive inflation rate. Put differently, at the natural rate, the marginal benefit of surprise inflation, leading to more employment, exceeds the marginal cost of inflation.

If policy commitments are ruled out and wages are chosen before observing the current price level, credibility imposes a binding incentive constraint on policy. To satisfy the incentive constraint, the equilibrium inflation rate must be optimal for the government when it takes wages and thus inflationary expectations as given. This happens when the following first-order condition is satisfied at the point $\pi = \pi^e$:[5]

$$L_\pi(\pi, x) = - L_x(\pi, x). \qquad (1.5)$$

To derive (1.5) we have taken $\pi^e(p^e)$ as given in (1.3) and set the derivative of (1.4) with respect to π equal to zero (we use also that $dx/d\pi = dx/dp = 1$ according to (1.1).) The left hand side of (1.5) is the

---

[4] Besides actual inflation, the government presumably also dislikes expected inflation as well as the variance of inflation. Adding these terms to (1.2) would not change the nature of the results. On this point, see Grossman [68].

[5] Throughout the monograph, subscripts denote potential derivatives. Thus, $L_\pi = \partial L(\cdot)/\partial \pi$, $L_x = \partial L(\cdot)/\partial x$.

marginal cost of inflation. The right hand side is the marginal gain of (unexpected) inflation, that takes the form of higher employment. Equilibrium policy under discretion equates the marginal cost and the marginal gain of inflation, at the point where the chosen rate of inflation is fully expected: $\pi^e = \pi$. In this equilibrium, employment is still at the natural level and inflation is positive.

The normative lesson is that commitments are better than discretion: The government is better off if it can precommit to the rule of zero inflation. As we have seen, equilibrium employment is the same in the two monetary regimes, but inflation is lower if commitments are possible. Thus the outcome under discretion is only third best.

1.3.4. Monetary Policy: An Overview

The first Part of the monograph (Sections 2 through 5) deals with the now rather voluminous literature on monetary policy. This literature largely relies on the example we have just analyzed and on extensions of it. We shall also extend the simple model in various directions, both with respect to the economics of the problem and with respect to the underlying game theory.

Section 2 introduces stochastic shocks into the model of monetary policy. In this setup discretionary equilibria lead to higher average inflation without higher average employment or lower employment variability. We demonstrate how the notions of credibility and equilibrium policy may be formulated more precisely in game theoretic terms. We also discuss institutional reforms that change the incentives of policymakers such as giving independence and secrecy to central banks, or that combine rules and discretion, such as monetary constitutions with escape clauses.

Section 3 takes up the idea that a policymaker who worries about his long-run reputation in fighting inflation may have incentives to abstain from policy surprises in the short run. We use the theory of repeated games to show that this is indeed a possibility if the policymaker values the future enough. Nevertheless, we find the reputation idea problematic, since it raises the difficulty of multiple equilibria.

Section 4 again investigates whether reputation can substitute for commitments in supporting a low-inflation policy as an equilibrium. But here, private agents have incomplete information about the costs and benefits in the policymaking process, so the policy of a new government cannot be perfectly predicted. Over time policy is observed and private agents learn about the 'type' of government, however. The learning process affects government incentives and is the basis of the reputational mechanism. In this section, we draw on recent developments in the theory of signalling games.

Section 5 models political aspects of monetary policy in more detail than the previous sections. We discuss equilibrium policy when there are competing policymakers that are motivated both by ideology and by a desire to be elected. We show how the political process adds new short-run incentives to pursue divergent policies, as well as new long-run costs of acting myopically. Among the specific topics that we address are the causes and effects of 'political business cycles' in a world of forward-looking voters.

Perhaps we should add a qualifier at this point. The model we rely on in Part I is really very *ad hoc*. What drives the model is the assumed objective for monetary policy, a loss function like (1.4). In the literature, different authors have fairly loosely referred to such a loss function as representing either a true 'Social welfare function' or a 'Popularity index'. But both interpretations are very unclear about the links between the government objective and the private objectives. If the loss function is really a Social welfare function, then its particular form squares badly with the private objectives in the model. And if the loss function is a Popularity index, the model fails to specify the behavior of voters and alternatives offered by the political opposition. Despite this lack of 'microfoundations', we believe that there is definitely something to learn from the model. We shall therefore go on using it without further apology in the next few sections. But our emphasis, in Section 5, on models that explicitly incorporate the political aspects of monetary policymaking is largely motivated by the critical remarks we have just made.

1.4. The taxation of capital

A useful introduction to some problems in dynamic tax policy is given by a simple model of capital taxation.[6] This model is dynamic and has explicit microfoundations; hence, it does not suffer from the criticism

---

[6] The model of capital taxation reminds one of the two-period model in Fischer [55]. It is a simplified version of the model in Kotlikoff, Persson and Svensson [79].

raised above. In particular, here we can make meaningful welfare comparisons.

1.4.1. *The Model*

Consider a two-period economy inhabited by an atomistic representative consumer. In the first period, the consumer receives an exogenous endowment, e, and decides how much to consume and how much to invest in a linear production technology. Thus, his first period budget constraint is:

$$c_1 + k \leqslant e, \tag{1.6}$$

where c_1 denotes first period consumption and $k \geqslant 0$ denotes investment.[7] In the second period, the consumer decides how much to consume and how much to work; labor time, denoted by l, causes disutility. His disposable income in the second period consists of the returns to investment net of taxes plus his labor income, also net of taxes, less a lump sum tax, ω. Thus, his second period budget constraint is:

$$c_2 \leqslant R(1 - \theta)k + (1 - \tau)l - \omega, \tag{1.7}$$

where $R > 1$ is the gross return to investment, the gross return to labor (the wage) is unity, θ is the tax rate on capital income, and τ is the tax rate on labor income. For simplicity, suppose that the consumer maximizes a linear utility function of the form[8]

$$u(c_1, c_2, l) = c_1 + c_2 - \mu l. \tag{1.8}$$

The following inequality constraints apply: $c_1, c_2 \geqslant 0$ and $\underline{l} \leqslant l \leqslant \overline{l}$.

The government sets tax rates so as to maximize consumer welfare, subject to the government budget constraint:

$$g \leqslant \tau l + \theta R k + \omega; \tag{1.9}$$

g being the (predetermined) amount of public expenditure.

The first order conditions of the consumer yield optimal savings and labor supply decisions:

---

[7] The restriction to no borrowing ($k \geqslant 0$) could be relaxed without affecting the results.

[8] A similar argument goes through with a less special non-linear utility function. However, it is harder to come up with simple analytic solutions in that more general case.

$$l = \bar{l} \quad \text{if } (1 - \tau) \geqslant \mu$$
$$l = \underline{l} \quad \text{if } (1 - \tau) < \mu$$
$$k = e \quad \text{if } R(1 - \theta^e) \geqslant 1 \qquad\qquad (1.10)$$
$$k = 0 \quad \text{if } R(1 - \theta^e) < 1,$$

where θ^e is the period-2 tax rate on capital income expected in period 1. Thus, labor supply and investment are decreasing functions of the tax rates. Moreover, because of the linear utility function both labor supply and investment have corner solutions. The consumer is at the upper corner only if the after-tax return is above (or equal to) the marginal rate of substitution. Tax rates above $(1 - \mu)$ and $(R - 1)/R$ drive labor supply and investment to the lower corner. The associated excess burdens are $(1 - \mu)\,(\underline{l} - \bar{l})$ and $(R - 1)e$, the difference between the marginal rates of transformation and substitution $\times$ the elastic part of the supply curve.

1.4.2. *The First Best*
Let us now turn to optimal tax policy. Suppose first that the government can set the lump sum tax ω at any level. Then, the optimal policy is clearly to collect everything through the lump sum tax, so as to avoid any tax distortions.[9] $\omega = g$, $\theta = \tau = 0$. With this tax policy, the government can achieve the first-best outcome without any excess burdens. Clearly, no incentive to surprise the private sector exists in this case.

1.4.3. *Commitment: The Second Best*
Next, suppose lump sum taxes are not feasible (so that $\omega = 0$ must hold). But in period 1, before any investment decision is made, the government can commit to a tax structure for period 2. To get an interesting optimal tax problem, we assume that $(R - 1)e/R + (1 - \mu)\bar{l} < g < \underline{l}$ and $g < Re$. Maximum tax revenue when tax rates are still non distortionary is not sufficient to finance government consumption (but fully taxing minimum labor supply or maximum savings is). Further, we assume that the excess burden associated with labor supply is lower than the excess burden associated with investment: $(1 - \mu)(\bar{l} - \underline{l}) < (R - 1)e$. This makes it optimal to tax labor

---

[9] Other equivalent tax structures exist, which exploit the fact that any $\theta \leqslant (R - 1)/R$ and any $\tau(1 - \mu)$ are also non distortionary. All of these equivalent structures lead to the same allocation.

income rather than capital income. An equilibrium tax policy under commitment is a combination of (θ, τ) that satisfies.[10]

$$\theta \leq (R - 1)/R$$
$$\tau = [g - \theta \operatorname{Re}]/\underline{l}.$$

(1.11)

The consumer's welfare is lower than with lump sum taxes. The equilibrium policy imposes an excess burden on the economy, in the form of a labor supply lower than at the first best. In other words, we are in a second-best situation.

1.4.4. Discretion: The Third Best

Finally, consider a discretionary regime in which the government cannot commit in period 1 to a specific tax policy for period 2. Instead the consumer chooses how much to invest, given his expectations about the future tax policy. And then, in period 2, the government sets θ and τ. In this discretionary environment, the tax policy in (1.9) is not credible and cannot be an equilibrium. To see why, suppose that the private sector, expecting $\theta^e \leq (R - 1)/R$, invested k = e (as indicated by (1.8)). But in period 2, bygones are bygones: Once the investment decision has been made, the tax on capital is like a lump sum tax. Hence, the government would find it optimal to surprise the private sector setting $\theta = 1$, so as to reduce the tax on labor income below $(1 - \mu)$ and to eliminate the excess burden in labor supply. By doing so, the government would achieve a higher welfare than with the policy in (1.9). Like surprise inflation in the previous subsection, a surprise tax on capital provides an aditional policy instrument, that moves the economy from the second towards the first best. Also, like in the previous subsection, the incentive to surprise is due to a conflict of interest between the government and the representative consumer. Each consumer is atomistic and rationally regards aggregate variables (and in particular the tax revenue) as unaffected by his decisions. This is why a tax on labor above $(1 - \mu)$ and a capital tax above $(R - 1)/R$ are distortionary: When the tax rate is raised, the private sector finds it optimal to respond by reducing the level of economic activity. The government on the other hand faces a budget constraint defined on

---

[10] There are different equivalent tax structures taxing capital at different rates below $(R - 1)/R$. They all lead to the same allocation.

economy-wide aggregates; hence it perceives that the individual responses to the tax rate create an excess burden. By surprising consumers, it reduces their response to the tax rates, and hence it reduces the excess burden. In equilibrium policy surprises are ruled out. Consumers realize that any positive investment would be fully taxed next period if the government is not committed. Hence, the only equilibrium in the regime with discretion must involve $\theta^e = \theta \geq (R - 1)/R$ and $k = 0$. The government is forced to rely exclusively on the distortionary labor income tax. But this policy induces two excess burdens instead of one. On top of the labor supply distortion, profitable investment opportunities are also lost (recall that $R > 1$) without any gain in tax revenue.[11] Again the government is left in a worse situation than in the equilibrium with commitments. Thus, the temptation to get to the first best drives the economy away from the second best and to a third best. As before, rules are better than discretion, since with discretion the government loses control of the market expectations.

1.4.5. Fiscal Policy: An Overview
The second Part of the monograph (Sections 6 through 9) deals with fiscal policy. Unlike in the first Part, all the models we deal with have structural dynamics (state variables). They also have explicit micro-economic foundations, which make the welfare comparisons of equilibrium policy in different environments more convincing. The approach in these sections borrows as much from public finance as from traditional macroeconomics.

Section 6 takes up the theme from the example in this subsection. We discuss the credibility problems of policies with moderate taxation of wealth. Even though these policies are desirable in the long run, they create the temptation to impose large 'capital levies' on already accumulated wealth. We show how a lack of commitment in wealth taxation may lead to multiplicity of equilibria, some of which have very low levels of savings. And we show how the results from capital taxation carry over to debt repudiation and to surprise inflation.

---

[11] It is, of course, only the simple linear structure of the utility function that allows us to rank equilibria simply by counting the number of distortions. Any less stylized model, like the models in Part Two, would have a second-best equilibrium with the tax distortions smoothed out across all the available tax bases.

Different institutions that may act as substitutes for commitment in wealth taxation are discussed in Section 7. We demonstrate that a particular 'capital structure' of the outstanding government debt may eliminate the public finance incentives for surprise inflation. We also discuss how a policymaker who values income distribution in addition to efficiency may put a check on the temptation to impose capital levies. Finally, we demonstrate how 'implicit social contracts' between successive generations may introduce a disincentive to overtax capital.

Section 8 shows that the credibility problems in fiscal policy are not exclusively tied to capital levies: They remain even if only labor can be taxed in each time period. Once again, a particular capital structure of the government debt may reduce the incentive for policy surprises and reduce the welfare losses associated with equilibrium policy under discretion.

Section 9 is devoted to politically oriented models of fiscal policy. In particular, we concentrate on public debt policy. We show how a political desire to bind the spending decisions of future governments—with potentially different objectives—may affect the current government's debt policy. Under certain circumstances the equilibrium policy has a definite bias towards debt issue. Similarly, in a setup where the public debt may redistribute income from future to current generations, the political equilibrium may have a deficit bias.

1.5. Discussion

All of the forthcoming sections have a common theme. The government is treated like all the other economic agents: Its behavior is the solution to a well-defined optimization problem. The task of the theory of economic policy is to spell out in detail the objectives and constraints that define the government optimization problem. Solving this problem yields a positive theory of economic policy. The positive analysis in turn leads to normative suggestions about how to modify the incentives and constraints that define the policy problem, so as to obtain more desirable government policies in equilibrium.

This analytical task is more difficult—but also more exciting —because many of the government constraints are incentive constraints. The incentive constraints reflect either the strategic interaction of the government with the rest of the economy or the nature of the political process. Much of the current research in the theory of macroeconomic policy deals with the question of how these incentive constraints shape government policy, and how they can be relaxed by means of appropriate institutional design. We conclude with a statement about what we don't do in this monograph. In recent years reseachers in several areas of economics have started analyzing incentive constraints on economic policy. Here we only focus on monetary and fiscal policies. Among the most important topics not covered in this book are: international trade policy, international economic policy coordination, external debt repayment and, more generally, policies towards economic development. Several of the concepts and methods illustrated in the subsequent sections can also be applied to these other areas of economic policymaking, even though the specific economic and institutional content of the models would differ.

1.6. Notes on the literature

The first three articles that used a game-theoretic approach to model macroeconomic policy were Hamada [71], Kydland and Prescott [85], and Calvo [29]. These papers set the stage for the large literature that has developed in the 80s and is the subject matter of this monograph. Recent surveys of this literature can be found in Blackburn and Christensen [25], Rogoff [116], Persson [103], Chari, Kehoe and Prescott [37] and Alesina and Tabellini [11]. Surveys of the recent literature on international policy coordination and external debt are Canzoneri and Henderson [34] and Crawford [40], respectively. The political economy literature on trade policy is surveyed by Baldwin [19], whereas credibility in trade policy is discussed in Staiger and Tabellini [123].

Part I

2. COMMITMENT VERSUS DISCRETION IN MONETARY POLICY

2.1. Introduction

This section analyzes in more detail the issue of commitments versus discretion in monetary policy. The section studies an economy subject to random shocks. We investigate how to design monetary institutions that aim at overcoming the credibility problem introduced in the previous sections. We consider two aspects of a monetary regime: having an independent and secretive central bank; and formulating simple targeting procedures with escape clauses. Both aspects combine elements of commitments and discretion: They enable society to achieve a low average inflation rate, while at the same time preserving some flexibility to respond to unforeseen circumstances.

The remainder of this subsection sets out the basic model. In Sections 2.2 and 2.3 we define the notions of 'equilibrium policy' and 'credibility' and we show once again that equilibrium policy leads to worse outcomes under discretion than under commitment. The institutional reforms are discussed in Section 2.4. A concluding subsection takes up possible extensions of the analysis and summarizes the main points.

The model we use is basically the same as in Section 1, and like there we restrict the analysis to a one-shot game with no political conflict. The behavior of the private sector is still summarized by an expectations-augmented Phillips curve. As in Section 1, expected inflation is a shorthand for nominal wage growth, since the optimal wage is changed one for one with expected inflation. Throughout this section we allow for supply shocks. Thus employment is

$$x = (\pi - \pi^e) - \epsilon, \tag{2.1}$$

where ϵ is a shock observed by the central bank when setting policy but not by the private sector when setting wages; ϵ is symmetrically distributed, with mean 0 and variance σ. This specification of equation (2.1) implies that there is scope for welfare improving stabilization policies.

The reason is the same as in Fisher (1977) and the subsequent rational expectations literature: Labor contracts are not state-contingent (for reasons we do not explain) and the government has an information advantage, since monetary policy can react on short notice, once the supply shock has been realized, whereas wages cannot.

For simplicity, we take the loss function minimized by the authorities to be quadratic in both inflation and employment:

$$L(\pi, x) = E\,[\pi^2 + \lambda(x - \chi)^2]/2, \lambda > 0, \chi > 0, \qquad (2.2)$$

where E is the expectations operator, χ denotes the target level of employment and λ is a relative weight. As in Section 1, the target level of employment exceeds the natural level: $\chi > \bar{x} = 0$.[12]

As in Section 1, the policy instrument is the inflation rate (price level) in the current period. But since the model is stochastic, the policymaker chooses a *policy rule*, rather than a policy action. A policy rule is a mapping from the policymaker's information set to the set of possible policy actions (a state-contingent strategy in game theoretic terms). Because the model is linear-quadratic, we restrict our attention to policy rules that are linear in the observed realization of ϵ:

$$\pi(\epsilon) = \bar{\kappa} + \kappa\epsilon. \qquad (2.3)$$

The next two subsections describe the optimal choice of the coefficients $\bar{\kappa}$ and κ, in two different policy environments: one in which the policymaker commits to a choice of $\bar{\kappa}$ and κ in advance, before nominal wages are set, and this choice is known to private agents when they set wages; and another in which the choice of $\bar{\kappa}$ and κ is made after—or simultaneously with—the determination of nominal wages. We will refer to this second environment by saying that the policy plan is chosen under discretion. Since private agents are atomistic, each agent disregards any effect of his own choices on policy.[13] Then there is no meaningful distinction between the case when policy is chosen after wages and the case when policy is chosen simultaneously with wages.

---

[12] Here is a point where the lack of microfoundations becomes troublesome: One could well argue that target employment χ should not be a constant, but shift with ϵ for efficiency reasons. Allowing this to happen would change the results of Section 4 below.

[13] We use 'atomistic' to mean that each private agent is small enough to ignore the effect of his own choices on economy-wide variables. This may be formally represented by letting the private agents form a continuum. The precise technical term for this representation is to describe the private sector as 'atomless'.

The representative private wage setter also chooses a rule, setting nominal wages contingent on the available infomation. In the discretionary regime the private information set is void, since the realization of ϵ is not observed. Hence, there is no relevant distinction between a rule and an action for setting nominal wages (private strategies are not state-contingent). In the commitment regime, on the other hand, the information set of the private sector includes the government choice of $\bar{\kappa}$ and κ. Hence, in that regime, the wage strategy is contingent on these two coefficients.

2.2. Equilibrium policy with commitments

Suppose that the government can commit to a policy rule of the form (2.3) before nominal wages are set. What is the equilbrium choice of $\bar{\kappa}$ and κ? Even though often in practice such commitments cannot be made, the answer to this question provides a benchmark for comparing policy outcomes.

In this environment, two conditions define the equilibrium: (i) For any government policy rule, the nominal wage is optimal for wage setters given that policy rule. (ii) Given the 'reaction function' of wage setters as defined in (i), the government policy rule is optimal for any realization of ϵ. In the literature this equilibrium notion is referred to as Stackelberg equilibrium, with the government as the dominant player.[14]

The equilibrium can be computed by working backwards. First, we compute the optimal wage as a function of $\bar{\kappa}$ and κ. Optimality here is equivalent to rational inflationary expectations.[15] Since ϵ is not observed by the private sector, condition (i) and equation (2.3) say that wage setters should form their expectations by setting $\pi^\epsilon = \bar{\kappa}$. Then, we can compute the optimal government policy rule. To do that we

---

[14] Note that nominal wages are required to be optimal for any policy rule and not just for the equilibrium policy rule. This rules out implausible equilibria. In the terminology of game theory, the equilibrium is a Subgame perfect Nash equilibrium in an extensive form game with the government moving first. We discuss Subgame perfection and related concepts more extensively in Section 3.

[15] In a game theoretic context like the present one, the notion of rationality is by no means unambiguous. By rational expectations we here mean unbiased predictors of equilibrium inflation. Stronger notions of rationality are extensively discussed in Sections 3 and 4.

substitute $\pi^e = \bar{\kappa}$ in equation (2.1) and plug the resulting expression for x into the loss function (2.2). We also plug (2.3) into (2.2). The rewritten loss function is then defined over $\bar{\kappa}$ and κ. From the first order conditions with respect to these parameters, we obtain the equilibrium state-contingent policy rule with commitments:

$$\pi(\epsilon) = \bar{\kappa} + \kappa\epsilon = \frac{\lambda}{1 + \lambda}\epsilon. \qquad (2.4)$$

It follows that equilibrium employment in this regime is:

$$x = -\frac{1}{1 + \lambda}\epsilon. \qquad (2.5)$$

Thus, the equilibrium policy rule in the commitment regime exploits the trade-off between inflation and unemployment. The government accepts that it has to create some inflation in order to cushion negative supply shocks and, according to (2.5), the supply shock ϵ affects employment less than one for one.

Any inflation that occurs in this equilibrium is fully unexpected. Since expected inflation cannot stabilize output and the government can commit policy, the optimal rule is chosen so as to have zero expected inflation in equilibrium. That is, $\bar{\kappa} = 0$. The equilibrium policy rule thereby involves 'biting-the-bullet' considerations: To create positive inflation surprises when the gains of higher employment are particularly large (when ϵ is positive and large), there has to be negative inflation surprises when the losses of lower employment are particularly small (when ϵ is negative and large in absolute value). The negative inflation surprises are needed to keep down expected average inflation that gets embodied into wages.

The unexpected inflation that occurs is definitely consistent with rationality, since it is due exclusively to the informational advantage enjoyed by the government. Without this informational advantage—or if the rule could not be made contingent on ϵ—the optimal rule would dictate zero inflation, as in Section 1.

2.3. Equilibrium policy with discretion

Consider now the more realistic discretionary monetary regime, where it is impossible to commit policy in advance. The equilibrium here is defined by the usual Nash conditions that both players select a best response to the strategy of the opponent. Thus: (i) Given the equilibrium government policy rule, the nominal wage is optimal for wage setters. (ii) Given the equilibrium nominal wage, the policy rule is optimal for the government, for any ϵ. The macroeconomics literature dealing with one-period models like the present one refers to this Nash equilibrium sometimes as the 'time consistent' equilibrium, sometimes as the 'discretionary' equilibrium.

There is a central difference between the equilibrium in the discretionary regime and the equilibrium in the commitment regime of the previous subsection. There, the government controlled π^e and nominal wages via its policy rule; but here, the government has to take π^e and hence the nominal wage as given. As explained in Section 1, this imposes a 'credibility constraint', or an incentive compatibility condition, on the government: Namely, the government must have no *ex post* incentive to deviate from the equilibrium policy rule and create surprise inflation.

The equilibrium policy rule is computed in a few steps. First, insert (2.3) into (2.1). This reveals that, from the governmen's point of view, employment is determined according to:

$$x = \bar{\kappa} + \kappa\epsilon - \pi^e - \epsilon. \tag{2.6}$$

Next, insert (2.6) and (2.3) into (2.2) and take the first order conditions with respect to $\bar{\kappa}$ and κ, for given π^e. It follows that the equilibrium policy rule must satisfy:

$$\pi + \lambda(-\chi - \epsilon + \pi - \pi^e) = 0. \tag{2.7}$$

Equilibrium condition (i) implies that private rational expectations are formed on the basis of (2.7), given the available information (see Footnote 13). Since the private information set does not include the realization of ϵ, we take unconditional expectations in (2.7) and obtain:

$$\pi^e = \lambda\chi. \tag{2.8}$$

Now, equations (2.7) and (2.8) together yield the equilibrium policy rule:

$$\pi(\epsilon) = \bar{\kappa} + \kappa\epsilon = \lambda\chi + \frac{\lambda}{1+\lambda}\epsilon. \tag{2.9}$$

The equilibrium level of employment is still given by equation (2.5) in the previous subsection.

If we compare this discretionary equilibrium with the commitment equilibrium, we see that the inability to commit results in a higher inflation rate, but leaves employment unaffected. The policy rules (2.9) and (2.4) differ by the constant $\lambda\chi$; this is the inflationary bias under discretion. As explained in Section 1, this bias arises because the government loses control of private sector expectations. Given the government objective, commitments are clearly better than discretion.

This finding is often referred to in the literature with statements like 'the optimal monetary policy rule is not credible (or is time inconsistent)' and 'the credible (or time consistent) rule is suboptimal'. Such statements are unclear and potentially misleading. Both policy rules—(2.4) and (2.9)—are equilibrium policy rules and both are optimal for the government. But they correspond to different policy environments. If commitments can be made, then the policy rule (2.4) is relevant, and credibility is not an issue. If commitments cannot be made, then (2.9) is relevant, and credibility is an issue. The statement that welfare is higher under (2.4) than under (2.9) really says that it would be desirable to have a commitment technology.

2.4. Changing monetary institutions

Real world policymakers cannot enter into binding policy commitments. The normative conclusion of the previous subsection may nevertheless serve as an argument for trying to set up institutions that push the discretionary equilibrium policy in the direction of the commitment policy. When thinking about such institutions, an important issue is what type of policy rules can realistically be enforced. Contingent rules of the form of equation (2.3) may be difficult to enforce, since they are contingent on private information of the government. This point is discussed more extensively in Section 3. Moreover, in a more complex stochastic environment, the optimal contingent rule may be difficult to characterize, or may be time variant. For example, some events—like wars, asset market crashes or big movements in energy prices—occur sufficiently seldom that their statistical distributions are not known. In these circumstances, it is hard to specify contingent rules. As a consequence, the real world choice is often between full discretion or institutions that support simple (non-contingent) rules—such as a k-percent rule for the money supply or a fixed exchange rate regime. But a choice between simple rules and discretion is generally ambiguous. Simple rules means to abandon activist stabilization. And discretion means to accept a higher average equilibrium rate of inflation. Which of these costs is higher generally depends on parameters in the economy. This point can be illustrated with the help of our simple model. The best non-contingent rule is to have zero inflation, $\pi = 0$, which yields no employment stabilization: $x = -\epsilon$.

Inserting these two expressions into the government objective (2.2) and taking expectations, yields the expected loss under the simple rule

$$L^s = (\sigma + \chi^2)\lambda/2. \tag{2.10}$$

Similarly, we can use (2.6) and (2.9) to determine the expected loss under discretion

$$L^d = [\bar{\kappa}^2 + \beta\sigma + \lambda\chi^2]/2, \tag{2.11}$$

where $\beta \equiv \lambda/(1 + \lambda)$. Thus, the difference between the losses is

$$L^d - L^s = [\bar{\kappa}^2 - \sigma/(1 + \lambda)]/2. \tag{2.12}$$

Equation (2.12) reveals that discretion can be better than the simple rule. This happens if the variance of the supply shock is so large that the expected gain from more stabilization (captured by the second term) outweighs the expected loss from more inflation (captured by the first term).

In the remainder of this subsection we discuss some institutional reforms that may improve the equilibrium outcome under discretion. We take up three issues that have been addressed in the existing literature: changing the degree of central bank independence; maintaining secrecy about the policy targets; and formulating policy targets with 'escape clauses'.

2.4.1. Central Bank Independence

According to equation (2.8), equilibrium inflation in the discretionary regime is increasing in the weight, λ, that the government attributes to employment. Intuitively, a higher λ raises the temptation to surprise the private sector with unexpected inflation, thereby making the credibility constraint more binding. Equilibrium inflation must go up, so that a larger marginal cost to inflate matches the larger temptation.

On the other hand, a higher λ makes the government engage in a more activist stabilization policy. From equation (2.5), we see that the variance of employment is decreasing in λ: A higher λ raises the cost of employment fluctuations, which leads to more stabilization of employment. This discussion suggests an institutional reform designed to improve the trade-off between inflation and employment variability. The reform requires a richer description of the policymaking process, however. So far we have made no distinction between society's preferences over different macroeconomic outcomes and the institution or individuals that actually set the policy instruments. Let us now make a distinction between two different bodies: The 'government'—which formulates society's true preferences—and the 'central bank'—which carries out monetary policy. In that setup, suppose that the weight on employment that enters the government true loss function (2.2) is $\tilde{\lambda}$. Suppose further that the government can appoint an independent central banker that minimizes a loss function equivalent to (2.2), but with an individual weight λ, possibly different from $\tilde{\lambda}$. What value of λ for such an independent central banker would be optimal for the government?[16]

To answer this question, first insert discretionary equilibrium employment and inflation ((2.5) and (2.8)) in the government's loss function, which thus is written as a function of λ: $L(\lambda)$. Then differentiate with respect to λ, taking $\tilde{\lambda}$ as given.

$$L_\lambda(\lambda) = \lambda_\chi^2 + \sigma(\lambda - \tilde{\lambda})/(1 + \lambda)^3. \qquad (2.13)$$

Consider the expression in (2.13). At the point $\lambda = \tilde{\lambda}$, the last term on the right hand side drops out, so $L_\lambda(\tilde{\lambda})$ is positive. Moreover, at the point $\lambda = 0$, the first term drops out and $L_\lambda(0)$ is negative. It follows that the optimal value of λ (where $L_\lambda(\lambda)$ is zero) is positive but smaller than $\tilde{\lambda}$.[17]

In words, it is optimal to appoint a 'conservative' central banker, someone who dislikes inflation more than society does. But it is not optimal to appoint an 'ultra conservative' central banker, someone who only cares about inflation. Intuitively, under discretion inflation is

---

[16] Rogoff [115] asked and answered this question. This subsection develops his analysis in the context of our model.

[17] The second-order conditions are always fulfilled.

too high whereas employment is set optimally (given the informational constraints and the lack of other policy instruments). At the margin, it is therefore optimal to accept some additional employment variability, in exchange for a reduction in inflation.

But even though a conservative central banker can be viewed as a substitute for commitments, it is an imperfect substitute: The expected loss under commitment is lower than under discretion with an optimally chosen central banker. One can view the appointment of an independent central banker as a way of getting a piece each of discretion and of the simple rule that we discussed earlier in this section.[18]

The finding, that appointing a conservative independent central banker is welfare improving, may contribute to explain the current monetary arrangements in many industrial countries. However, the finding also raises a natural question. Why can society find a way to commit to having an independent central bank, but not to a specific monetary policy rule? We return to this question in our discussion in Section 2.5.

2.4.2. Secrecy

So far, we have assumed that the realization of the shock ϵ is private information of the policymaker. However in principle he could publicly reveal his information to the private sector.[19] What is the optimal information structure from the viewpoint of the policymaker?

In the context of this model, it is easy to show that secrecy is beneficial. If wage setters could observe the realization of ϵ, they would anticipate that the government incentives to inflate have changed, and they would set nominal wages accordingly. Hence, the policymaker would be unable to create unexpected inflation. To show the result formally, we assume that ϵ is known to wage setters when they set wages. It is then

---

[18] Actually, in the context of the model there is an even better way to choose a central banker. Suppose the set of possible central bankers differed in their individual employment targets — the χ-parameter in our model — rather than in their weights on deviations from a given target. Choosing a central banker with $\chi = 0$ would then eliminate the inflation bias altogether and reproduce the commitment outcome under discretion.

[19] This raises the interesting question of how can the policymaker be induced to reveal the correct information. This question has recently been addressed by Stein [124]. He shows that, by making imprecise announcements, the policymaker can credibly reveal some ranges for the privately observed variable.

easy to repeat the same steps as in Section 2.3 to determine equilibrium inflation and employment under discretion:

$$\pi = \lambda(\chi + \epsilon)$$

$$x = -\epsilon.$$

(2.14)

Even though average equilibrium inflation is the same as with secrecy, the policymaker loses his capacity to stabilize employment by revealing his private observation of ϵ. Inserting (2.14) in the expected loss function (2.2) and comparing the resulting expression with the expected loss under secrecy (given by (2.11)), it is easy to see that the expected loss is higher when ϵ is revealed. Intuitively, secrecy about ϵ enables the policymaker to surprise wage setters in periods when the marginal gain of unexpected inflation is unusually high, and revealing ϵ eliminates this possibility.[20]

We should reiterate, however, that even though this point is generally valid, the model is really inadequate to address the welfare consequences of secrecy. Since the model lacks microfoundations, it cannot spell out the nature of the conflict between the policymaker and the rest of the economy. Our current model assumes two things: The natural rate of employment, $\bar{x} - \epsilon$, is affected by the shock, while the policy target, χ, isn't. Both assumptions may be questioned. For one, if the private sector knew the realization of ϵ, it may demand a different real wage. This may reduce the change in the natural rate and weaken the argument in favor of secrecy. For another, the shock could affect the employment target of the policymaker and the natural rate in the same manner, which would again weaken the argument for secrecy. The only general argument in favor of secrecy is that it enables the policymaker to time its policy surprises when they are most valuable to him.

2.4.3. Rules with Escape Clauses

As we mentioned in Section 2.4.1, one can interpret the appointment of a conservative central banker as combining a simple rule with discretion. In this subsection we discuss an alternative method of achieving the same result. Namely, the formulation of simple rules with explicit escape clauses.[21] In the absence of a complete state-contingent rule, you

---

[20] Cuikerman and Meltzer [42] further investigate this idea in a more elaborate model.

[21] The idea that we develop in this subsection is largely borrowed from Flood and Isard [56].

want a policy that follows a simple rule in 'normal times'—when there are no major shocks—but is discretionary in 'abnormal times'—when shocks are large. A good example of a real world policy rule of this type is the fixed exchange rate system under the Bretton Woods agreement. The rule was even codified in the agreement: Countries were required to keep fixed parities against the dollar and parity changes were not allowed except in 'fundamental disequilibrium'. The Bretton Woods system is thus an example of a simple rule with an 'escape clause'. The European Monetary System is another one.

Consider a regime in which the central bank follows the simple rule of zero inflation when the supply shock is small in absolute value and acts discretionally when its absolute value is large. We do not specify exactly how the central bank can be induced to act in this way; but one possibility is that the government imposes a cost on the central bank for breaking the simple rule. The central bank then would find it optimal to stick to the rule unless the gains from deviating are large enough; that is, unless the supply shock is large enough. Alternatively, the escape clause could be explicitly codified in a targeting procedure as under the Bretton Woods agreement, or under a strict procedure of targeting intermediate monetary aggregates.

Let q be the probability that the escape clause is invoked and a discretionary policy is followed. The simple rule is followed with probability $1 - q$.[22] Wages are formed before observing the realization of ϵ, and hence before knowing whether the escape clause will be invoked or not. Hence, private expected inflation is

$$\pi^e = qE(\pi^d) + (1 - q)E(\pi^s) = q\bar{\kappa}/(1 + (1 - q)\lambda), \qquad (2.15)$$

where π^d and π^s denote inflation under discretion and under the simple rule, respectively. The rightmost expression is obtained by taking expectations of the central bank's first order condition under discretion and recalling that $\pi^s = 0$. We see that as long as there is positive probability that the rule will be followed, so that $q < 1$, expected inflation is lower than in the purely discretionary regime, and is increasing in q. That is, making the escape clause very narrow (making q small) has the advantage of reducing expected inflation.

The equilibrium policy when the escape clause is triggered is

$$\pi^d = \gamma\bar{\kappa} + \kappa\epsilon, \qquad (2.16)$$

---

[22] Thus, for some thresold $\mu > 0$, q is defined as: $q \equiv \text{Prob} \, (-\epsilon \leqslant -\mu \text{ or } \mu \leqslant \epsilon)$.

where $\gamma \equiv (1 + \lambda q)/[(1 + \lambda)(1 + \lambda(1 - q))]$ is a positive number below unity (if $q < 1$), and where $\bar{\kappa}$ and κ have the same values as in subsection 2.3. Because inflationary expectations are lower, the central bank does not have to inflate as much as under pure discretion: It is a surprise in itself that the shock triggers the escape clause. For that reason, if the clause is triggered equilibrium employment is higher than under pure discretion:

$$x^d = \pi^e(1 - q)/q - \epsilon/(1 + \lambda). \tag{2.17}$$

For small shocks, the simple rule is followed and inflation is zero. But employment is

$$x^s = -\pi^e - \epsilon. \tag{2.18}$$

When there is a positive probability that the escape clause is triggered, inflationary expectations are positive, and are reflected in wages. Zero inflation then generates a negative inflationary surprise and employment below the natural rate, even if the supply shock is zero. Thus combining a rule with an escape clause has a cost: There is a tendency for underemployment in normal times, when the rule is followed. This indicates that, if q is positive, it should not be too high. That is, the escape clause should be saved for truly exceptional events.

We now ask whether it is indeed optimal to have a rule with an escape clause. This question is equivalent to asking whether the optimal value of q is inside the (0, 1) interval. First we derive the expected loss from a rule with an escape clause as a function of q: $L(q) \equiv qL^d(q) + (1 - q)L^s(q)$, where $L^d(q)$ and $L^s(q)$ are the conditional expected losses under the escape clause and under the simple rule, respectively.[23]

We take the derivatives of $L(q)$ with respect to q at the extreme points $q = 1$ and $q = 0$.[24] First, we get

---

[23] From (2.16) through (2.18) and the definition of the government loss function, one can show (after tedious but straightforward calculations) that the expected loss is

$$L(q) = \chi^2 + \sigma^s(q) + q(\beta\sigma^d(q) - \sigma^s(q)) +$$

$$\left\{ q\frac{(1 + \lambda q)^2 + [(1 - q)(1 + \lambda)]^2}{[(1 + \lambda)(1 + \lambda(1 - q))]^2} + (1 - q)\frac{q^2}{[1 + \lambda(1 - q)]^2} \right\} \bar{\kappa}^2.$$

where $\sigma^s(q)$ and $\sigma^d(q)$ denote the conditional variances of ϵ, when ϵ falls into the rules and discretionary regions respectively.

[24] It follows from the conditional variances properties that at these extreme points

$$L_q(1) = \sigma_q^d(1) + \beta\sigma + \bar{\kappa}^2(\lambda + \kappa) > 0. \tag{2.19}$$

As explained in Footnotes 23 and 24, $\sigma_q^d(1) < 0$. Hence, it is never optimal to have pure discretion. This result follows from the same logic that underlies the result on the conservative central banker in subsection 2.4.1. In a purely discretionary regime, inflation is too high whereas employment stabilization is done correctly. Hence, in this regime it is optimal to trade off one distortion against the other, reducing average inflation at the price of a marginally higher employment instability. A reduction of q below 1 achieves precisely this. We also get

$$L_q(0) = -\sigma + \bar{\kappa}^2\nu, \tag{2.20}$$

where $\nu \equiv (1 + (1 + \lambda)^2)/(1 + \lambda)^4$ is a positive number. Thus a rule with an escape clause is also better than a simple rule if the supply shocks are large enough, as measured by their (unconditional) variance σ.

2.5. Discussion

Our findings in this section once again established that equilibrium policy in a regime with discretion has an inherent inflationary bias relative to the equilibrium policy with commitments. It is therefore useful to try and set up institutions such that the equilibrium under discretion approaches the commitment outcome. With an explicitly stochastic framework, we argued that supporting complicated state-contingent policy rules is probably unrealistic. Institutions must therefore aim to combine rules and discretion. In this spirit, our results in Section 2.4 provide a rationale for two monetary arrangements that are common in many countries. First they suggest that there may be a gain in delegating monetary policy decision to an independent central bank. The central bank should be conservative to reduce expected inflation. And it should be secretive to retain some capacity to engage in stabilization policies. Naturally, the model from which these prescriptions are derived is overly simplistic in other important respects. In particular, it neglects the negative repercussions that secrecy of monetary policy might have on financial markets or on the functioning of political and bureaucratic institutions.

When q = 0: $\sigma^d(0) = \sigma_q^d(0) = 0$, $\sigma^s(0) = \sigma$, and $\sigma_q^s(0) < 0$

When q = 1: $\sigma^d(1) = \sigma$, $\sigma_q^d(1) < 0$, and $\sigma^s(1) = \sigma_q^s(1) = 0$.

Second, our results identify an important role for fixed exchange rate agreements, like the European Monetary System or Bretton Woods. The requirement that major exchange rate realignments be approved by all countries in the agreement is equivalent to the rule with escape clauses discussed in Section 2.4. The enforcement mechanism is provided by the international sanctions that would be imposed on a country breaking the agreement.[25]

These considerations, however, also raise some difficult questions. Why does the international agreement specify a range of values for the exchange rate, rather than for other policy variables, like the money supply? Or why would it be easier to commit to preserve an independent central bank than to comply with a specific rule for monetary policy? A possible answer to the second question is that lack of information may constitute a commitment technology. This technology may work in preserving the independence of a central bank, but not in enforcing compliance to a policy rule: In order to implement a policy rule, society has to be informed of how to apply the rule; but once the information is available, the temptation to deviate from the rule is inescapable. By appointing an independent central bank, on the other hand, society can remain uninformed about how to run monetary policy at any specific point in time, and avoid the temptation to deviate.

However, if society stays uninformed, it may not be able to induce the central bank to generate the desired policy outcomes, as in any standard principal agent model. An interesting topic for future research is how to design a monitoring scheme for an independent central bank, or for enforcing simple rules with escape clauses.[26]

Having a truly independent central bank also raises some other interesting issues. Specifically, suppose that an independent central bank controls monetary policy, while other government agencies—like the treasury—control fiscal policy or trade policy. In such a situation, problems of policy coordination between different government institutions can easily arise, and some of the welfare comparisons between rules and discretion that were presented above can be reversed.

---

[25] Giavazzi and Pagano [63] discuss the European Monetary System from this point of view.
[26] Interesting papers by Stein [124] and by Lohman [90] make some progress on these issues.

To discuss these problems is, however, beyond the scope of this monograph.[27]

In this section we have discussed institutions that may support desirable low inflation policies under discretion. Much of the literature on monetary policy has taken a different course. Instead of focusing on institutions, the literature has focused on the idea that reputation may substitute for commitments in supporting desirable policies. In the next section we turn to precisely this issue.

2.6. Notes on the literature

Already Barro and Gordon [22] introduce uncertainty in their seminal paper on monetary policy, although uncertainty enters somewhat differently than here. The discussion about the benefits of an independent central bank—in the context of the recent theory of macroeconomic policy—was started by Rogoff [115]. Cukierman and Meltzer [42] discuss secrecy of policy. A good discussion of monetary rules with escape clauses is found in Flood and Isard [56]. Lohmann [90] analyzes what incentive structure to impose on central banks, and Stein [124] asks how the policymaker can credibly reveal his private information. Giavazzi and Pagano [63] discuss the role of the European Monetary System in providing credibility to the monetary authorities. Finally, Alesina and Tabellini [9] study the problem of monetary and fiscal policy coordination in a deterministic version of this model.

3. REPUTATION AND SEQUENTIAL RATIONALITY

3.1. Introduction

We have argued that the inflation bias associated with a discretionary monetary regime is a strong reason to consider reforming the institutions that shape monetary policy. Nonetheless, we may have overstated the case against discretion. In Section 2 we looked only at a one-shot policy game. But in practice, monetary policy is an ongoing process,

---

[27] Alesina and Tabellini [9] study a non-stochastic version of the model in this section, but add a fiscal authority that controls a fiscal instrument. They show that it is still beneficial to have an independent central bank. But they also show that some of the results in the model (in particular the fact that rules dominate discretion) are not robust when there are policy coordination problems.

with many repeated interactions between the government and the private sector. These repeated interactions provide a possible link between current policy and future expected policy. Suppose the private sector interprets high inflation today as a sign of high inflation in the future and sets future wages accordingly. This introduces a trade-off for the policymaker: Unexpectedly high inflation today not only brings about current employment gains, but it also brings about higher expected inflation tomorrow, which raises the cost of the current policy surprise. A policymaker that worries enough about the future might therefore resist the temptation of inflate today.

The recent literature often refers to this intuitive idea as a story about 'reputation' in monetary policy. Our first purpose in this section is to review this literature. In particular, we shall investigate whether and how reputation can be a substitute for commitments in sustaining an equilibrium with low inflation. To address this issue, we have to extend our monetary policy model to a multiperiod framework. The second aim in the section is more methodological: We discuss the appropriate game-theoretic methodology to model equilibrium policy in a multiperiod setting.

In this section we maintain the assumption that the private sector is fully informed about the policymaker's preferences and his capability of making policy commitments; that is, we consider only games of complete information. The next section extends the analysis to situations where the private sector is not fully informed about all aspects of the policymaker; that is, to games of incomplete information.[28]

Throughout the rest of this section we formulate our multiperiod model of monetary policy. Section 3.2 looks at equilibrium policy when the government and the private sector interact over a finite horizon. We introduce the key concept of sequential rationality and use it to show that reputational considerations have no force in this setup. They may have force, however, if the horizon is infinite. This is demonstrated in Section 3.3. In Section 3.4, we briefly take up some

---

[28] A game is said to be of incomplete information if some players do not know some of the *characteristics* of their opponents (such as their objective funcions). The game is said to be of imperfect information if some players do not observe the *actions* of some of their opponents, or of nature. Hence, the game studied in the previous section is of imperfect (but complete) information. As shown by Harsanyi [73], this distinction is convenient but artificial, since a game of incomplete information can always be transformed into one of imperfect information.

additional ideas that have been treated in the literature. Section 3.5 critically evaluates what we have learned.

In the new multiperiod framework, all agents care about their payoffs throughout the game. Thus, each agent in the private sector sets the nominal wage so as to maximize the discounted present value of the sum of his one-period payoffs (expected real wage bills; see Section 1.3.1). As in previous sections, the optimal nominal wage in each period changes one for one with the expected price level. Hence, we can still describe the private sector by means of the expectations-augmented Phillips curve given in (2.2). For now, we assume that there are no shocks to the economy. We discuss what happens when this assumption is relaxed in Section 3.4.

In the multiperiod setup the government minimizes a loss function of the following form:

$$\mathscr{L} = \sum_{t=0}^{T} \delta^t L_t, \qquad 0 < \delta < 1, \tag{3.1}$$

where δ is a discount factor and L_t is the one-period loss function for period t. It is convenient to simplify the one-period loss function further relative to (2.2), making it linear rather than quadratic in employment:

$$L_t = L(\pi_t, x_t) = \pi_t^e/2 - \lambda x_t, \qquad \lambda > 0. \tag{3.2}$$

The linearity simplifies the description of the equilibrium under discretion for the one-shot game. Repeating the procedure in Section 2, it is easy to see that in the one-shot game the optimal inflation rate for the government is independent of the nominal wage and is given by:

$$\pi = \lambda. \tag{3.3}$$

In game-theoretic terms the government has a dominant strategy.[29] Therefore, in the one-shot game, wages are set based on inflationary expectations that comply with (3.3): $\pi^e = \lambda$. As before, equilibrium employment is at the natural rate $x = \bar{x} = 0$. That the one-shot game can be solved in such a simple way considerably simplifies the analysis of its multiperiod extension.

---

[29] A strategy is said to be dominant for a player if it yields the highest payoffs to that player irrespective of the strategies chosen by the other players in the game.

Two central assumptions are maintained throughout most of the section: (i) The private sector is atomistic, so that wage setters neglect the impact of their individual decisions on aggregate variables; (ii) Before taking any action in the current period, everybody observes policy and aggregate variables—such as employment and the average wage—in the previous period. However, the actions of single individuals cannot be observed, neither by (other) single individuals nor by the government.[30] These two assumptions make the game we study 'anonymous'.[31] Anonymity, though obvious for most macroeconomic problems, is often left implicit in the literature on economic policy. Yet it plays an important role in ruling out some implausible equilibria, as we will see in Footnote 41 below. Finally, we assume that agents have perfect recall: Once they acquire some information, they never forget it.

In line with the anonymity assumption, we define the 'aggregate history' of the game at t as the sequence of policies and aggregate variables—determined by individual actions of private agents—from the beginning of the game up to period t − 1. The aggregate history should be distinguished from the traditional definition of the history of the game. The latter is the sequence of actions selected by all the players in all previous periods. Such a history may be appropriate for games with a few players, but it is not observable in our setup because of the anonymity assumption.

Despite its multiperiod structure, the game we are about to study is static in the following sense: The actions available to the government and to wage setters in each period and the corresponding payoffs are independent of the outcome in all previous periods. However, the information set of the players changes over time, since it contains the aggregate history of the game up to the current period. This updating of the information sets introduces an important strategic time dependence, because the strategies selected in a given period can now be made conditional on the outcome in previous periods. It is this strategic time dependence that gives a role to reputation.

---

[30] If the private sector is assumed to form a continuum, our explicit assumption that aggregate or average variables can be observed means an implicit formal assumption of measurability.

[31] Here we use anonymity in the sense of Green [66].

3.2. Reputation with a finite horizon

We look at a discretionary policy environment where the monetary policy game is repeated a finite, but potentially large, number of times, T. Discretion has the same meaning as in Section 2: In any given period the government chooses the policy rule simultaneously with (or after) the private nominal wage strategies are chosen. In this multiperiod framework, a *policy rule* chosen in period t specifies a sequence of inflation rates, one for each period from t until the end of the game, as a function of the aggregate history up to that period. Similarly, a *wage strategy* specifies a sequence of nominal wages, one for each period until the end of the game, also as a function of the aggregate history up to that period. All agents including the government are free to reoptimize in each period; in other words, commitments to a sequence of actions are ruled out.[32]

3.2.1. Nash Equilibrium and Reputation

A Nash equilibrium is a government policy rule and a collection of wage strategies, one for each wage setter, that satisfy two conditions. In each period: (i) Given the equilibrium policy rule and the equilibrium wage strategies of the other private agents, the wage strategy is optimal for each private agent. (ii) Given the equilibrium wage strategies, the policy rule is optimal for the government.

It is easy to show that the discretionary equilibrium of the one-shot game is also a Nash equilibrium of the repeated game. Suppose that in every period each private agent sets nominal wages as in the equilibrium of the one-shot model, irrespective of the aggregate history. In any period expected inflation is then $\pi^e = \lambda$ (see equation (3.3) above). This strategy is clearly optimal for wage setters if, in every period, the government also follows the one-shot equilibrium policy rule given by (3.3), $\pi = \lambda$. But given that π^e does not depend on the aggregate history, it is indeed optimal for the government to stick to

---

[32] In the terminology of game theory, a wage strategy and a policy rule are closed-loop strategies. If the players were not reoptimizing at the beginning of each period, their strategies could only depend on the information available at beginning of the game; hence, they would not depend on the aggregate history of the game. In this case, they would be called open-loop strategies. The government's policy rule in a multi-period analysis of a policy regime with commitments could thus be modeled as an open-loop strategy. We will come back to the distinction between open-loop and closed-loop strategies in our analysis of dynamic models in Part II of the monograph.

the one-shot equilibrium policy rule in every period, irrespective of the aggregate history. Hence, both equilibrium conditions are satisfied. But it turns out that there are several other Nash equilibria as well. We now investigate one of them, in which the equilibrium inflation is zero except in the last period.

Consider the following wage strategy (since there is a one-to-one correspondence between the optimal nominal wage and the expected price level, this strategy can be expressed as a sequence of inflationary expectations):

$$\text{In period 0:} \quad \pi_0^e = 0$$

$$\text{In period t:} \quad \pi_t^e = \begin{cases} 0 & \text{if } \pi_{t-1} = 0 \\ \varphi\lambda & \text{otherwise} \end{cases} \qquad (3.4)$$
$$0 < t < T$$

$$\text{In period T:} \quad \pi_T^e = \begin{cases} \lambda & \text{if } \pi_{T-1} = 0 \\ \varphi\lambda & \text{otherwise} \end{cases}$$

for some $\varphi > 1$. A strategy like (3.4) is called a 'trigger strategy'. Each private agent starts by setting wages on the expectation of zero inflation. If his expectations are fulfilled, he continues to set wages consistent with zero expected inflation up to period $T - 1$. Otherwise, he revises wages and expectations upwards, beyond the one-shot equilibrium inflation rate (since $\varphi > 1$). In the last period, the nominal wage is set on the basis of positive expected inflation, which depends on the outcome in period $T - 1$. This wage strategy can be thought of as incorporating an implicit 'reputation' mechanism: As long as the government has the reputation of sticking to zero inflation, expected inflation is indeed zero. But deviating from the zero inflation rule destroys the government reputation and leads to higher expected future inflation.

This wage strategy is optimal for private agents in equilibrium if their expectations are fulfilled. Therefore, to show that (3.4) is a Nash equilibrium strategy, we need to prove that—given this strategy—the government does not face any incentive to defect from (3.4) and create unexpected inflation. We shall do this by backward induction.

In period T, we are left with a one-shot game. Here, the dominant strategy of the government is to choose inflation according to (3.3), irrespective of π_T^e and irrespective of the aggregate history. Hence, the wage strategy is optimal only if the aggregate history has $\pi_{T-1} = 0$; since if $\pi_{T-1} \neq 0$, (3.4) dictates $\pi_T^e = \varphi\lambda \neq \pi_T$, which is suboptimal for wage setters.

Go to period $T - 1$, and suppose that $\pi^e_{T-1} = 0$. If the government does not fulfill these expectations, it would clearly set $\pi_{T-1} = \lambda$, according to the one-shot dominant strategy in (3.3). That would create surprise inflation and higher employment by $(\pi_{T-1} - \pi^e_{T-1}) = \lambda$; against this gain, there would be the cost of positive inflation. Relative to following the zero inflation rule, the government would be able to reduce its loss in period $T - 1$ by

$$L(\lambda, \lambda) - L(0, 0) = -\lambda^2/2. \qquad (3.5)$$

This net gain in period $T - 1$ is the '*temptation*' to defect from the zero inflation rule and surprise the private sector with unexpected inflation. But in addition to this current net gain, the government would lose its reputation and bear the future cost of higher expected inflation. According to the wage strategy, π^e_T increases from λ to $\varphi\lambda$ if $\pi_{T-1} \neq 0$ is observed. And this leads to lower employment in period T by $(\pi_T - \pi^e_T) = (1 - \varphi)\lambda$, which causes a net loss, relative to following the rule. This net loss, discounted to period $T - 1$, is:

$$\delta[L(\lambda, (1 - \varphi)\lambda) - L(\lambda, 0)] = \delta(\varphi - 1)\lambda^2. \qquad (3.6)$$

The loss represents the cost of losing the reputation, and is the '*enforcement*' mechanism that discourages defection.

In period $T - 1$, there is thus a trade-off between higher employment today and lower employment tomorrow. For the government not to defect in period $T - 1$ and fulfill the private sector expectations, the future costs of low employment must be sufficiently high. That is, the right-hand side of (3.6) must exceed (in absolute value) the right-hand side of (3.5).[33] If this condition is satisfied, we can repeat the same argument for all previous periods. The government finds it optimal to fulfill the expectations in (3.4) in every period, playing $\pi_t = 0$, $t < T$, and $\pi_T = \lambda$. Thus the wage strategy (3.4) is optimal in equilibrium for each wage setter and (3.4) is a Nash equilibrium strategy.

Intuitively, the Nash equilibrium condition forces the government to take *current* expected inflation as given. But the government realizes that *future* wages and inflationary expectations depend on the aggregate history and therefore on current policy. This mechanism of expectation formation creates incentives for the government to

---

[33] This yields the condition $\varphi \geq (1 + 2\delta)/2\delta$.

preserve its 'reputation' for fighting inflation. If these incentives are large enough, the government resists the temptation to inflate, and the equilibrium policy has zero inflation up to period T − 1. Naturally, several other equilibria can also be sustained by means of similar trigger strategies.

3.2.2. *Sequential Rationality*

Our last example showed that, for an equilibrium aggregate history of zero inflation, it was optimal for all agents to continue along the zero (actual and expected) inflation path up to period T − 1. But we did not investigate whether the equilibrium wage strategy and the equilibrium policy rule were optimal for an aggregate history off the equilibrium path. Had we done so, we would have found a negative answer: The wage strategy (3.4) is not optimal for a non-equilibrium aggregate history, since after a government deviation it prescribes a nominal wage which incorporates excessive expected inflation, and thus leads to employment below the natural rate (recall the employment term $(1 - \varphi)\lambda < 0 = \bar{x}$ in (3.6)). But this did not lead us to reject the wage strategy (3.4) and the corresponding policy rule as Nash equilibrium candidates. The reason is that Nash equilibrium only requires that the strategy of each player be an optimal response to the equilibrium strategy of the other players. Off-equilibrium events are disregarded, because they occur with zero probability in equilibrium. The key property of a Nash equilibrium is that it is self enforcing, but only in the sense that continuation of the equilibrium aggregate history is optimal for all the players.

This points to an important weakness of Nash equilibrium in a multi-period setting: It does not require rational behavior subsequent to zero probability events. This omission is important because zero probability events are not exogenous in a game, but depend endogenously on the strategies of the players. As illustrated by the two equilibria in the previous subsection, an event which has probability zero in one equilibrium may not have zero probability in another.

Consider again the zero inflation equilibrium in Section 3.2.1. One may argue that the government should not take the wage strategy (3.4) as given, unless it is optimal for wage setters. The government should ask how a rational wage setter would respond in the future to a policy of unexpected inflation today. The answer ought to be that the wage path prescribed by (3.4) is not credible: Given that there is unexpected inflation today, (3.4) entails an overprediction of future inflation. A rational private agent observing unexpected inflation in period $T - 1$—and knowing the government's trade-off between employment and inflation—must set $\pi_T^e = \lambda$ irrespective of past aggregate history, since that policy is a dominant strategy for the government. But then, the government would find it optimal to inflate in period $T - 1$ as well. Repeating the same argument for period $T - 2$ and earlier periods leads us to reject (3.4) as a candidate for equilibrium.

This backward induction argument can be formalized by the concept of sequential rationality. We say that a Nash equilibrium is *sequentially rational* if the equilibrium strategy for each agent is optimal for *all* aggregate histories of the game, given the equilibrium strategies of other agents. Everyone must find it optimal to continue along his equilibrium strategy even if the aggregate history is off the equilibrium path. Thus, sequential rationality coincides with the requirement that the strategies yield a Nash equilibrium starting from any possible aggregate history of the game.[34] In fact, we have already used the notion of sequential rationality—without explicit acknowledgement—in our Stackelberg equilibrium in Section 2. There, we indeed required that the wage strategy be optimal for *any* government policy rule, not just for the equilibrium policy rule.

What we have labeled sequential rationality is a special case of an equilibrium concept, known in the game-theoretic literature as *Perfect bayesian equilibrium*. This concept is discussed more extensively in the next section. The macroeconomic literature that has tried to be explicit about the underlying game theory has typically used a slightly different equilibrium concept, namely *Subgame perfect equilibrium*. A subgame is a specific branch of the game tree, that starts from a node with a particular history. In a Subgame perfect equilibrium, the strategies must yield at Nash equilibrium starting from any subgame. But we have already argued that in the typical macroeconomic context the

---

[34] By this definition we assume that the government evaluates any combination of individual decisions that lead to the same aggregate outcome in the same way. In particular, the government does not have to form any beliefs about which individual agents have caused an observed aggregate deviation from the equilibrium path. This makes sense in our set-up, where private agents are homogenous and the government's payoff depends only on aggregate outcomes. If anonymity was combined with heterogeneity among private agents and a government interested in outcomes for specific (groups of) individuals, we would have to be more careful in specifying how beliefs are formed over aggregate off-equilibrium events.

private sector is atomistic, so agents cannot observe the detailed history of the game, only the aggregate history. Strictly speaking then, proper subgames do not exist and we cannot really talk about subgame perfection.[35]

In this finite horizon model of monetary policy, there is only one sequentially rational equilibrium. It is the equilibrium of the one-shot game, described by equation (3.3). This follows from the backward induction argument that we used above. Since the last period is like a one-shot game, any sequentially rational equilibrium strategy must have $\pi_T = \pi_T^e = \lambda$, irrespective of the aggregate history. But then the equilibrium of period $T - 1$ cannot affect the future. So period $T - 1$ is also like a one-shot game, irrespective of the aggregate history. And so on. Hence, the reputation mechanism breaks down.[36]

3.3. Reputation with an infinite horizon

In the previous subsection, we rejected the reputational equilibrium on the basis of backward induction. The last period played a central role in our argument, so the finite horizon was very important. This subsection investigates whether there are sequentially rational reputational equilibria in an infinite horizon version of the same model.

The assumption of an infinite horizon can be justified in two ways: The termination of the game may be random and the players' discount

---

[35] A *proper* subgame must satisfy three properties: (a) It must begin with an information set that contains only one node; (b) If a node is in the subgame, so are all its successors; (c) All information sets of the subgame are information sets of the initial subgame. These conditions are not satisfied if the history of the game is not in the information sets of the players. Chari and Kehoe [36] provide an insightful discussion of this point. Observe that the argument does not apply to the Stackelberg equilibrium in Section 2. In a single-period game where the government moves before the private sector, a proper subgame is well identified, since the policy is observed by everyone. Hence, the Stackelberg equilibrium defined in Section 2 is a Subgame perfect equilibrium. See also the comment of Footnote 34.

[36] Under certain circumstances, there may be sequentially rational reputational equilibria even if the policy game has a finite horizon. Suppose that the one-shot game has more than one Nash equilibrium, say one with low inflation and one with high inflation. This could happen if the loss function L_t was not convex. Wage setters could then sustain a sequentially rational equilibrium policy of low inflation for all periods before the last one, by reverting to wages that match the high expected inflation equilibrium if they observe high inflation. Here wage setters indeed revert to a sequentially rational strategy; that is, a strategy that is rational for any agregate history, given that the government expects it. In this setup there would actually be a multiplicity of such equilibria. Rogoff [116] discusses this point in more detail.

factors reflect their (subjective) termination probabilities. Alternatively, we may interpret the players as collective bodies—in our context a central bank, and a set of trade unions—rather than as individuals. If the individuals operating in these bodies overlap with one another, it can be shown that under reasonable hypotheses a last period never comes about, even if each individual has a certain and finite horizon. Intuitively, these bodies reach decisions according to some collective procedure such as bargaining or majority voting. Any reasonable procedure is likely to give at least some weight to individuals whose term of office is not about to expire. Hence the collective body never faces a last period problem.[37]

As in the finite horizon framework, it is straightforward to show that with an infinite horizon there is a sequentially rational Nash equilibrium where all agents select the equilibrium strategies of the one-shot game in every period. That is, $\pi_t = \pi_t^e = \lambda$ for all t. The question we pose in this subsection is whether there also exist other equilibria with lower inflation, and in particular with zero inflation.

3.3.1. Temptation and Enforcement

Consider the following wage strategy, analogous to (3.4) in the previous subsection:

$$\text{For } t = 0: \quad \pi_0^e = \gamma\lambda,$$

$$\text{For } t > 0: \quad \pi_t^e = \begin{cases} \gamma\lambda & \text{if } \pi = \pi^e, = t-1, \ldots, t-I \\ \varphi\lambda & \text{otherwise,} \end{cases} \tag{3.7}$$

where $\varphi \geq 1$ and $\gamma \leq 1$. Unlike in (3.4), if in any period private agents see the government defect from the inflation rate they expected, they expect high inflation for the I subsequent periods.

The wage strategy in (3.7) is a sequentially rational equilibrium strategy if the expectations in (3.7) are correct for any aggregate history of the game. In other words, (3.7) is a sequentially rational best response to:

$$\text{For } t = 0: \quad \pi_0 = \gamma\lambda,$$

$$\text{For } t > 0: \quad \pi_t = \begin{cases} \gamma\lambda & \text{if } \pi = \pi^e, = t-1, \ldots, t-I \\ \varphi\lambda & \text{otherwise,} \end{cases} \tag{3.8}$$

---

[37] See Cremer [41] and, in the context of this monetary policy model, Tabellini [127].

To verify whether (3.7) and (3.8) constitute a sequentially rational equilibrium, we need to show that the government policy rule in (3.8) is optimal for any aggregate history, given that wages are set according to (3.7). This in turn requires an investment in some additional notation. If the government does not deviate from (3.8), it always fulfills private expectations. Its loss in period t then becomes $L_t = L(\pi_t^e, 0) = (\pi_t^e)^2/2$. The losses in period t, if $\pi_t = \pi_t^e = \gamma\lambda$ and $\pi_t = \pi_t^e = \varphi\lambda$, are, respectively:

$$L^0 \equiv L(\gamma\lambda, 0) = (\gamma\lambda)^2/2$$
$$L^P \equiv L(\varphi\lambda, 0) = (\varphi\lambda)^2/2. \tag{3.9}$$

In (3.9), L^0 is the government's one-period loss when it behaves according to the equilibrium policy rule with low (possible zero) inflation and is expected to do so. And L^P denotes the one-period loss when the government 'bears the punishment' and expectedly accommodates high nominal wage increases in the I periods following a deviation from the equilibrium policy rule.

Next, consider an unexpected deviation. The optimal deviation, in any period t and irrespective of π_t^e, is the dominant one-period policy $\pi_t = \lambda$. If $\pi_t^e = \gamma\lambda$, then the deviation creates surprise inflation and employment above the natural rate (as long as $\gamma < 1$). The one-period loss becomes

$$L^S \equiv L(\lambda, (1 - \gamma)\lambda) = \lambda^2/2 - \lambda^2(1 - \gamma). \tag{3.10}$$

If $\pi_t^e = \varphi\lambda$, on the other hand, a deviation means a refusal to accommodate high nominal wage increases with high actual inflation. Then the deviation creates surprise deflation and employment below the natural rate (as long as $\varphi > 1$). The one-period loss becomes

$$L^R = L(\lambda, (1 - \varphi)\lambda) = \lambda^2/2 + \lambda^2(\varphi - 1). \tag{3.11}$$

With these preliminaries, we return to the question of whether the policy rule (3.8) is a sequentially rational equilibrium strategy, when wages are set according to (3.7). If so, the government should have incentives to stick to (3.8), both when $\pi_t^e = \gamma\lambda$ and when $\pi_t^e = \varphi\lambda$. Thus, we have to check two distinct incentive compatibility conditions.

First, suppose $\pi_t^e = \gamma\lambda$ and we are along the equilibrium path. The one-period gain from an unexpected deviation (the 'temptation') is $L^0 - L^S$. The cost of the deviation (The 'enforcement') is high expected and actual inflation for I subsequent periods. Discounted to period t, this cost is $\Sigma_{i=1}^{I}\delta^{i}(L^{P} - L^{0})$. Thus, our first incentive compatibility condition is that

$$L^{0} - L^{S} \leqslant \sum_{i=1}^{I}\delta^{i}(L^{P} - L^{0}). \tag{3.12}$$

If (3.12) holds, the government has no incentive to create unexpected inflation along the equilibrium path, since the temptation is lower than the enforcement. This inequality is the analog of the Nash condition in Section 3.2.1. But there is one important difference. There, the enforcement had expected inflation higher than actual inflation, and employment below the natural level. Here, the enforcement has high actual and expected inflation, but no loss of employment. The government's trade-off thus entails higher employment today versus higher inflation in the future. This difference in enforcements comes from the sequential rationality requirement, which imposes optimality of the wage strategy (and hence no unexpected inflation) on non-equilibrium paths.

Next, suppose that $\pi_{t}^{e} = \varphi\lambda$ and we are off the equilibrium path, following a government deviation from the policy rule in the previous period. Sequential rationality requires that the government finds it optimal to accommodate the high wage increases with high inflation. This yields the second incentive compatibility condition:

$$L^{P} - L^{R} \leqslant \delta^{I}(^{P} - L^{0}). \tag{3.13}$$

The left hand side is the temptation to refuse accommodating high nominal wage increases in the current period, and instead surprise the private sector with unexpected deflation. The right hand side is the enforcement, which now consists in prolonging the period of high expected and actual inflation for one more period, namely to include period $t + I$.[38] If (3.13) holds, the government is willing to 'participate in the punishment' so as to keep it as short as possible. And then the

---

[38] Note that this future punishment is discounted to period t by δ^{I}. In this first period of the punishment phase the incentive to deviate is largest. A deviation in a later period would prolong the punishment phase with more than one period and impose a larger enforcement. Therefore it is enough to check that (3.13) holds to verify that it does not pay to deviate at any point in the punishment phase. A similar argument shows that it is enough to check a deviation in a single period, as opposed to repeated deviations for a finite or infinite number of periods.

wage strategy in (3.7) is indeed sequentially rational, since the private sector's expectations are fulfilled even out of equilibrium. We can view (3.12) as the Nash condition, and (3.13) as the condition imposing sequential rationality.

3.3.2. Properties of Equilibrium

Making use of (3.9)–(3.11), conditions (3.12) and (3.13) can be simplified to:

$$\delta(1 - \delta^I)/(1 - \delta) \geqslant (1 - \gamma)^2/(\varphi^2 - \gamma^2) \qquad (3.12)'$$

$$\delta^I \geqslant (1 - \varphi)^2/(\varphi^2 - \gamma^2). \qquad (3.13)'$$

It is easy to obtain four results from these two inequalities: (i) An infinitely long 'punishment period' ($I \to \infty$) can only be an equilibrium if $\varphi = 1$; that is, only if wages are set as in the one-shot Nash equilibrium after a deviation. Intuitively, a government is willing to participate in a harsh punishment only for a finite time period. But if $I < \infty$, then $\varphi > 1$ can be part of an equilibrium, even though it involves a phase in which the government is worse off than in the one-shot Nash; (ii) If the punishment lasts only one period ($I = 1$), then the zero inflation equilibrium ($\gamma = 0$) can only be enforced if $\varphi > 1$ (since for $I = 1$ (3.12)' reduces to $\varphi \geqslant \sqrt{1/\delta}$). For I sufficiently large, on the other hand, $\gamma = 0$ can be enforced even if $\varphi = 1$; (iii) The higher the discount factor δ, the lower the critical values of φ and I; (iv) There are many combinations of the three parameters φ, δ and I that are consistent with the zero inflation equilibrium.

Even though the results are model specific, they suggest some general principles: The reputational forces are stronger the larger is the upward revision of inflationary expectations after a deviation from low inflation, and the longer the loss of confidence lasts. Both serve to raise the cost of future inflation relative to the benefits of current employment, as does, of course, a higher government concern for the future.

We wanted to show that a zero inflation equilibrium could be enforced through reputation. In a sense, we overachieved our goal. The zero inflation equilibrium can indeed be enforced with appropriate values for φ, I and δ in (3.12)' and (3.13)'. But, given δ, the combinations of φ and I that can enforce the zero inflation equilibrium form a continuum. Moreover, other combinations of φ, I and δ can enforce equilibria with any other inflation rate. This is particularly disturbing, because φ and I—like γ but unlike δ—are choice variables in the game, not exogenous parameters. To argue that a particular equilibrium is reached, one therefore has to argue that the government and all the private agents coordinate on one particular combination of φ, γ and I that satisfies (3.12)' and (3.13)'. This seems a formidable task. Moreover, even if this paramount coordination problem were solved, the multiplicity of equilibria seriously reduces the predictive contents of the theory. We return to these difficult issues in Section 3.5.

3.4. Reputation and uncertainty

So far this Section has abstracted from uncertainty, which was a big issue in Section 2. Suppose we returned to the model with supply shocks of that section. How would that alter our results on reputational incentives in monetary policy? The general answer is that reputational equilibria are still possible. But the nature of these equilibria depends on how well private agents can monitor the information available to the government and its policy instruments. We discuss two alternative cases below. A formal analysis of reputational equilibria under uncertainty very quickly becomes non-trivial, however. We shall therefore keep the discussion at an intuitive and non-formal level.

3.4.1. *Perfect Monitoring*
Consider the model of Section 2, with supply shocks and a quadratic objective over employment, so that the benefits of employment stabilization vary with the realization of the supply shock. But let the interaction between private agents and the government occur over an infinite horizon. In each period the timing is the same as in the discretionary regime of Section 2: Wages at t (and hence π_t^e) are determined before observing policy π_t and the supply shock ϵ_t, but after observing ϵ_{t-1} and π_{t-1} perfectly. (Wage setters could either observe ϵ_{t-1} directly or infer it by observing employment x_{t-1}.) Policy is set after observing the current supply shock, ϵ_t.

Thus the aggregate history at t includes the sequence of supply shocks up to period $t - 1$. A trigger strategy for wages (like 3.7) above) could be made conditional not only on previous policy, but also on previous supply shocks. In principle, we can then find trigger strategies that support state-contingent policy rules with lower expected inflation than in the one-shot discretionary policy game. However, we conjecture that the equilibrium policy rule under commitment—given in

(2.4)—could *not* be supported in a reputational equilibrium, except if the suport of the distribution of the supply shock is bounded and sufficient small.[39] Suppose wage setters had a trigger strategy for wage setting of the same type as (3.7). That is, they set wages on the basis of zero expected inflation as long as the government does not defect from the rule in (2.4), but after observing a defection they set wages based on expectations corresponding to the discretionary equilibrium policy rule in (2.8) for the next I periods. Superficially, this looks exactly like the situation in Section 3.3. But there is one important difference. In the case without shocks the temptation to deviate from the rule is constant across time periods, as is the enforcement. In the case with supply shocks, the enforcement would still be constant over time (as long as the shocks were serially uncorrelated), since it would be based on expected future outcomes. The temptation to deviate from the rule would not be constant, however; it would depend on the realization of the supply shocks. Indeed if the support for the distribution of ϵ_t was unbounded, the temptation could be very large in certain periods. Hence, in periods with large shocks the reputational force could be insufficient to prevent deviations from the equilibrium policy rule under commitment.

The above discussion suggests that perhaps the best one could hope for is a reputational equilibrium where the policymaker sticks to a rule with low expected inflation in normal times (when shocks are small) but acts in a discretionary manner in abnormal times (when shocks are large). This sounds very much like the rule with an escape clause that we discussed in Section 2. Thus, our conjecture is that such rules might be supported as trigger strategy equilibria; whereas fully state-contingent rules like (2.4) would not. In such an equilibrium we would observe temporary episodes of high unexpected inflation in the face of large shocks. These episodes could not be punished by a subsequent reversion to high expected inflation. Since wage setters can perfectly monitor the realization of the shock, they don't feel 'cheated' when the government invokes the implicit escape clause. Empirical episodes of devaluations for countries under a fixed exchange rate regime may be investigated along these lines.

[39] Our conjecture and the discussion in this subsection is based on Rotemberg and Saloner [120]. Canzoneri and Henderson [34] and de Kock and Grilli [46] applied their results to international coordination in monetary policy.

3.4.2. *Imperfect Monitoring*

The wage strategies discussed in Sections 3.3 and 3.4.1 are all contingent on the aggregate history observable to all private agents. However, if the policy rule was contingent on variables *not* perfectly observable by the private sector, trigger strategies of this kind are no longer operational: Wage setters can no longer tell with certainty whether the government cheated in the past or not. In this case, private agents are said to have imperfect information. Is there any role for reputation in this context?[40]

To answer this question, suppose that the government still observes ϵ_t in period t, but private agents do not observe ϵ_t even in period t + 1 or later. (For this to happen, either there has to be an additional source of uncertainty or the private sector cannot observe employment x_t and infer ϵ_t indirectly). As before, the wage in period t is chosen not knowing the policy in that period, but having observed the policy in the previous period. These information assumptions are quite plausible. In the real world, the government process for elaborating its information is often judgemental. The government forecasts about the future state of the economy are therefore private information of the policymaker, even if the government and the private sector have access to the same sources of information.

In this setup, (perfect) observation of previous supply shocks do not enter the aggregate history observable to private agents. Hence, trigger strategies like those discussed in Section 3.4.1 are no longer possible. Consider, however, a trigger strategy conditional on something that private agents can observe, namely previous government policies. Specifically, suppose that wages are set on the basis of zero expected inflation, until an episode of particularly high inflation—say inflation above some number $\bar{\pi}$—is observed in the previous period. After observing inflation above $\bar{\pi}$, wages and expected inflation go to the level associated with the one-period discretionary equilibrium for the next I periods. One can show that this kind of trigger strategy can support an equilibrium policy rule with low inflation in normal times but high inflation after abnormal times.

This points to a difference between equilibria with perfect and

---

[40] Our discussion in this subsection is inspired by the paper on price wars in oligopoly by Green and Porter [67]. Canzoneri [33] applies the Green–Porter model to reputation in monetary policy, using a model similar to ours.

imperfect monitoring. With perfect monitoring, a large adverse supply shock is met with high unexpected inflation but no subsequent 'punishment' phase. With imperfect monitoring, on the other hand, a large adverse shock is followed by a sequence of high actual and expected inflation. This is because the imperfect monitoring gives the government an incentive to blame high inflation on unfortunate (but unobservable) shocks. The inflationary episodes are necessary to induce the government to continue implementing the equilibrium policy rule in the future, even if the government never actually cheats in equilibrium. These 'punishment periods' with high inflation make the equilibrium inflation rate serially correlated, even if the shocks in the economy were serially uncorrelated.

Of course, the multiplicity issue and the associated coordination problems that we discussed under certainty apply here, too. If anything they seem more serious, since all agents have to coordinate on strategies that support complicated state-contingent outcomes. This coordination problem is one of the issues we take up in the next section.

3.5. Discussion

In the introduction to this section, we asked whether reputation can substitute for commitments in sustaining an equilibrium with low inflation. Our answer has been: No, if the policymaker interacts with the private sector over a finite horizon (except in the special case mentioned in Footnote 36); Yes, maybe, if the policymaker interacts with the private sector over an (effectively) infinite horizon. But in the latter case, the results point to some difficulties in this approach to modelling reputation. We now turn to a discussion of these difficulties.

3.5.1. *Too Many Equilibria*
The first difficulty is the multiplicity of equilibria that we have already mentioned several times. Multiplicity raises two problems. First, there is the problem of how the government and all private agents can coordinate on one of these many equilibria.[41] Second, the theory has

---

[41] In his survey of reputational models of monetary policy Rogoff [116] provides an extensive and insightful discussion of this coordination problem. As we have noted, the reputation models 'substitute a coordination problem for a cooperation problem'. It may be argued that the coordination problem would be less severe if we replaced the anonymity assumption with the hypothesis that wages are set by a centralized trade

very little predictive content if we cannot single out a particular equilibrium with well-defined characteristics. Thus a satisfactory positive theory of monetary policy and reputation would somehow have to drastically narrow down the class of equilibria.

Multiplicity of equilibria is something that plagues all application of game theory.[42] The game theory literature seems to be going in two somewhat different directions in trying to resolve the multiplicity issue: One is the approach of 'equilibrium refinements', the other is the approach of 'equilibrium selection'. Both approaches have the same goal, namely to predict a unique equilibrium point that the players will choose. The distinction between the two approaches is therefore quite subtle, but we believe it lies in a different conception of what beliefs are relevant.

The theory of equilibrium refinements basically tries to narrow down the number of equilibria by imposing stricter equilibrium conditions. A set of strategies is 'strategically stable' (or self-enforcing) if, in any actual play of the game, no player can increase his payoffs by unilaterally changing his strategy. The theory of equilibrium refinements studies the beliefs of a rational player about the consequences of a unilateral deviation from the candidate equilibrium. The player's beliefs concern the responses of the other players to his deviation, but not the candidate equilibrium, which is taken as given. By imposing stricter individual rationality requirements, the theory of equilibrium refinements hopes to single out a unique 'strategically stable' equilibrium that rational players would implement. The requirement of 'sequential rationality' is an example of a refinement (of Nash equilibrium). We saw that sequential rationality was successful when the horizon was finite, but not when the horizon was infinite. In the next section, we will illustrate other refinements that can successfully reduce the number of equilibria in finite horizon games of incomplete information, and discuss the notion of sequential rationality in these games.

The theory of equilibrium selection basically recognizes that there

---

union. However, this argument is not persuasive. If the private sector is non-atomistic, the government can play trigger strategies too, contingent on the nominal wage. As shown in Carraro [35], this would open the door to additional equilibria (in particular, to equilibria in which inflation is zero and yet employment is above the natural rate).

[42] Our comments in this and the following paragraphs are largely provoked by some insightful comments by John van Huyck on an earlier draft.

are many possible equilibria and analyzes how the players in the game will select one of them. Here, the focus is on how rational players behave in a situation of 'strategic uncertainty'; that is, when they do not know which equilibrium strategies their opponents will choose. Thus, the players' beliefs do not take a particular candidate equilibrium as given, but also concern the selection criteria of their opponents. One (yet unformalized) example of selection criteria is the theory of 'focal points'.[43] This theory argues that for some reason—that sometimes may be thought of as 'culture' or 'social custom'—one particular equilibrium is more 'natural' than the other ones and that the players therefore will select it. In the context of our model of monetary policy it could be argued—and has been argued—that the zero inflation equilibrium is a natural 'focal point' of the game, and the best candidate amongst the several equilibria. Therefore, the argument goes, the government can announce the zero-inflation equilibrium and credibly coordinate the strategies of private agents. Counter to this, one may argue that there is nothing special about zero. But leaving that issue aside, the argument is still not persuasive, at least if we insist on sequential rationality. The reputational equilibria in Section 3.3 also rely heavily on the 'punishment phase', when wage setters revise their inflationary expectations upwards. How do wage setters coordinate on a choice of φ, γ and I? Clearly no focal point exists here.

Another example of a selection criterion is what game theorists refer to as 'renegotiation proofness'. This criterion basically requires equilibrium strategies to yield a Pareto-optimal outcome at all nodes of the game tree, particularly at nodes following off-equilibrium events. One can show that the reputation mechanism described in the previous sections is not renegotiation-proof. Thus, in our monetary policy model, renegotiation proofness picks out the discretionary equilibrium of the one-shot game as a unique equilibrium, even with an infinite horizon.[44]

---

[43] The classical book by Schelling [121] first launches the idea about focal points.

[44] Matsuyama [93] discusses the application of renegotiation proofness to this monetary policy model in more detail. He shows that the definition of renegotiation proofness proposed by Farell and Maskin [52] indeed picks out the one-shot discretionary equilibrium as the unique equilibrium of the infinitely repeated game. But he also considers another — perhaps less plausible — definition of renegotiation proofness proposed by Pearce [100]. Applying this alternative definition of renegotiation proofness to the same monetary policy model leads to drastically different results.

3.5.2. Reputation and Credibility

The multiplicity problem is not just a technical problem. In a sense, it reflects a difficulty with the whole idea that reputation can be modelled in a setting of complete information. If agents have complete information, why should they revíse their expectations of inflation upwards after a policy surprise? Thinking about equilibrium selection suggests a tentative answer to this question. Upon observing an inflationary policy, private agents may conclude that the economy is converging to another (high inflation) equilibrium. In other words, the trigger-strategies in (3.8) can be interpreted as a revision of private beliefs about the selection criteria of the government.

Nevertheless, this interpretation is not without difficulties. First of all, the theory of equilibrium selection is still very much in its infancy. And however attractive it would be to have such a theory, we believe that the literature is far from the stage where we can deduce robust conclusions in particular applications.[45] Second, and perhaps more important, the specific form of the trigger strategy in (3.8) is difficult to reconcile with this interpretation. According to (3.8), any policy surprise, not just unexpected inflation, yields an upward revision of expectations. This property of the equilibrium, though non-sensical, is crucial to ensure that the equilibrium is sequentially rational. Moreover, this property makes it impossible to discuss how a policy-maker, who does not yet have a reputation for fighting inflation, can *acquire* it. To analyze how a reputation can be acquired we have to go to a setup with explicit uncertainty and learning about the policy-maker's type. In the next section we will do precisely that by leaving the complete information model for a model with incomplete information.

Let us end by discussing what we have learned about another question: What should we mean by credibility of government policy? In Section 2 we identified credibility in a one-shot game with the Nash equilibrium condition. A major theme of this section has been that the Nash equilibrium condition may be too weak in a multiperiod setting. In more familiar macroeconomic terms, Nash equilibria are perfect foresight (rational expectations) equilibria, in the sense that expectations are self-fulfilling in equilibrium. If one were content with

---

[45] See Harsyani and Selten [74] for a recent attempt to construct a general theory of equilibrium selection. Van Huyck, Battalio and Beil [135] provide experimental evidence on equilibrium selection.

assuming a backward-looking rule of thumb for expectations formation, the fact that expectations are not falsified may be considered sufficient. But if one takes seriously the idea that private agents are rational and have complete information of the government objective for policy, then the Nash concept runs into trouble in a multiperiod setting. Moreover, from a practical point of view, a theory based on Nash equilibria has very low predictive power because it allows such a plethora of equilibria.

We have argued that a more plausible requirement in a multiperiod framework is to impose sequential rationality. Namely, the requirement that the equilibrium satisfies the Nash condition subsequent to all possible aggregate histories. Sequentially rational equilibria are perfect foresight (rational expectations) equilibria in the wider sense that expectations are correct also outside of equilibrium. But as we claimed in discussing the multiplicity of equilibria under an infinite horizon, even this requirement may be insufficient to nail down a satisfactory equilibrium. Moreover, sequential rationality is very difficult to reconcile with some recent evidence from experiments.

Perhaps a general lesson to take away from this section is that there is no unique notion of credibility. The appropriate definition of credibility (or time consistency) depends on the economic context. This conclusion is further reinforced by the results presented in the next section.

Unfortunately, this ambiguity of what is meant by credibility is reflected in the several different definitions that have been offered in the literature. The original articles by Kydland and Prescott and by Calvo do not define time consistency with reference to explicit game theoretic notions. Hence, their definitions are not widely applicable. In a multiperiod context, researchers—to the extent that they have tried to be precise about the underlying game theory—have generally identified credibility with subgame perfection. However, as we noted in Section 3.2, a policy game is typically anonymous. In such a game, a proper subgame is not well defined, and hence subgame perfection does not strictly apply: Our definition of sequential rationality is really the analog of subgame perfection in anonymous games of this kind. What we defined as a sequentially rational Nash equilibrium is a special case of Perfect Bayesian equilibrium. We discuss this equilibrium concept, as well as some of its refinements, more extensively in the next section.

3.6. Notes on the literature

The game theoretic literature discussed in this section is presented and surveyed in more detail in Friedman [57] and Tirole [133]. Other relevant surveys that discuss the industrial organizations applications of this literature, are Shapiro [122] and Fudenberg and Tirole [61]. The model of reputation in this section was applied to monetary policy for the first time by Barro and Gordon [23]. Reputation with imperfect monitoring in this monetary policy model is studied in Canzoneri [33]. Rogoff [116] surveys the literature on reputation in monetary policy and extensively discusses the multiplicity problem. Chari and Kehoe [36] and Chari, Prescott and Kehoe [37] point out that policy games are typically anonymous, and further discuss the notion of sequential rationality in such games.

The model of reputation we have dealt with has been extensively used in the macroeconomic policy literature. Grossman and van Huyck [69] and Barro [20] apply it to the choice of the inflation tax. Grossman and van Huyck [70] analyze the external debt repayment policies of a small open economy in a stochastic setting with perfect monitoring. Atkeson [13], in a similar setup, allows for imperfect monitoring, following the approach pioneered in Abreu, Pierce and Stacchetti [1]. Finally, Levine [86] extends the reputation model of this section to a simple dynamic framework.

4. REPUTATION AND SIGNALLING

4.1. Introduction

In this section we relax the assumption that private agents have complete information about the policymaker. There are several reasons for investigating what happens in situations of incomplete information. An obvious reason is that even though some countries have independent central banks with a long history, individual policymakers who shape monetary policy have finite incumbencies. Therefore, private agents may be uncertain about the preferences over policy outcomes of a newly appointed policymaker. Furthermore, in some countries central banks are not independent, but very much influenced by the current government. The weights in the inflation-employment trade-off of a newly elected government may also be uncertain to the private sector. Or, more generally, there might be incomplete information about the government's attitudes and its bargaining position vis-à-vis the different interest groups lobbying for different policies. In these cases it is realistic to assume that private agents do not have perfect information about the new government when it takes office. As policy is observed over time, however, the private sector gradually gathers information and learns about the actual priorities in policymaking.

Such private learning motivates a second approach to modelling reputation in monetary policy. In our view, the resulting model of reputation is richer and more relevant than that of Section 3. As in the previous section, the basic idea is that surprise inflation in the current period generates higher expected inflation in the future through a loss of government reputation. In contrast to the previous section, however, the expectations of the private sector now reflect learning in a situation of genuine uncertainty about the policymaker's 'type'. Different policymakers have different weights in the inflation-employment trade-off, which is a crude but simple way of capturing the idea that different policymakers have different objectives.

Quite apart from developing a good theory of reputation in monetary policy, there is an additional reason to study models in which the private sector is uncertain about the policymaker's type. Such models can be seen as an attempt to analyze 'changes in the policy regime,' and the consequences of such changes for private behavior, as well as the feedback of private behavior on government incentives.

Which beliefs are rational, and how rational individuals revise their beliefs as they observe policy are two key issues. The analysis of these issues makes the reputation models in this section easier to interpret and perhaps more appealing from an economic point of view than the models in Section 3. The approach also raises new and difficult conceptual issues, even when the time horizon is finite. Throughout the section we therefore use a model in which the government and the private sector interact over a finite horizon.

Consider a two-period version of our simple deterministic model of monetary policy. We denote the two periods as 1 and 2. The two-period horizon can be interpreted as the incumbency of a newly appointed policymaker. The private sector is atomistic and its behavior is described by the usual Phillips curve, equation (1.1). The government minimizes the discounted sum in (3.1), where the single period loss function is linear in employment as in (3.2).

A central assumption in the section is that when the policymaker enters office and the game begins, wage setters do not know the true value of the weight λ in the government loss function, (3.2). The government can be one of two types: 'tough', with $\lambda = \underline{\lambda}$; or 'weak', with $\lambda = \bar{\lambda} > \underline{\lambda}$. That is, a tough type assigns a greater relative weight to inflation than a weak type. At the start of the game the private sector assigns a prior probability q_1 to the event that the government is tough ($\lambda = \underline{\lambda}$), and $(1 - q_1)$ to the complementary event that the government is weak ($\lambda = \bar{\lambda}$).[46] This initial prior is common to all private agents, and is common knowledge amongst all the players in the game (including the government).[47] Naturally, the government knows its own type. Thus, the game is one of incomplete information (see Footnote 28 in Section 3).

In this framework, monetary policy signals government preferences. By observing policy in period 1, wage setters can learn something about the true value of λ. We assume that private prior beliefs, q_1, are revised according to Bayes' rule. Period 2 nominal wages are then set on the basis of the posterior beliefs, q_2.

The equilibrium in this model is a set of strategies and posterior beliefs that satisfy the following three intuitive conditions: (i) In every period, the wage strategy of each wage setter is optimal, given his beliefs in that period, given the equilibrium policy rules and given the other equilibrium wage strategies. (ii) In every period, the policy rule is optimal for the government, given its type and given the equilibrium wage strategies of the private sector. (iii) Given the equilibrium policy rules followed by the two types of government, the posterior beliefs of the private sector are derived from the prior and the observation of government policy in period 1. The derivation is based on Bayes' rule, when it applies. An equilibrium satisfying these three conditions is called a *Perfect bayesian equilibrium*.

---

[46] We think of these initial beliefs as an objective parameter that reflect, say, the previously observed frequency of non-inflationary governments or other relevant historical information. Thus, the information the private sector has about the government's type beforehand leads to a unique value for q_1. If q_1 were not a parameter but an arbitary belief, there would be a large number of equilibria.

[47] A statement is 'common knowledge' if all the players in the game know that this statement is true, everybody knows that everyone else knows, and so on *ad infinitum* (see Aumann [16] for a precise definition of this notion).

Does this equilibrium concept incorporate the sequential rationality requirement from the previous section? The answer is ambiguous. Yes, in the sense that the wage strategies must be optimal for any beliefs, given these beliefs. No, in the sense that the equilibrium concept specifies how to 'rationally' revise these beliefs only along the equilibrium path. Off-equilibrium events have a zero prior probability of occuring, and thus Bayes' rule does not pin down posterior beliefs outside of equilibrium. This is why we include the qualifier 'when it applies' in condition (iii). Any posterior belief is admissible subsequent to a non-equilibrium history, according to this condition. Hence, the equilibrium concept is incomplete: It leaves room for arbitrary *beliefs* off the equilibrium path, in the same way as the Nash equilibrium without the sequential rationality condition leaves room for arbitrary *actions* off the equilibrium path. Several equilibrium refinements have been proposed in the literature to cope with this problem. Some of them are discussed in Section 4.3 below.

According to condition (ii) in our equilibrium definition, the government takes into account the effect of its current policy on wage setters' future beliefs, and hence on future expected inflation. This is the source of the reputational effects in this model. Any government would like to establish a reputation of being tough, so as to reduce expected inflation in period 2. One central question in this section is whether these incentives are strong enough to sustain an equilibrium with low inflation in period 1. Section 4.2 studies the incentives of the weak type to mimic the tough type. Section 4.3 emphasizes the incentives of the tough type to signal its identity. And Section 4.4 discusses what we have learned.

4.2. Mimicking

Throughout this section we assume that $\lambda = 0$. This implies that the tough government type always plays $\pi_t = 0$ in every period, irrespective of private beliefs.[48] Hence, only the weak type has an active strategic role.[49]

---

[48] In this case, the two government types can be interpreted as reflecting two different institutional environments (rather than two possible governments with different preferences over inflation and employment). Specifically, we can think of the following situation. A government with true preferences $\lambda = \bar{\lambda}$ announces beforehand that it will

4.2.1. *Private Learning*

Let $\tilde{\rho}_t = \text{Prob}(\pi_t = 0 : \lambda = \bar{\lambda})$ be the period-t probability assigned by the private sector to the event that the weak type tries to masquerade as being tough by playing zero inflation. (We show below when he has an incentive to do so.) If the weak type does not masquerade as being tough, we shall find that he is going to carry out his one-shot optimum policy, which we know is given by $\pi = \bar{\lambda}$. Recall that $q_1 = \text{Prob}(\lambda = 0: t = 1)$ denotes the (exogenous) private prior beliefs at time 1.

If the private sector observes the policy $\pi_1 = 0$ or $\pi_1 = \bar{\lambda}$, Bayes' rule suggests how to rationally update these prior beliefs. In these cases, Bayes' rule says

$$q_2 = \text{Prob}(\lambda = 0: \pi_1) = \frac{q_1 \, \text{Prob}(\pi_1 : \lambda = 0)}{\text{Prob}(\pi_1)}. \tag{4.1}$$

The posterior probability is given by the prior multiplied by the conditional probability to observe the policy π_1 given that the government is tough ($\lambda = 0$), divided by the unconditional probability to observe the policy π_1. Clearly, if the policy $\pi_1 = \bar{\lambda}$ is observed, (4.1) gives

$$q_2 = \frac{q_1 0}{(1 - q_1)(1 - \tilde{\rho}_1)} = 0, \tag{4.2a}$$

since the tough type would choose $\pi_1 = \lambda$ with probability 0. But if zero inflation is observed, (4.1) gives

$$q_2 = \frac{q_1}{q_1 + (1 - q_1)\tilde{\rho}_1}, \tag{4.2b}$$

since the tough type chooses zero inflation with probability 1 and the weak type chooses it with probability $\tilde{\rho}_1$. In equilibrium $\tilde{\rho}_1$ must be

---

play $\pi_t = 0$ in each period. Deviating from the announced policy imposes a fixed cost in each period. But the private sector does not know how large this cost is. For a tough government, the cost in prohibitive; hence the announcement is binding and the government is forced to behave as if $\lambda = 0$. For a weak government the cost is negligible, and the government is free to behave according to its true preferences, $\lambda = \bar{\lambda}$.

[49] Our model in this section can be seen as a two-period version of the multi-period model of strategic entry deterrence in Kreps and Wilson [83]. The first application of Kreps's and Wilson's analysis to monetary policy was formulated independently by Backus and Driffill [17], Stella [125], and Tabellini [126].

equal to the true probability ρ_1 chosen by a weak government in period 1. In the next subsection, the optimal value of ρ_1 is derived by solving the weak government's decision problem in period 1, taking $\tilde{\rho}_1$ in (4.2) as given.

If some policy other than $\pi_1 = 0$ or $\pi_1 = \bar{\lambda}$ is observed, Bayes' law does not apply. This is because other inflation rates are off-equilibrium events that have zero probability. Our equilibrium concept does not give any guidance on how beliefs should be revised here. But since the tough type always set inflation at zero, we shall make the natural assumption that private agents set $q_2 = 0$, if they observe a π_1 different from 0 or $\bar{\lambda}$. (In the more general setup of Section 4.3, it is more difficult to resolve how beliefs are revised in the face of off-equilibrium events.)

Our assumption about off-equilibrium beliefs together with (4.2) can be combined with the equilibrium requirement $\tilde{\rho}_1 = \rho_1$ to obtain a complete description of the private learning process:

$$q_2 = 0 \quad \text{if } \pi \neq 0$$
$$q_2 = q_1/(q_1 + (1 - q_1)\rho_1) \quad \text{if } \pi = 0. \tag{4.3}$$

The private beliefs q_2 are a sufficient statistic for the aggregate history of the game in period 1. Furthermore, they provide a natural measure of government reputation. If a positive inflation rate is observed in period 0, then the reputation of being tough is destroyed and $q_2 = 0$. If, on the other hand, zero inflation is observed, then the government could really be tough; or it could simply pretend to be so in order to maintain or enhance its reputation. The appropriate inference is then described by the second line in (4.3).

4.2.2. Temptation and Enforcement

With the learning process in (4.3), it is clear that if a weak type considers inflating at all, the optimal inflation rate is $\pi = \bar{\lambda}$. By inflating the weak government reveals its true identity anyway, and then the best policy is the short run optimal inflation rate from equation (3.3). Hence, the weak type either plays $\pi_t = 0$ (with probability ρ_t), or $\pi_t = \bar{\lambda}$ (with probability $(1 - \rho_t)$). It follows that expected inflation is:

$$\pi_t^e = (1 - q_t)(1 - \rho_t)\bar{\lambda}. \tag{4.4}$$

Equation (4.4) illustrates clearly that a higher government reputation (a higher value of q_t) reduces expected inflation. This is the source of the government reputational incentives.

In the last period (period 2), the weak government has no incentive to maintain its reputation. Hence it always plays $\pi_2 = \bar{\lambda}$. Thus, $\rho_2 = 0$ and $\pi_2^c = (1 - q_2)\bar{\lambda}$. Employment in the last period is thus $(\pi_2 - \pi_2^c) = q_2\bar{\lambda}$, so the weak government loss is:

$$L(\bar{\lambda}, q_2\bar{\lambda}) = \bar{\lambda}^2(1/2 - q_2) = V(q_2), \qquad (4.5)$$

where we have expressed the government loss as a function of q_2 to emphasize that the equilibrium loss for the weak government is a function of its reputation. Not surprisingly, the derivative $V_q(q_2) = -\bar{\lambda}^2$ is negative: The higher is government reputation, the lower is expected inflation; hence the higher is employment and the smaller is the loss.

Next, consider period 1. Now, the weak government trades short-term benefits of unexpected inflation against long-term costs of losing its reputation. Figure 4.1 illustrates how the government evaluates these benefits and costs, for given inflationary expectations π_1^c. If the government plays the short-run optimal inflation rate $\pi_1 = \bar{\lambda}$, then (by

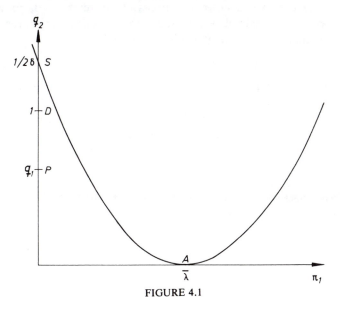

FIGURE 4.1

(4.3)) its reputation is completely destroyed: $q_2 = 0$. This leaves the weak government at point A. The U-shaped indifference curve depicts all the combinations of π_1 and q_2 that give the same overall loss as point A.[50] Because a higher reputation reduces the government loss, any point above the indifference curve is preferred to A, but A is preferred to any point below the curve.

Recall that the loss function L is linear in employment. Therefore expected inflation in period 1, π_1^e, does not affect the shape of the indifference curve (even though it determines its vertical position). Moreover, the indifference curve is flat at point A, because the current marginal gain of higher unexpected inflation is zero when $\pi_1 = \bar{\lambda}$. To the left of point A, the marginal gain is positive, and so the indifference curve is downward sloping. The opposite is true to the right of point A. Finally, it can be shown that $q_2 = 1/2\delta$ at point S, where the indifference curve intersects the vertical axis. The position of point S relative to point D (where $q_2 = 1$) and P (where $q_2 = q_1$) plays a central role in the next subsection, in characterizing the equilibrium. Here point S is drawn above D, but this need not always hold.[51]

This trade-off between the short-run benefits of inflation and the long-run costs of losing the reputation can also be expressed algebraically, using the concepts of temptation and enforcement. By running the short-run optimal policy in period 1, the weak government reduces its loss compared to a policy of zero inflation by:

$$L(\bar{\lambda}, (\bar{\lambda} - \pi_1^e)) - L(0, - \pi_1^e) = - \bar{\lambda}^2/2. \qquad (4.6)$$

This is exactly the same expression as the temptation in Section 3, and the economic considerations involved are also the same. Against this current benefit, the government has to balance the future cost of losing its reputation. Using (4.5), this cost can be written as:

$$\delta[V(0) - V(q_2)] = \delta\bar{\lambda}^2 q_2. \qquad (4.7)$$

This loss plays the same role as the enforcement described in Section 3. However, here it is due to a genuine change of beliefs rather than to an artificial 'punishment' by wage setters.

---

[50] Combining (4.3), (4.5), and the weak government's first period loss, the equation of the indifference curve is: $L(\pi_1, \pi_1 - \pi_1^e) + \delta V(q_2) = L(\bar{\lambda}, \bar{\lambda} - \pi_1^e) + \delta V(0)$.

4.2.3. *Equilibrium Policy*

The equilibrium policy in period 1 is obtained by comparing (4.6) and (4.7). Three cases can be distinguished, and the case which will occur depends on the parameter values:

(a) If $\delta < 1/2$, the reputational incentives are not strong enough, and the weak government chooses the discretionary equilibrium policy $\pi_1 = \bar{\lambda}$ with certainty. This equilibrium is called *separating*, since the two types separate out and policy in period 1 is fully revealing. To confirm that $\pi_1 = \bar{\lambda}$ is an equilibrium, consider whether the weak type has any incentive to deviate. In this equilibrium, wage setters expect $\rho_1 = 0$. Hence, a deviation of the weak government (playing $\pi_1 = 0$) would lead the wage setters to infer that they face a tough type: According to (4.3), $q_2 = 1$ if $\pi_1 = 0$ is observed (since $\rho_1 = 0$). In terms of Figure 4.1, a deviation would put the government at point D. But if $\delta < 1/2$, D lies below the indifference curve (since S is above D). Hence, it does not pay to deviate and $\pi_1 = \bar{\lambda}$ is indeed the equilibrium policy for the weak government. This graphic argument can be confirmed by comparing (4.7) and (4.6) at the point $q_2 = 1$: The temptation exceeds the enforcement even if reputation is maximal. In this separating equilibrium, there is surprise inflation in period 1 (recall from (4.4) that $\pi_1^e = (1 - q_1)\bar{\lambda} < \bar{\lambda}$ here) and fully anticipated inflation in period 2 if the government is weak. But there is surprise deflation in period 1 and fully anticipated zero inflation in period 2 if the government is tough.

(b) If $\delta > 1/2q_1$, the reputational incentives are strong enough to sustain $\pi_1 = 0$ with certainty. This equilibrium is called *pooling*, because both types play zero inflation; the observed policy thus does not convey any information about the identity of the government. To confirm that this is an equilibrium, consider whether it pays for the weak type to deviate. Here wage setters expect $\rho_1 = 1$. The equilibrium policy $\pi_1 = 0$ does not add anything to the government reputation. From (4.3), $q_2 = q_1$ if $\pi_1 = 0$ is observed and $\rho_1 = 1$. In terms of Figure 4.1, the weak government is at point P in this pooling equilibrium. A deviation, which destroys the reputation, takes the weak type to point A. But when $\delta > 1/2q_1$, P lies above the indifference curve through A (since S lies below P) and it does not pay to deviate by creating unexpected inflation. Again, the graphical argument can be confirmed by replacing q_2 with q_1 in (4.7) and comparing the resulting expression with (4.6). Then one sees that the temptation is smaller than the enforcement, which makes it optimal to mimic the tough type. In this pooling equilibrium there is zero actual and anticipated inflation in period 1 whatever the identity of the actual government. Since the identity of the government is not revealed, period 2 has a positive inflation surprise if the government is weak, and a negative surprise if the government is tough.

(c) Finally, if $1/2 \leqslant \delta \leqslant 1/2q_1$, the weak type chooses a mixed strategy: It sets $\pi_1 = 0$ with probability ρ_1 and $\pi_1 = \bar{\lambda}$ with probability $(1 - \rho_1)$. This equilibrium is called *semi-separating*, since a policy of zero inflation is not fully revealing (even though it contains some information). The equilibrium probability ρ_1 is such that the weak type is indifferent between inflating and not inflating (that is, it equates (4.6) and (4.7)).[52] In terms of Figure 4.1, this equilibrium occurs if S falls in between D and P. The mixed strategy is chosen so that q_2 takes the value corresponding to point S if $\pi_1 = 0$ is observed.

4.2.4. *General Comments*

These equilibria illustrate that reputation can sustain low-inflation monetary policy, even in a finite-horizon setup. This is more likely to happen the higher is a new government's reputation when it enters office at the start of the game (the larger is q_1), and the lower is its discount rate (the higher is δ). Moreover, given the parameter values and the initial beliefs, the equilibrium is unique.[53]

It is interesting to note how private expectations are formed in these equilibria. The inflationary expectations reflected in nominal wages are indeed rational in the traditional sense: They are unbiased forecasts of inflation given the information available when wages are set. But the uncertainty about government types leads to a 'peso problem' in expectations formation at some point along each of the equilibrium paths.[54] Furthermore the peso problem has real effects. In the pooling

---

[51] The indifference curves of the tough type could also be drawn in Figure 4.1. They would be vertical straight lines (since employment and thus expected inflation receive zero weight). Hence, for the tough government, the vertical axis coincides with the indifference curve corresponding to the minimum loss.

[52] Inserting (4.3) in (4.7) and equating the resulting expression with (4.6), we obtain that ρ_1 must satisfy: $\rho_1 = q_1(2\delta - 1)/(1 - q_1)$.

[53] The multiplicity may reappear, however, if the government loss function $L(\cdot)$ is non-linear in employment.

[54] The 'peso problem' refers to a situation when there is positive probability for a discrete policy shift to occur in a particular period of time. Rational expectations may

equilibrium, the peso problem arises in period 2. The private sector has learned nothing from observing policy in period 1 and sets wages based on expectations $\pi_2^e = (1 - q_1)\bar{\lambda}$. If the government is weak, there is surprise inflation and employment above the natural rate, while there is surprise deflation and employment below the natural rate if the government is tough. In the separating equilibrium, the peso problem arises in period 1, when wage setting is based on $\pi_1^e = (1 - q_1)\bar{\lambda}$. Here too, there is surprise inflation with a weak government and surprise deflation with a tough government. But in this case the private sector learns the government's true type from observing policy in period 1, so the economy is in a perfect foresight equilibrium in period 2.

An extension to more than two periods is not difficult. In such a model the phase when the weak policymaker chooses a mixed strategy may typically last several periods. This has led some commentators to argue that the reputational model is not satisfactory. Mixed strategy equilibria are not very plausible, particularly in the case of economic policy: By construction, the government has no clear incentive to select the unique probability assignment for the mixed strategy which is consistent with equilibrium. However, it is easy to change the model slightly so as to get rid of the mixed strategy equilibrium—by having a continuum of government types, or by modeling the private sector as a non-atomistic player who moves before the government.[55]

A more forceful criticism of the model is that only one government type, the weak government, acts strategically. A tough government that cared about employment, however little, would realize that wage setters perceive the incentives of the weak type to pool by choosing a low inflation rate in period 1. And the tough government would try to separate out by choosing an even lower inflation rate, since its loss in period 2 is lower if inflationary expectations are lower. We investigate this case in the next subsection.

---

therefore appear biased *ex post* if a policy shift does not occur during a particular sample period. The name refers to the positive devaluation probability of the Mexican peso in 1974 that caused a positive and variable forward premium in the foreign exchange market during the period in which the peso was pegged to the US dollar. Early references are Krasker [80] and Lizondo [89]. See also Obstfeld [99].

[55] Rogoff [116] shows how to introduce a continuum of government types in the monetary policy model, while Tabellini [128] models the private sector as non-atomistic. If the private sector is risk averse and discounts the future, it always prefers the pooling equilibrium to the mixed-strategy equilibrium. If it is non-atomistic, it will set wages so as to remain in the pooling stage rather than in the mixed-strategy stage.

4.3. Signalling

Suppose that the tough type also cares about employment, but less than the weak type. Thus: $0 < \underline{\lambda} < \bar{\lambda}$. Then the tough government may try to signal its preferences in period 1 to reduce future expected inflation and hence raise future employment.[56] This makes it more difficult for the weak type to masquerade as being tough. In this section we ask if the reputational incentives can remain strong enough to sustain an equilibrium with low inflation in period 1 even if the tough government tries to signal its type.

The learning process of wage setters is similar to that described in (4.1). Suppose that in equilibrium the *tough* type never sets π_1 above a certain threshold $\hat{\pi}$, and let $\rho_1 = \text{Prob } (\pi_1 \leqslant \hat{\pi} : \lambda = \bar{\lambda})$ now be the equilibrium probability that the *weak* type abstains from inflating above the threshold. We can then specify the private learning process in equilibrium as:

$$q_2 = 0 \quad \text{if } \pi_1 > \hat{\pi}$$
$$q_2 = q_1 / (q_1 + (1 - q_1)\rho_1) \quad \text{if } \pi_1 \leqslant \hat{\pi}. \tag{4.8}$$

As before, q_2 is a sufficient statistic for the aggregate history of the game, and can be interpreted as a measure of government reputation. If inflation above the threshold $\hat{\pi}$ is observed, then wage setters infer that they face a weak government. Otherwise, their beliefs are revised according to Bayes' rule.

The general form of this learning process is quite plausible. However, it cannot be derived exclusively from Bayes' rule, without an auxiliary hypothesis (as we discussed in Section 4.2, Bayes' rule does not apply outside of equilibrium). Moreover, we will emphasize below that it is not immediately obvious how to choose the threshold—and the choice may generate multiple equilibria.

In the last period (period 2) both government types always play their short-run optimal inflation rate: $\pi_2 = \lambda$, where $\lambda = \bar{\lambda}$ and $\lambda = \underline{\lambda}$ if the government is weak or tough, respectively.

---

[56] Again, the inspiration for the model comes from the industrial organization literature and most closely from Milgrom and Roberts [94]. Their model was applied to monetary policy by Vickers [136]. We now interpret the private sector uncertainty as referring to relative weight assigned by the government to inflation versus employment, rather than to the cost of deviating from a previous announcement, as suggested in Footnote 48.

In period 1, both types trade off the short-run benefits—or costs—of inflation against its long-term consequences on their reputation. Both types would like to convince wage setters that they are tough. The weak type is prepared to mimic tough policies by choosing low inflation. And the tough type is prepared to signal its true identity with an even more restrictive monetary policy.

This trade-off between the short-term and long-term consequences of period 1 policy is illustrated in Figure 4.2. There are now two indifference curves, one for each government type. The indifference curve to the left, which goes through point B, belongs to the tough government. The two indifference curves intersect the vertical axis at the points $q_2 = \lambda/2\delta(\bar{\lambda} - \lambda) < 2\delta$ (point S') and $q_2 = \bar{\lambda}/2\delta(\bar{\lambda} - \lambda) < 2\delta$ (point S"). Since $\bar{\lambda} > \underline{\lambda}$, point S" always lies above point S'. However, each point can be either above or below 1 and q_1. As in the previous subsection, the position of S' and S" relative to 1 and q_1 is crucial in determining which equilibrium will occur.[57]

4.3.1. *Separating Equilibrium*

Suppose that both S' and S" lie above the point $q_2 = 1$ in Figure 4.2. A necessary and sufficient condition for this to be true is

$$\underline{\lambda} > \frac{2\delta}{2\delta + 1}\bar{\lambda}. \tag{4.9}$$

If (4.9) holds, there always exists a separating equilibrium in which the weak type chooses its short-run discretionary policy, $\pi_1 = \bar{\lambda}$, and the tough type signals its true identity by adopting the policy $\pi_1 = \hat{\pi}$. Inflationary expectations in this equilibrium are formed rationally:

$$\pi_1^e = q_1 \hat{\pi} + (1 - q_1)\bar{\lambda}. \tag{4.10}$$

This separating equilibrium is illustrated in Figure 4.2. The solid horizontal lines depict the learning process in (4.8). In this equilibrium the weak government chooses $\pi_1 = \bar{\lambda} > \hat{\pi}$; hence, $\rho_1 = 0$. So if wage setters observe $\pi_1 \leq \hat{\pi}$ they infer that they face a tough type, because

---

[57] The equation of the indifference curves now is:

$$L(\pi_1, \pi_1 - \pi^e) + \delta V(q_2) = L(\lambda, \lambda - \pi_1^e) + \delta V(0)$$

for $\lambda = \bar{\lambda}$ and $\lambda = \underline{\lambda}$ respectively. The expression for $V(q_2)$ is no longer given by (4.5) in the text, but is: $V(q_2) = \lambda^2(1/2 - (\bar{\lambda} - \underline{\lambda})/\bar{\lambda}q_2)$, again with $\lambda = \bar{\lambda}$ and $\underline{\lambda}$ respectively. This expression is obtained by noting that here: $\pi_1^e = q_2\underline{\lambda} + (1 - q_2)\bar{\lambda}$.

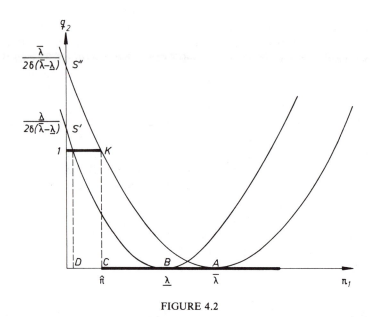

FIGURE 4.2

(4.8) says that $\pi_1 < \hat{\pi}$ should make them set $q_2 = 1$ if $\rho_1 = 0$. And conversely, if $\pi_1 > \hat{\pi}$, wage setters infer that the government is weak ($q_2 = 0$). Point K—with coordinates ($\pi_1 = \hat{\pi}$, $q_2 = 1$)—lies on the weak government's indifference curve in the figure.[58] Thus the tough type is at point K and the weak type at point A.

To confirm that this is indeed an equilibrium, we must show that neither type would like to choose a different policy, given private learning in (4.8). Consider the tough type first. A more restrictive policy, $\pi_1 < \hat{\pi}$, would not add anything to its reputation since $q_2 = 1$ already at $\pi_1 = \hat{\pi}$. But a more restrictive policy would be suboptimal in the short run, since it would create additional surprise deflation and lower employment further below the natural rate. A more expansionary policy, $\pi_1 > \hat{\pi}$, would reduce the short-run loss of underemployment, but it would destroy the tough government's reputation: The tough government would find itself on the bottom solid

---

[58] This condition defines $\hat{\pi}$ as:

$$\hat{\pi} = \bar{\lambda}[1 - \sqrt{2\delta(\bar{\lambda} - \underline{\lambda})/\bar{\lambda}}].$$

segment of Figure 4.2, where $q_2 = 0$. It is clear from Figure 4.2 that the long-run cost dominates the short-run benefit, since point K is above the indifference curve of the tough type, and therefore preferred to any point on the bottom solid line. Thus, the tough type has no incentive to deviate.

Consider now the weak type. Any inflation rate $\pi_1 > \hat{\pi}$ other than $\pi_1 = \bar{\lambda}$ would clearly be suboptimal because it would not bring about any reputational gains on top of being short-run suboptimal. Mimicking the tough type's policy, $\pi_1 = \hat{\pi}$, would induce wage setters to infer that they face a tough government, which would take the government to point K, where $q_2 = 1$. But by construction, point K is on the indifference curve of the weak type which goes through A. Therefore, the weak government gains nothing by mimicking the tough type, since the cost of masquerading as tough just outweighs the benefit.[59]

This is not the only separating equilibrium. Any $\hat{\pi}$ in between points C and D in Figure 4.2 can also be sustained as a separating equilibrium. (To see this the reader can repeat the same steps as above.) Unlike in the previous section, however, these other equilibria can be ruled out as economically implausible. More precisely, they can be ruled out on the basis that they are founded on implausible off-equilibrium beliefs on the part of wage setters.

Suppose a deviation from a particular equilibrium is observed. Suppose further that, for one of the two types, the deviation is always dominated. By this we mean that the deviation yields a higher overall loss than the equilibrium policy, irrespective of how private beliefs are revised after the deviation. Revising their beliefs after this deviation, the wage setters should not attribute it to the type for which the deviation is dominated. This restriction on beliefs is known as *Elimination of weakly dominated strategies*. It singles out that particular separating equilibrium where the tough type signals its type at the lowest possible cost. In Figure 4.2, any inflation rate π_1 to the left of point C is dominated by $\pi_1 = \bar{\lambda}$ for the weak type, irrespective of what wage setters infer. Hence, observing π_1 to the left of C, they should never attribute it to the weak type. This leaves the threshold inflation rate, π, as the only

---

[59] We use the convention that the weak type chooses not to mimic when he is indifferent about mimicking and separating. If the reader does not like this convention there is another separating equilibrium just to the left of point K on the solid line segment between K and 1, where the weak type strictly prefers to separate out.

candidate for a separating equilibrium, since that point allows the tough type to signal its type at the lowest possible cost.[60]

4.3.2. *Pooling equilibrium*

Restricting private beliefs by eliminating weakly dominated strategies is not sufficient to eliminate other equilibria that are non-separating. Figure 4.3 illustrates a pooling equilibrium that can exist for the same parameter values. Again, the solid line depicts the learning process of private agents. Now however the threshold $\hat{\pi}$ corresponds to point B, where $\hat{\pi} = \underline{\lambda}$, (rather than point C) of the diagram. The equilibrium has both government types choosing the policy $\pi_1 = \underline{\lambda}$. Since nothing can be learned by observing this policy, $q_1 = q_2$ in equilibrium and the period 2 expected inflation rate is: $\pi_2^e = q_1 \underline{\lambda} + (1 + q_1)\bar{\lambda}$.

To confirm that this is an equilibrium, consider whether any type would prefer to deviate, given the private learning process. For the

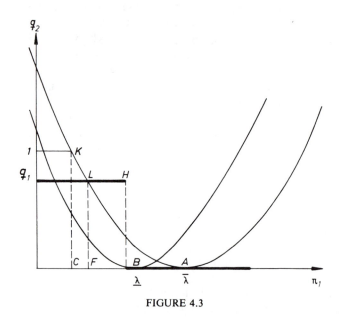

FIGURE 4.3

---

[60] If the difference between $\bar{\lambda}$ and $\underline{\lambda}$ is large enough the tough government may actually be able to separate out by choosing its short-run equilibrium policy $\pi = \underline{\lambda}$. In this extreme case signalling costs nothing.

weak government, the only sensible deviation would be $\pi_1 = \bar{\lambda}$. This would take it to point A, which is clearly dominated by point H. Hence, a deviation does not pay for the weak government. A tough type would also not gain by deviating, since it already pursues its short-run optimal policy and there is nothing it can do to signal its true identity. Hence, we have an equilibrium.

This equilibrium cannot be eliminated by removing dominated strategies, as was done in the previous subsection.[61] But consider the following additional restriction on off-equilibrium beliefs, known as the *Intuitive criterion*. Suppose that at point K the tough government is better off than at point H. Then: (i) The tough government would like to choose the policy π_1 corresponding to point K if that would convince wage setters that it is tough (for then it would achieve point K that dominates point H). And (ii): The weak government would never gain from choosing the policy π_1 corresponding to point K (or any lower inflation rate) irrespective of the inference drawn by wage setters (since K lies on the weak type's indifference curve through A). Given (i) and (ii), it is natural to require that wage setters infer that they face a tough government if they observe π_1 corresponding to point K (or any lower inflation rate). This requirement thus makes us reject this pooling equilibrium.

Whether or not point K is better than point H for the tough type (and hence whether or not condition (i) is satisfied) depends on parameter values. Specifically, if the inequality in (4.9) is violated and if q_1 is sufficiently close to 1, then point H can be preferred to point K by the tough type. In this case, the pooling equilibrium cannot be rejected. Whether or not the separating equilibrium also exists when (4.9) is violated again depends on parameter values. Mixed strategy equilibria also cannot be ruled out.

4.3.3. *General Comments*
We see that despite the possibility of signalling the equilibrium can be either pooling or separating, even when we impose economically meaningful restrictions on off-equilibrium beliefs. But a separating equilibrium occurs for a larger set of parameter values than in Section

---

[61] The removal of dominated strategies has been used implicitly in singling out point H amongst several other pooling equilibria (all those corresponding to points in between H and L).

4.2. Referring to Figure 4.2 and 4.3, a separating equilibrium is more likely the higher are the points S' and S" and the lower is q_1 (and vice versa for the pooling equilibrium).

That a higher reputation at the start makes the pooling equilibrium more likely is very intuitive. With a higher reputation, the incentives to mimic are higher for a weak type, since the cost of losing the reputation and increasing expected inflation is also higher. At the same time the incentives to signal are lower for a tough type, since separating out would not reduce expected inflation much because the initial reputation is already high.

That the separating equilibrium is more likely with higher S' and S" may seem counter-intuitive. The positions of the points S' and S" depend on the discount factor δ and on how different the two types are from each other. If the types are similar—if $\bar{\lambda}$ and $\underline{\lambda}$ are close—then S' and S" tend to be lower down the vertical axis. Separation is therefore more likely when the two types are similar than when they are very different. A tough government with a low $\underline{\lambda}$—so that $\bar{\lambda}$ and $\underline{\lambda}$ are far apart—does not care much about employment. Therefore it does not care much about future expected inflation and is unwilling to bear the costs of signaling. Hence, the pooling equilibrium is more likely. The same is true, but for the opposite reason, if the two types are different because $\bar{\lambda}$ is high. In that case, the weak type has large incentives to mimic: since the weak type cares a lot about employment, the value of having lower future expected inflation is particularly high and this makes the pooling equilibrium more likely.

In the above discussion we have assumed that the two types have the same discount rates. A natural extension is to allow different discount factors: δ^T and δ^W (T for tough and W for weak). Then δ^T above (below) δ^W would make the separating (pooling) equilibrium more likely. This is because the benefits of signalling (mimicking) do not occur until period 2, but the cost is borne in period 1.

Leaving the game-theoretic subtleties aside, the signalling model of this section has similar empirical predictions as the mimicking model of the previous section. Namely, when the private sector has incomplete information about the policymaker, inflationary expectations reflect this uncertainty. To the extent these expectations are incorporated in nominal contracts in labor markets or asset markets, monetary policy has real effects until the private sector has learned the policymaker's type by observing policy.

4.4. Infinite horizon and multiplicity of equilibria

In the complete information framework of Section 3, having an infinite horizon brings about a plethora of equilibria. This is actually less of a problem in the incomplete information framework of this section, provided that we retain the assumption of an atomistic private sector. With incomplete information, having an infinite horizon may narrow down the set of equilibrium outcomes. If the private sector is atomistic, it always plays its short-run best response to the policy rule, conditional on its beliefs. Thus the government is the only player in the game who has an incentive to mimic or signal. In this case, we can appeal to some recent results in game theory which bound the equilibrium outcomes that can occur in infinite repetitions of this game.[62]

Specifically, suppose that the incomplete information structure is sufficiently rich, in the following sense: At the start of the game, private agents assign a positive probability to the event that the government is 'almost committed' to zero inflation (that the true value of λ lies in a neighborhood of zero), their prior is otherwise unrestricted. It can then be shown that if the discount factor δ is sufficiently close to 1, all equilibria of the infinite horizon game must have almost zero inflation in almost every period.[63]

This result can easily be understood in light of the results of the previous two sections. When the horizon is infinite, the incentives to mimic are at their strongest. Moreover, given that there never is a last period in which the 'weak' types separate out, no policymaker type ever faces any incentive to signal. Hence, the pooling equilibria where everybody pools in a neighborhood of zero inflation are the only equilibria that survive.[64]

4.5. Discussion

We want to discuss four issues in this subsection: (i) How do the reputation models of this section compare with those of Section 3? (ii)

---

[62] This subsection draws on an argument presented in a more general setting by Fudenberg and Levine [59].

[63] There are no requirements placed upon the specific beliefs that can support these equilbria. Whatever the beliefs are, the limiting result stated in the text is true.

[64] This result fails to hold if wage setters are non-atomistic. In this case, we know from Fudenberg and Maskin [60] that the multiplicity of equilibria again is pervasive.

How effective is the reputation mechanism in reducing the equilibrium rate of inflation? (iii) What are the empirical implications of the incomplete information models of monetary policy? (iv) What have we learned about how to impose the credibility constraint in discretionary policy regimes?

4.5.1. Which Model of Reputation?

The answer to this question is controversial. However, in our opinion, the incomplete information model of reputation is more appealing than that of Section 3 for several reasons. First, the expectation formation mechanism that creates the reputation incentives corresponds to a well-defined learning mechanism. We can interpret this mechanism and discuss its plausibility from an economic point of view, while we cannot choose in this way between the different trigger strategies of Section 3.

Second, the multiplicity problem seems more pervasive under complete information, at least if we retain the assumption that the private sector is atomistic. With complete information, whenever there is a reputational equilibrium, there are also many other equilibria. Multiplicity is endemic to that approach to reputation. This is not true of the incomplete information model. With incomplete information and a finite horizon, sequential rationality plus reasonable restrictions on beliefs typically rule out all but one (reputational) equilibrium.[65]

Nevertheless, in a certain sense the multiplicity of equilibria reappears even in this incomplete information framework. Equilibrium refinements only put restrictions on how the beliefs are revised, not on how the initial beliefs come about. Even though the equilibrium is often unique given the prior beliefs, these priors are unrestricted.

---

[65] Our signalling model of monetary policy may have overemphasized the importance of the equilibrium refinements. The model is very special, with only two types of policymakers and with policy perfectly observable. A more general model might have a continuum of government types, and/or it may have imperfect monitoring of policy. These two extensions would make the set of off-equilibrium events considerably smaller. This would reduce the arbitrary features of the model, since it is only for the off-equilibrium events that the private learning process is not well defined. Both extensions have recently been investigated in the literature, by Driffill [47] and by Hoshi [78]. The upshot of these analyses is that the general features of the equilibria discussed in the previous pages are robust. In particular, enlarging the set of government types generally makes the pooling equilibrium easier to sustain. And allowing for imperfect monitoring tends to weaken the reputational incentives, since it makes reputation less sensitive to government policy.

And, as shown above, these priors often determine whether the equilibrium is pooling or separating, or whether there is mimicking or signalling. Nonetheless, it may be easier to choose among prior beliefs (on grounds of historical plausibility for instance) than it is to select one of several equilibria in a complete information game. Moreover, the sensitivity of the equilibrium to the prior beliefs diminishes in the infinite horizon versions of incomplete information models. Going to the infinite horizon strengthens the incentives to pool if there is incomplete information. This limits the range of equilibrium outcomes, at least if the private sector is atomistic.

The question of how to choose between finite and infinite horizon models is difficult to answer; it is probably easier to address it with reference to a particular policy problem and a particular institutional setup than in the abstract. We will return to this issue in a more specific setup in Section 5.

4.5.2. *Is Reputation a Substitute for Commitments?*

Here, too, one must consider different dimensions. With an infinite horizon, the answer seems to be a qualified yes. The qualifications were discussed in the previous subsection and have to do with whether or not the private sector is atomistic and with the size of the government discount factor. Note also that here we have neglected the impact of stochastic shocks.

If the horizon is finite, things are a bit more complicated. But on an average, the reputation mechanism described in this section seems to create strong incentives for low inflation. When signalling is absent, as in Section 4.2, only the weak government has reputational incentives. If the incentives are strong enough, a pooling equilibrium with zero inflation can be sustained in period 1 or, more generally, in the early part of its incumbency. Moreover, the incentives to pool become stronger as the policymaker's horizon lengthens. When signalling is present, as in Section 4.3, both government types have reputational incentives. This makes the pooling equilibrium more difficult to sustain, since now the tough government is willing to separate out by signalling its identity through a recessionary monetary policy. The signal must involve a lower inflation than would otherwise be chosen. So even though signalling may break the reputational incentives for the weak government, it tends to reduce the inflationary bias of the tough government.

The cost of signalling is that employment falls below the natural rate. By evaluating the policymaker's losses in the various equilibria as a function of its type, it can be shown that 'on average' the presence of incomplete information reduces the losses.[66] In a sense, this finding reinforces our previous arguments about secrecy in central banking, although the reason is somewhat different. In Section 2, secrecy was valuable basically because it provided an additional policy instrument. Here, secrecy is valuable because it changes government incentives: It tends to make non-inflationary policies more desirable and hence more credible.

4.5.3. What Empirical Implications?

Our third question concerns the empirical implications of these incomplete information models of monetary policy. Even though precise empirical analysis based on such models is very scant,[67] some general implications seem robust. First, if the time horizon of a government coincides with its tenure in office, one should never observe inflation falling in the later part of a new government's incumbency. This is because the reputational incentive is strongest in the early part, as shown in Sections 4.2 and 4.3. Of course, this argument abstracts from uncertainty and the effects of elections. Second, the incomplete information model leads us to expect some monetary surprises—that may result in employment fluctuations—in each government incumbency. The surprises may occur at different points of the incumbency, when the new government reveals its true identity. This can happen either early (the separating equilibrium) or late (the pooling equilibrium). Maybe this can help explain the empirical regularity that the inflation surprises occurring in the US seem to be highly concentrated in the earlier part of presidential administrations.[68]

The models of reputation presented in this section also have a troublesome and perhaps counterfactual property. Once lost, a reputation can never be regained. This occurs because the private sector can perfectly monitor government action. As was noted in Footnote 65, with imperfect monitoring the equilibria would become

---

[66] See Vickers [136].

[67] See Driffill [48] for a survey of empirical work based on reputational models of monetary policy.

[68] See Alesina [5] for a documentation of this fact, and for a different political explanation that we take up in the next section.

more realistic: the government reputation would move more smoothly and it could never be totally destroyed.

4.5.4. *Reputation and Credibility*

Finally, the results in this section reinforce the general conclusions from Section 3, about how to model the requirement that equilibrium policy be credible. In the incomplete information framework, the credibility concept gets specific content only with reference to a particular equilibrium refinement. That is, the specific meaning of credibility is tied to a specific requirement of how the players ought to 'rationally' revise their beliefs. So, again, credibility can only be defined with reference to a specific economic context. More generally, the requirement of credibility is very much linked to the notion of rational expectations, and of what constitutes a rational system of beliefs about government policy. But it may be hard to be precise about what beliefs are rational without a more detailed model of the policymaking institutions.

This is an additional reason to go further in modelling the details of the politico-economical decision process. In this spirit, the next section discusses more politically oriented models of monetary policy.

4.6. Notes on the literature

As for Section 3, the analytical tools used in this section were originally formulated in the industrial organization literature. Tirole [133] again provides an excellent introduction to the concepts presented here at about the same level of difficulty. The model of reputation in Section 4.2 is an application of the Kreps and Wilson [83] and Milgrom and Roberts [94] papers on the chain store paradox. Models of monetary policy or exchange rate policy, similar to the one in Section 4.2, are analyzed in Backus and Driffill [17], [18], and Barro [21] for an atomistic private sector, and in Horn and Persson [77], Tabellini [126] and Tabellini [128] for a centralized trade union.

The model of signalling in Section 4.3 is an application of Milgrom and Roberts [95], who studied limit pricing in oligopoly. Equilibrium refinements for games of incomplete information are discussed and illustrated by Cho and Kreps [38], who specifically discuss signalling games, and by van Damme [134] and Tirole [133]. Vickers [136] studied the monetary policy model of Section 4.3. Milgrom and

Roberts [96] analyze multiple signals, also in an industrial organization context. Persson and van Wijnbergen [109] study a version of the signalling model of Section 4.3 in which the policymaker chooses a stabilization program with multiple signals (the second signal being wage controls). Driffill [48] contains a survey of signalling models of monetary policy. Finally, the infinite horizon results mentioned in Section 4.4 are due to Fudenberg and Levine [59].

5. ELECTIONS AND MONETARY POLICY

5.1. Introduction

The results in Sections 3 and 4 are very sensitive to small details of the model specification, such as the rules of the game, the information sets of the players, and the particular form of the government loss function. This sensitivity is a feature of most game theoretic models, and it can be both a blessing and a drawback. It is a drawback if the model is derived from arbitrary assumptions. It is a blessing, however, if it forces the economist to limit the arbitrariness of his assumptions, for instance by being precise about economic institutions. Indeed, one of the recognized advantages of game theory is that it provides a framework and a formal language for modeling institutions.

In this section we add political institutions and political conflict to our simple monetary policy model. The general theme of the section is that political institutions add new strategic interactions between the government and the rest of society. In particular, we focus on elections and on the interaction between the government and the voters. Elections have two main effects. On one hand, they impose new incentive constraints on the government: the policies chosen by the incumbent are partially shaped by his desire to win the elections, and hence to please the voters. On the other hand, elections may lead to changes in government, and thus create uncertainty about future economic policies.

For simplicity, we identify the central bank with a branch of government throughout the section. Thus, we assume that the central bank responds to electoral incentives as the administration would. This assumption is really the extreme opposite of our approach in previous sections, where the policymaker was assumed to be totally insensitive to electoral influences.

In Section 5.2 we illustrate how elections create new temptations to surprise, and how these temptations can induce a political business cycle. As in Section 4, policy signals government type, although here, the signal is directed to the voters rather than to the wage setters. Section 5.3 explores a second distortion induced by elections: Excessive policy volatility. Unlike in the previous subsection, alternative political candidates have different ideologies and pursue different policies once in office. Hence, elections can cause policy shifts and create policy uncertainty. Finally, Section 5.4 considers the role of elections in correcting pre-existing distortions. In particular, we show that elections can reinforce the reputational incentives of a government, because voters can 'punish' a government who created policy surprises by voting it out of office. This enforcement mechanism can strengthen the credibility of policy announcements and bring about equilibria with low inflation. Thus, this section offers an example of how political incentive constraints can offset the credibility constraints and substitute for a commitment technology. The section concludes with a discussion of positive and normative implications in Section 5.5.

5.2. Political business cycles

If voters are irrational and backward looking it is easy to fool them. This is essentially the view in the traditional 'political business cycle' theory.[69] The prediction of the theory is that policymakers overstimulate the economy before elections and contract it after elections to reduce inflation. This trick is used in every election; voters never learn from the past and governments never lose credibility. The empirical evidence is mixed, but mildly consistent with the predictions. The theory is inconsistent with forward-looking voting behavior, however. Why would a rational individual ever assign any weight in his voting decision to what a government does before the elections, when what matters is what it will do after the elections? In this section we formulate a model that generates equilibrium political business cycles even with forward-looking voters.[70]

---

[69] See Lindbeck [88] and Nordhaus [98].

[70] This section is based on ideas presented in Cukierman and Meltzer [43], Rogoff and Sibert [118], and Rogoff [117].

5.2.1. *A Political Model*

The model is a modified version of the two period signalling model in Section 4. A policymaker who is in office in period 1 is called 'the incumbent'. Elections are held at the end of period 1. Voters can either re-elect the incumbent, or they can elect 'the opponent'. The opponent is drawn at random from the population.

Voters are rational and forward looking: They elect the policymaker who minimizes their expected loss in period 1. For simplicity, they are assumed to all have the same loss function (the notation is as in previous sections):

$$\mathcal{L} = E\left[\sum_{t=1}^{2} \delta^{t-1}L(\pi_t, x_t)\right],$$

$$L(\pi_t, x_t) = \pi_t^2/2 - \lambda x_t, \ 0 < \delta < 1, \lambda > 0. \tag{5.1}$$

All the candidates have the same objectives. They care about inflation and employment, just like the voters do.[71] In addition, they enjoy being in office. Candidate c minimizes the loss function:

$$\mathcal{L}^c = E^c\left[\sum_{t=1}^{2} \delta^{t-1}(L(\pi_t, x_t) - Kz_t^c)\right]. \tag{5.2}$$

In (5.2), $L(\cdot)$ is defined in (5.1), K denotes the gains from being in office, and z_t^c is a dummy variable that is equal to one if c is in office at time t and is equal to zero otherwise. The c superscript on the expectations operator indicates that expectations are conditional on the information available to candidate c. The index c can take either of two values: i, for the incumbent; and o, for the opponent.

Candidates differ in their 'competence,' that is, in their abilities to solve policy problems. For example, one candidate may be particularly able (or unable) to cope with a shock to the price of oil, or to enact effective labor market legislation, or to negotiate with trade unions. We assume that a candidate's competence is reflected in the natural level of employment that this candidate can bring about. Specifically, if candidate c is in office at time t, employment is

---

[71] That the loss function in (5.1) is linear in employment simplifies the analysis considerably. If the loss were nonlinear in employment, the political motives for monetary policy would be confounded with stabilization motives. Similar results would continue to hold, but the analysis would become much more complicated.

$$x_t = \pi_t - \pi_t^e + \epsilon_t^c, \tag{5.3}$$

where ϵ_t^c is a measure of c's competence. We assume that $\epsilon_t^c = \mu_t^c + \mu_{t-1}^c$, where μ_t^c is a random variable, which reflects shocks to c's competence. The competence of a government is random, since it depends on the nature of the policy problems that the government faces: A candidate may be particularly good at dealing with trade unions, but particularly bad at dealing with a tariff war. Competence—though random—is partially lasting: If yesterday's policymaker was particularly able, chances are that he will also be able tomorrow, either because the external environment changes slowly, or because his ability to deal with different problems is positively, if not perfectly, correlated. Hence, we assume that competence is a moving average. As will be shown below, this assumption is important, because it enables the voters to make informed guesses about the future competence of an incumbent by looking at his previous policy performance.

For all c, the random variables μ_t^c are assumed to be distributed as follows

$$\mu_0 = 0$$

$$\mu_t^c = \begin{cases} \bar{\mu} > 0 \text{ with probability } \rho \\ \underline{\mu} < 0 \text{ with probability } 1 - \rho \end{cases}, t = 1, 2. \tag{5.4}$$

In (5.4) μ_0 is an initial level of competence inherited from the past. We assume that $0 < \rho < 1$ and that the unconditional expectation of μ_t^c is $E[\mu_t^c] = \rho\bar{\mu} + (1 - \rho)\underline{\mu} = 0$. When the voters elect a government for period 2, they essentially select the variable $\epsilon_2^c = \mu_2^c + \mu_1^c$. Clearly, since all the voters are identical, their goal is to elect the most competent government. Since elections take place at the end of period 1, and μ_2^c is realized only in period 2, this goal is achieved by voting for the candidate with the highest perceived realization of μ_1^c.

Voters cannot observe the competence of the opponent. Thus, whoever the opponent is, $E(\mu_1^0) = 0$. If the competence of the incumbent is known—that is, if $\epsilon_1^i = \mu_1^i$ is observed by voters before the elections—then the political equilibrium is obvious: The incumbent wins the elections if $\mu_1^i = \bar{\mu}$, and loses if $\mu_1^i = \underline{\mu}$.

We instead consider the more plausible and interesting case when the incumbent's competence in period 1 is not observed by the voters. Specifically, we impose the following timing assumptions. At the beginning of period 1, the realization of μ_1^i is observed by the incumbent. Then, wages and inflation (π_1^e and π_1) are set and the resulting level of employment, x_1, is observed by everybody. Next, elections take place. But policy and the policymaker's competence are only observed with a lag. That is, π_1 and μ_1 are not observed by the voters until period 2, after the elections. In period 2 the sequence of events is repeated, except that there are no more elections.

The assumption that employment can be observed before inflation may appear odd to some readers. But remember that we are using the shortcut of letting the policymaker set π directly, rather than a monetary instrument. As we argued in Section 3, in a more realistic setting all the information upon which monetary policy is based may not be immediately observable to the private sector. This makes it difficult to determine exactly how expansionary a given monetary policy is, or was intended to be. Furthermore, in the setup with nominal contracts considered here, quantities will generally react before prices.

Under these timing assumptions, employment can signal the incumbent's competence. The incumbent has an incentive to bring about a high level of employment before the elections, in order to make the voters believe he is competent (that $\mu_1^i = \bar{\mu}$). The voters understand these incentives. Thus, we have a signalling game, similar to that of the previous section. But here the signal is directed to the voters rather than to wage setters and it occurs through employment rather than through inflation.[72]

5.2.2. *The Value of Being Reelected*

As in Section 4, all the action takes place in period 1. In period 2 the government has no incentive to signal, and thus in equilibrium:

$$\pi_2 = \lambda = \pi_2^e, \tag{5.5a}$$

$$x_2 = \epsilon_2^c. \tag{5.5b}$$

Therefore, the voters' expected loss in period 2, given that c has won the election, is:

---

[72] If the timing was reversed, and employment rather than inflation was observed after the elections, the incumbent would still face the incentive to signal. But now the signal would be through low inflation, and political business cycle would bring about low inflation before the elections, and a recession just afterwards.

$$L^c \equiv E(\lambda^2/2 - \lambda\mu_1^c), c = i, o, \tag{5.6}$$

(the expectation in (5.6) refers to μ_1^c). With this notation and the definition in (5.2), we can express the incumbent *net gain from being re-elected* as:

$$W(\mu_1^i) \equiv -[L^i - K - L^o] = \lambda\mu_1^i + K \tag{5.7}$$

where we have used $E^i(\mu_1^o) = 0$.

We assume that the value of being in office is sufficiently large that even an incompetent incumbent (that is, one for which $\mu_1^i = \underline{\mu}$) wishes to be re-elected. Hence, $K > -\lambda\underline{\mu}$. According to (5.7), however, the value of being re-elected is higher for a competent than for an incompetent incumbent. Intuitively, an incompetent incumbent expects employment to be lower if he is re-elected than if the opponent wins, and this reduces his net gain from re-election. The opposite is true if the incumbent is competent.

5.2.3. *The Cost of Signalling*
In period 1, the incumbent policymaker realizes that the probability of his re-election depends on his competence, as perceived by the voters. Thus, an incompetent government may have an incentive to mimic a competent one, by artificially increasing employment through unexpected inflation. And a competent government may also have an incentive to increase employment, so as to signal its true identity. These incentives to mimic or signal are traded off against the cost of excessive inflation in period 1. The incentives closely resemble those in the previous section, except that here the cost of signalling takes the form of high inflation, rather than low employment. Specifically, suppose that the incumbent wishes to bring about a given level of employment x_1 in period 1. From (5.3), he has to set inflation equal to:

$$\pi(x_1, \mu_1^i) \equiv \pi_1^e + x_1 - \mu_1^i. \tag{5.8}$$

For any given expected inflation rate, we can define the *net cost of signalling* (or mimicking) as:

$$C(x_1, \mu_1^i) \equiv L(\pi(x_1, \mu_1^i), x_1) - L(\lambda, \lambda - \pi_1^e + \mu_1^i) \tag{5.9}$$

where $L(\cdot)$ is defined in (5.1). This cost is the difference between the loss when monetary policy is set to achieve employment x_1 and the loss when the short-run discretionary policy is pursued. The cost depends on both the target level of employment and the incumbent competency, μ_1^i. In particular, a more competent incumbent faces a lower cost of signalling, since it has to inflate less in order to bring about a given level of employment.

We are now ready to analyze the equilibria of this game. As in the previous section, an equilibrium can be either separating or pooling (we neglect mixed strategy equilibria).

5.2.4. Separating Equilibrium

Consider first a separating equilibrium. Here the two government types accept different levels of employment and therefore, the equilibrium is fully revealing: The voters can discern with certainty whether the incumbent is competent or not by observing employment in period 1. Let $\rho_2 = \text{Prob } (\mu_1^i = \bar{\mu}: x_1)$ denote the posterior probability that the incumbent is competent. Following the approach of the previous section we can then postulate:

$$\rho_2 = 0 \quad \text{if } x_1 < x^s$$
$$\rho_2 = 1 \quad \text{if } x_1 \geqslant x^s, \tag{5.10}$$

where x^s is an appropriate threshold, and the s-superscript is a reminder that the equilibrium is separating.

In this equilibrium, the incompetent type does not attempt to mimic, and chooses the short-run optimal inflation rate: $\pi_1 = \lambda$. The competent type signals his identity by bringing about the level of employment x^s. For this to be an equilibrium, the following conditions must be satisfied: First, wage setters must forecast inflation correctly:

$$\pi_1^e = (1 - \rho)\lambda + \rho\pi(x^s, \bar{\mu}) = \lambda + \rho(x^s - \bar{\mu})/(1 - \rho), \tag{5.11}$$

where the right hand side has been derived from (5.8). Second, for the competent (incompetent) incumbent, the discounted net gain from re-election must exceed (not exceed) the cost of signalling:

$$\delta W(\bar{\mu}) > C(x^s, \bar{\mu}) \tag{5.12a}$$

$$\delta W(\underline{\mu}) \leqslant C(x^s, \underline{\mu}), \tag{5.12b}$$

where $W(\cdot)$ and $C(\cdot)$ are defined in (5.7) and (5.9), respectively.

The inequalities (5.12) define a range of admissible values for x^s all of which are consistent with equilibrium. As explained in Section 4, by removing beliefs that require dominated strategies we can restrict our

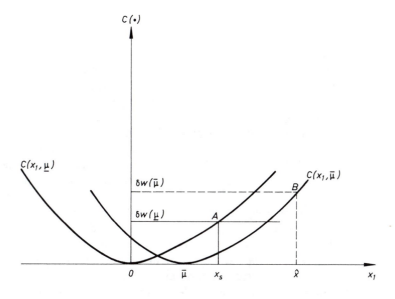

FIGURE 5.1

attention to the unique separating equilibrium where the competent type signals at the lowest possible cost. This equilibrium corresponds to the level of employment at which (5.12b) holds with equality.[73] This equilibrium is illustrated in Figure 5.1. The two parabolas represent the cost of signalling for the two government types as a function of x_1. Using the equilibrium expected inflation rate defined in equation (5.11), one can show that these costs are zero when $x_1 = 0$ for the incompetent type and when $x_1 = \bar{\mu}$ for the competent type.[74]

---

[73] If $\delta W(\underline{\mu}) < C(\bar{\mu}, \underline{\mu})$, that is, if the two incumbent types are sufficiently far apart, the separating equilibrium identified by the removal of dominated strategies is $x = \bar{\mu}$. In this case, neither type signals, and both choose $\pi_1 = \lambda$. In terms of Figure 5.1, this is the case when $\bar{\mu}$ lies to the right of point A.

[74] Specifically, exploiting (5.11), one can show that in the separating equilibrium:

$$C(x_1, \bar{\mu}) = \frac{1}{2}\left[\frac{x_1 - \bar{\mu}}{(1-\rho)}\right]^2$$

$$C(x_1, \underline{\mu}) = \frac{1}{2}\left[\frac{x_1}{(1-\rho)}\right]^2.$$

According to (5.12b), the equilibrium must lie to the left of point B, so that the value of re-election for the competent type—corresponding to the dotted line in Figure 5.1—exceeds the cost of signalling. And according to (5.12a), the equilibrium must lie to the right of point A, so that the condition is reversed for the incompetent type—for whom the value of re-election is given by the solid line. Our discussion in Sections 5.2.2 and 5.2.3 ensures that point B always lies to the right of point A, since the dotted line always lies above the solid line and the cost of signalling is always higher for the incompetent type. Hence, a separating equilibrium always exists. The equilibrium where the competent type signals at the lowest possible cost coincides with point A.[75]

Thus, a separating equilibrium has the following features: If the incumbent is competent, he unexpectedly inflates and creates a boom just before the elections, so as to signal his competence to the voters. If he is incompetent, he chooses the short-run optimal monetary policy. This creates an unexpected deflation and causes a recession. Hence, elections give rise to a business cycle. Moreover, an incumbent who creates a boom always wins the elections and an incumbent who causes a recession always loses. An outside observer of this pattern, unaware of the underlying signalling game, would be tempted to conclude that voters are naive. Obviously, this conclusion would be wrong. Voters realize that booms and recessions are deliberate signals of incumbent competence. They don't 'punish' policymakers for causing pre-election recessions or 'reward' policymakers for creating pre-election booms. On the contrary, their vote is forward-looking and based on correct perceptions about post-election outcomes.

5.2.5. *Pooling Equilibrium*
Next, consider a pooling equilibrium. Here, both types of incumbent choose the same employment. Voters beliefs are now described by:

---

[75] Formally, the region identified in Figure 5.1 corresponds to values of x_1 in the interval:

$$(1 - \rho)\sqrt{2\delta(\lambda\bar{\mu} + K)} + \bar{\mu} > x_1 > (1 - \rho)\sqrt{2\delta(\lambda\underline{\mu} + K)}.$$

The equilibrium where signalling occurs with the lowest possible cost is:

$$x^s = \text{Max}(\bar{\mu}, (1 - \rho)\sqrt{2\delta(\lambda\underline{\mu} + K)}).$$

$$\rho_2 = \rho \quad \text{if } x_1 \geq x^p$$
$$\rho_2 = 0 \quad \text{if } x_1 < x^p, \tag{5.10$'$}$$

where x^p is an appropriately defined threshold, and the p-superscript serves as a reminder of pooling equilibrium. Voters cannot learn anything about the incumbent competence: The incumbent and the opponent look identical to the voters. Hence, it is reasonable to assume that in a pooling equilibrium the probability that the incumbent will be re-elected is 1/2.

In contrast to the separating equilibrium, the roles of the competent and incompetent incumbents are reversed. The competent policymaker chooses monetary policy non-strategically and thus sets his short-run optimal inflation rate, $\pi_1 = \lambda$, which results in employment

$$x^p = \lambda - \pi_1^e + \bar{\mu}. \tag{5.13}$$

And the incompetent policymaker mimics his competent counterpart, by creating sufficient unexpected inflation so as to bring about $x_1 = x^p$.

In equilibrium, inflation forecasts must be rational:

$$\pi_1^e = \rho\lambda + (1 - \rho)\pi(x^p, \underline{\mu}) = \lambda + (1 - \rho)(x^p - \underline{\mu})/\rho, \tag{5.14}$$

where the right hand side has been derived from (5.8). Combining (5.13) and (5.14) yields that the equilibrium employment level is $x^p = 0$.

We now verify that this is an equilibrium. Given voter beliefs, there is nothing a competent incumbent can do to increase his chances of re-election. Hence, setting $\pi_1 = \lambda$ is optimal. An incompetent policymaker is choosing an optimal policy if the cost of mimicking is smaller than his expected net gain from re-election:

$$C(0, \underline{\mu}) < \delta W(\underline{\mu})/2. \tag{5.15}$$

This condition is illustrated in Figure 5.2. It can be shown that the cost of mimicking for the incompetent type is zero when $x_1 < 0$. Hence, condition (5.15) is equivalent to saying that point A in the figure must lie in the positive orthant. Clearly, this condition is satisfied if the value of being in office, K, is sufficiently large.[76]

In summary, a pooling equilibrium has the following features: Both

---

[76] Making use of (5.14), condition (5.15) can be stated as:

$$(\bar{\mu} - \underline{\mu})^2 < \delta(\lambda\underline{\mu} + K).$$

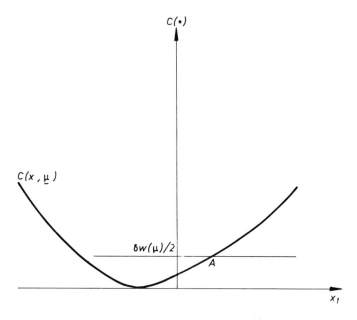

FIGURE 5.2

incumbent types choose the same level of employment. But now an incompetent incumbent brings about unexpected inflation, whereas a competent one causes unexpected deflation. Hence, this equilibrium too exhibits a politically induced cycle, although it is somewhat different than in the separating equilibrium: The competent type has a higher natural rate of employment than the incompetent type and actual employment is in between these two natural rates.

As in the previous section the pooling equilibrium can be ruled out for some parameter values by appealing to the Intuitive criterion. For other parameter values, both the pooling and the separating equilibrium can coexist.[77]

---

[77] The intuitive criterion states that the pooling equilibrium can be ruled out if:

$$\delta(\lambda\bar{\mu} + K) > \left[\frac{x^s - \bar{\mu}}{(1 - \rho)}\right]^2 + 2\lambda \left[\frac{\rho x^s}{1 - \rho} - \bar{\mu}\right]$$

where x^s is defined in Footnote 75. For some parameter values this condition can be violated even though the condition stated in Footnote 76 holds. In this case, both the pooling and the separating equilibrium coexist.

5.2.6. *Discussion*

The central point of this subsection is that elections may distort government incentives. In order to increase its chances of re-election, the government has an incentive to appear more competent then it really is and expand the economy. Since policy can create the appearance of competence in the short run, elections can induce the government to pursue distorted policies. In a separating equilibrium, the competent incumbent signals its identity by causing a pre-electoral boom. If he did not do so, he would be mistaken by the voters for an incompetent type, and would lose the elections. In a pooling equilibrium, the roles of the two types are reversed: it is the incompetent type who plays strategically, trying to give an appearance of competence at the price of subsequent inflation. Which equilibrium prevails depends on how the voters revise their beliefs when observing the state of the economy.[78]

The point that elections may distort government incentives is robust to extensions of the model, such as to a continuum of government types, to multiple signals, or to multiple periods. It is also applicable to a variety of policy problems besides monetary policy: for instance to the provision of public goods, or to the collection of government revenue. Moreover, it has empirical predictions, some of which are consistent with empirical evidence.[79]

5.3. Political polarization and volatility of policy

In Section 5.2 all voters and political candidates were alike in their preferences over macroeconomic outcomes. However, the candidates were 'office motivated' and their desire to be elected generated a conflict of interests between the voters and the government. If voters and candidates are not all alike in their policy preferences, they also become 'ideology motivated'. In that case elections may give rise to another distortion: They may enhance volatility of policy.

---

[78] It may appear that the pooling equilibrium in which only the incompetent implements a distorted policy, is more plausible. But in fact, the pooling equilibrium may well be the more fragile. If we introduced a random shock to the voters' preferences for either the incumbent or the opponent, as in Rogoff [117], then in the separating equilibrium the probability that the incumbent wins would be bounded away from zero and one. We conjecture that in this case the Intuitive criterion would always rule out the pooling equilibrium as it does in Rogoff [117].

[79] See Alesina [5] and the literature quoted therein.

This point is best illustrated in a simple one-period version of our usual monetary policy model.[80] Let the loss function of the ith voter be:

$$L^i = (\pi - \beta^i)^2/2 - \lambda x, \qquad (5.16)$$

where β^i is an individual specific parameter. Thus, different individuals prefer different inflation (or deflation, if $\beta^i < 0$) rates. These preferences may reflect the voters' interests in variables other than employment; for example, the preferences may reflect their net nominal position as debtors or creditors. Different parameterizations of disagreement among voters (for instance, over the weight λ) would yield analogous results.

At the beginning of the period, voters elect one of two candidates, who will be in charge of monetary policy. Let the candidates be called A and B, and suppose that their loss functions are given by (5.16), with $\beta^A = 0, \beta^B > 0$, which means they disagree about which policy to implement. The disagreement arises, for instance, because the two candidates are ideologically committed to a particular view of the world, or to the interests of a specific constituency. The values of β^A and β^B are known to the voters with certainty. The economy is still described by equation (5.3), except that now $\epsilon = 0$ since the candidates are equally competent.

For simplicity, we now assume that the elected government can enter into binding commitments. That is, we assume that wages are set after having observed monetary policy. Under this timing, there is no unexpected inflation and employment is at the natural rate, $x = 0$, irrespective of which candidate is elected. We discuss below what happens if the timing is reversed. Finally, we assume that the candidates can only set policy once in office. In other words, candidates cannot enter into a binding commitment to a policy platform at the time of elections (this assumption reflects a feature of all democratic societies). Then, denoting with π^c the inflation rate set by a government of type c, we have $\pi^A = 0, \pi^B = \beta^B > 0$.

Who wins the elections? Voters look forward and recognize the post-election incentives of the two candidates. All voters for whom $\beta^i < \beta^B/2$ vote for candidate A, and all voters for whom $\beta^i > \beta^B/2$ vote for candidate B. Let β^m be the median value of β in the population. Then, A wins if $\beta^m < \beta^B/2$, and B wins in the opposite case. More

---

[80] The model in this section is a variant of Alesina [4].

generally, if voter turnout is random, β^m is a random variable, with say a cumulative distribution $P(\beta)$. Then, the probability that A wins is $P(\beta^B/2)$. Exactly the same results would apply if the game was repeated any finite number of times.

This simple model has two interesting implications. First, with fully informed voters, the probability of winning the elections is independent of past policy performance, and only depends on the preferences of the voters compared to those of the candidates. In particular, there is no policy convergence towards the position of the median voter on the part of the incumbent or of the elected government. This result reflects the 'discretionary political regime'; that is, the inability of the candidates to commit to a policy before the elections. It would survive even if the candidates enjoyed being in office *per se*, as long as they retained some ideological preferences about policy. Policy announcements other than $\pi^A = 0$ and $\pi^B = \beta^B$ are simply not credible without commitment. If candidates could commit to policy platforms—as in the traditional political science literature—they would choose policies much closer to each other.[81]

Second, a byproduct of elections is policy volatility, the more so the more polarized are the two candidates in their policy preferences. This volatility results in a welfare loss for society as a whole. Because private agents are risk averse (since their loss functions are convex in inflation), everybody would be better off *ex ante* if the candidates could agree to always set $\pi = \beta$ irrespective of who won the elections, for some $\beta^B > \beta > 0$. (Which particular value of β depends on the probability that either candidate wins). However, this *ex ante* efficient policy cannot be enforced without commitments in a one-shot model.

The inefficiency has nothing to do with wage setters' expectations. But the inefficiency would be reinforced if wages were set before observing the election outcome, as in the 'discretionary economic regimes' of previous sections. For then, elections would also cause volatility in employment, besides volatility in inflation. In this case the equilibrium would be $\pi^A = \lambda$, $\pi^B = \lambda + \beta^B$, and $\pi^e = \lambda + (1 - P)\beta^B$. It can be shown that P, the probability that A wins, is still given by $P(\beta^B/2)$. Hence, A would always cause a recession, whereas B would always cause a boom. As in the previous subsection, elections would induce a cycle in output and employment. But it is a different cycle,

---

[81] See Calvert [28] and Wittman [138].

which occurs after rather than before the elections, and it is associated with government ideology rather than with competence.[82] Strictly speaking, in this model the volatility of employment is not costly, because of the linearity of the loss function in x, although it would become costly in a more general model.

With an infinite horizon, excessive policy volatility might potentially be reduced. The two candidates could enter into a cooperative agreement to achieve some policy convergence. Such an agreement could be enforced without binding commitments if the two candidates interacted over an infinite horizon. Deviations from the agreement could be punished by a reversion of the other candidate to a more extreme policy when in office. Alternatively, cooperation could be enforced by the voters, through trigger voting strategies similar to the wage strategies in Section 3. Naturally, as discussed extensively in Sections 3 and 4, cooperation could be difficult to sustain because of the many equilibria in this class of games.

Most of the results in this section go beyond a two-candidate system. In particular, they generalize to a setting where the voters vote directly on the policy. Two aspects are crucial. First, that the pivotal majority has to be unstable, for instance, because of shocks to voting turnout, or because of changes in the composition of the eligible voting population. Second, the alternating majorities have to be polarized in their preferences; for in this case, changes in the identity of the winning majority results in wide policy shifts.

In a dynamic environment changes in the identity (preferences) of the policymaker have other important consequences on the policymaker's incentives. The current government would now try to manipulate the state variables under his control so as to influence the policy choices of future governments with different preferences. This point is discussed more fully in Section 9. There we show that political instability and polarization result in suboptimal time paths of state variables such as public debt or aggregate capital.

---

[82] Alesina [4], [7] contrasts the empirical predictions of these two alternative political business cycle models; he finds that in the post-war period US data and the data of several European countries support the model with ideological policymakers of this subsection.

5.4. Elections and reputation

So far we have argued that elections create incentives to pursue distorted policies, and that they can enhance the temptation to create policy surprises. In this subsection we argue that elections can also have an opposite effect: They can provide an additional enforcement mechanism via reputational incentives.

5.4.1. *The model*

Consider an infinite-horizon version of the simple model in Section 5.3. At the beginning of each period, voters elect one of two candidates (A or B). Both candidates enjoy being in office and have the loss function defined in (5.1), $L(\pi_t, x_t)$, with regard to inflation and employment: However, the two candidates differ along other dimensions, which are not explicitly modeled here. The voters are forward looking and have complete information. They vote for the candidate who minimizes their own loss function. The loss function for voter i is:

$$\mathscr{L}^i = \sum_{t=0}^{\infty} \delta^t [L(\pi_t, x_t) - \theta^i z_t], \qquad (5.17)$$

where the dummy variable $z_t = 1$ if A is elected in period t and $z_t = -1$ if B is elected. Thus, all voters are alike in their preferences over inflation and employment. But they differ in the parameter θ^i: If $\theta^i > 0$, voter i is 'biased' in favor of candidate A, if $\theta^i < 0$ the voter is biased in favor of B. This bias can be interpreted as referring to other policy dimensions on which the candidates differ, and on which there is disagreement among the voters. The two candidates' loss functions are special cases of (5.17), with $\theta^A = K = -\theta^B$, where K is the value of holding office for both candidates.

The economy is described as in (5.3), except that here $\epsilon_t \equiv 0$. That is, both candidates are equally competent. Wages are set after having observed the election outcome for the current period, but in advance of policy. As usual, policy commitments are ruled out, both vis-à-vis voters and vis-à-vis wage setters.

As in Section 3, this infinite-horizon model admits many equilibria. But one class of equilibria stands out as particularly interesting. Suppose the following wage strategies were adopted:

$$\text{At } t = 0: \quad \pi_t^e = \gamma\lambda,$$

$$\text{At } t > 0: \begin{cases} \pi_t^e = \gamma\lambda & \text{if } \pi_{t-1} = \pi_{t-1}^e \ or \text{ if } z_t \neq z_{t-1} \\ \pi_t^e = \lambda & \text{otherwise.} \end{cases} \tag{5.18}$$

where $0 < \gamma < 1$. The wage strategy in (5.18) resembles the trigger strategies in Section 3 with one important difference: Wage setters revert to low expected inflation whenever the old government is replaced with a new one—that is, if $z_t \neq z_{t-1}$—irrespective of the policy implemented in the previous period. Thus a newly appointed government is 'given the benefit of doubt' if the previous government messed up the economy in the previous period. Of course, this assumption is largely arbitrary, but it is meant to capture electoral promises and, more generally, indicate that a change of government can break the continuity with the past and focus the economy's attention on a new set of policy proposals. Clearly, the expectations underlying this wage strategy may make sense in some political environments, but not in others. We now show that this new feature of (5.18) has striking implications for reputational equilibria.

5.4.2. *The Voters*
In equilibrium, the two candidates choose the same inflation rate. Hence, along the equilibrium path, the election outcome depends only on the distribution of θ^i in the population. Specifically, let θ^m denote the median value of θ. Following an equilibrium history, A is elected if $\theta^m > 0$, B is elected if $\theta^m < 0$. With shocks to voters' turnout, θ^m is a random variable. Suppose that the cumulative distribution of θ^m, $P(\theta)$, remains constant over time. Then, the equilibrium probability that A wins the elections is constant and given by

$$P \equiv 1 - P(0) \tag{5.19}$$

in each period. Following a non-equilibrium history, however—that is, if $\pi_{t-1} \neq \pi_{t-1}^e$—the two candidates are associated with different expected inflation rates and choose different policies. Suppose for concreteness that A is the incumbent in period t, and that $\pi_{t-1} \neq \pi_{t-1}^e$ (A cheated in the previous period). If A wins, wages are set on the basis of $\pi_t^e = \lambda$. Suppose that (5.18) is consistent with equilibrium (we show when this is true in the next subsection). Then, $\pi_t^e = \pi_t = \lambda$, $x_t = 0$ and the loss for voter i is $L(\lambda,0) - \theta^i = \lambda^2/2 - \theta^i$. If B wins, on the other hand, $\pi_t^e = \gamma\lambda$ and the equilibrium loss for voter i is $(\gamma\lambda)^2 + \theta^i$. Thus, the probability that A is re-elected after having cheated is:[83]

$$\tilde{P} \equiv -P(\lambda^2(1-\gamma^2)/4), \tag{5.20}$$

which is clearly smaller than P in (5.19) (since the function $P(\cdot)$ is increasing). An analogous result holds for candidate B.

In other words, an incumbent that created policy surprises loses votes. Voters realize that re-electing an incumbent who cheated means higher expected inflation, and hence lower social welfare, in the current period. Therefore, they are less likely to cast their vote for him. Note that voters are forward looking: They don't 'punish' a government for having cheated; on the contrary, cheating may temporary decrease the loss. But voters realize that policy surprises disrupt inflationary expectations, and electing a new government can be a way to stabilize those expectations.

5.4.3. *Equilibrium*

Consider now the incentives of a government (say of type A) that is in power at time t, after an equilibrium history (so that $\pi_t^e = \gamma\lambda$). The temptation to surprise is identical to that in Section 3.

$$L(\lambda\gamma, 0) - L(\lambda, \lambda(1-\gamma)) = \lambda^2(1-\gamma)^2/2. \tag{5.21a}$$

The enforcement now takes into account the change in the probability of re-election. Specifically, in this new environment, the enforcement is:

$$\delta[\tilde{P}(\lambda, 0) - L(\gamma\lambda, 0)) + K(P - \tilde{P})] \\ = \delta[\tilde{P}(\lambda^2(1-\gamma^2)/2 + K(P - \tilde{P})]. \tag{5.21b}$$

For (5.18) to be an equilibrium, the enforcement must exceed the temptation. Using (5.21) and (2.3), this incentive compatibility condition can be written as:

$$\delta K(P - \tilde{P}) > \lambda^2(1-\gamma)[(1-\gamma) - (1+\gamma)\delta\tilde{P}]/2. \tag{5.22}$$

Thus, if (5.22) holds, $\pi_t = \gamma\lambda = \pi_t^e$ in each period, and an inflation rate lower than the one-shot Nash can be enforced.[84] Clearly, (5.22) is more

---

[83] Equation (5.20) has been obtained by noting that voter i is indifferent between A and B when $(\lambda^2/2) - \theta^i = (\gamma\lambda)^2 + \theta^i$, which in turn implies $\theta^i = (\lambda^2(1-\gamma^2)/4)$.

[84] Since according to (5.18) wage setters revert to the one-shot Nash strategy in the event of a deviation, the sequential rationality condition is automatically satisfied.

likely to hold the higher is the value of holding office—the higher is K —and the more the future is valued—the higher is δ. Moreover, and more interestingly, (5.22) is less likely to be satisfied if $(P - \tilde{P})$ is small; that is, if cheating results in only a small drop in the probability of re-election.

The value of $(P - \tilde{P})$ can be small for two reasons. First, if P is close to zero, the probability of re-election is low for the incumbent even along the equilibrium path. In this case, the threat of being voted out of office for cheating becomes less fearsome, because the government has a very small probability of being elected anyway. Hence, the enforcement mechanism breaks down, since the government has little to lose.

Second, $P - \tilde{P}$ can be small if the distribution of θ^i in the population is very polarized. Recall from (5.19) and (5.20) that $P - \tilde{P} = P(\lambda^2(1 - \gamma^2)/4) - P(0)$ (if A is the incumbent), where $P(\cdot)$ is the cumulative distribution of θ^m. For a very polarized society, the cumulative distribution of the median is relatively flat (since the median is unlikely to be representative of a large fraction of the voters). Hence, $P - \tilde{P}$ is smaller than for a more homogeneous society. More intuitively, in a very polarized society the alternative candidates are perceived as being very different. Voters are therefore relatively immobile and unwilling to switch candidate and punish a government just because it created policy surprises. Hence, the political enforcement mechanism is less effective.

5.4.4. *Discussion*

Our simple political model of reputation yields some easily testable predictions: Equilibrium inflation should be higher in those countries or in those times in which the government is weak, in the sense of facing dim re-election prospects. It should also be higher if the electorate is very polarized, and hence immobile.

Naturally, our model admits many other equilibria. However, in this context multiplicity seems a little less disturbing. Credibility is enforced by the voters. But the vote is a non-strategic decision, in the sense that what is optimal for one voter does not depend on how the other voters behave. Hence, the coordination problem among voters is less formidable than among wage setters. True, the voting decision is a best response to the wage setters' strategy, and in this sense it is strategic. However, the precise form of the expectations formation rule becomes less important, and more plausible specifications of (5.18) can also sustain an equilibrium with low inflation. In particular, the low-inflation equilibrium survives if the wage formation rule reflects some form of bounded rationality on the part of wage setters, rather than being a sequentially rational strategy. What is essential is that: (a) unexpected policy actions change inflationary expectations; (b) voters perceive this change in expectations as negative; and (c) electing a new government stabilizes expectations. Finally, for many governments the threat of being voted out of office is likely to be more powerful than the fear of bringing about some adverse economic outcome.

5.5. Discussion

The research on political aspects of macroeconomic policy is still in its infancy. Thus, the results of this section are more preliminary and more likely to become quickly obsolete than the results of the previous chapters. A complete assessment of what has been learned from the literature and the previous subsections is still premature. But we can speculate on where this literature is likely to go. Two directions seem particularly fruitful.

On one hand, the models in this section are richer in institutional content and in testable predictions than most of the models discussed in the previous sections and therefore are particularly apt to stimulate empirical research. To some extent they have already done so. For instance, the empirical predictions of political business cycle models like those in Sections 5.2 and 5.3 have been investigated, both for the US and for some European countries.[85] Although the results are somewhat mixed, they seem to mildly support this generation of models rather than the old generation of political business cycles models based on backward-looking voters. In particular, the stylized fact about the US that we mentioned in Section 4—that inflationary surprises tend to occur after rather than before presidential elections—supports the model based on ideologically motivated candidates in Section 5.3.

On the other hand, models with political institutions lead naturally to normative questions of institutional design. For instance, an obvious question is whether the political business cycles due to ideologically motivated or office motivated politicians can be mitigated by

---

[85] See Alesina [4] and [5].

delegation of responsibility to a central bank. Another question is whether changes in the electoral system (such as in the timing of elections or in the degree of proportionality) can facilitate the political enforcement mechanisms or again mitigate the political cycles. These are difficult questions, since politically induced distortions may reflect other more primitive distortions. For instance, political business cycles may convey information to the voters, and trying to suppress them may be welfare reducing for society as a whole. As in many second-best situations, the analysis of institutional reform is a delicate, though very exciting, task for research.

On this note, we leave the politically oriented theory of monetary policy, as well as the theory of monetary policy, inflation and employment, in general. The next part of the monograph deals instead with fiscal policy. We return to a politically oriented theory of policy in Section 9.

5.6. Notes on the literature

The idea of a political business cycle was first discussed in the context of models with adaptive expectations, by Lindbeck [88] and Nordhaus [98]. The model of Section 5.2, where the business cycle reflects the signalling activity of the incumbent, is based on the research of Cukierman-Meltzer [42], Rogoff and Sibert [118], Rogoff [117] and Ferejohn [53].

Alesina [5] analyzes a model similar to that of Section 5.3, where political instability causes excessive policy volatility. The point that policy convergence to the median voter fails in the absence of precommitment is studied in Wittman [137]. Wittman [139] is a more recent survey of the literature on elections with ideological policy-makers. Alesina [3] and [4] investigate how to sustain cooperation between alternating ideological parties with different preferences. The idea that political alternation may be a cause of political business cycles is due to Hibbs [75]. Alesina [3] applies it to the monetary policy model of Section 5.3. The idea of Section 5.4, that elections can enforce reputation, is studied in Minford [97], though in a model quite different from that of this section. Several recent empirical papers on the topics of this section have been written. They are surveyed in Alesina [5].

Finally, Terrones [132] shows that endogenous timing of elections can mitigate political business cycles.

Part II

6. COMMITMENT VERSUS DISCRETION IN WEALTH TAXATION

6.1. Introduction

This section starts the second part of our monograph and our discussion of fiscal policy. Our general approach in this Part borrows from the methods of public finance. Namely, the models we study have explicit microeconomic foundations and lend themselves to meaningful welfare analysis. But our approach departs from the traditional public finance approach in that it includes a richer description of the policy environment. Traditional public finance is largely normative and, to the extent it deals with dynamic models, typically assumes that the policymaker can commit future policy. We are after a positive as well as a normative theory, and typically assume that policy can not be committed in advance. This leads to credibility constraints on the policymaker, similar to those that we studied in the first Part. Furthermore, we discuss policy environments where political considerations help shape policy and where the expected policies of future governments with different preferences impose additional, political, incentive constraints on current policymakers.

From a methodological point of view, there is an important difference between the models in Part II and the models of monetary policy in Part I. There, the models had no economic dynamics and the only links between time periods were the updating of the government's and the private sector's information sets. Here, the models do have economic dynamics, because there are state variables like capital or debt. Formally, we are therefore dealing with dynamic games, rather than with repeated games. The theory of dynamic games has not been able to derive many results on how to characterize solutions for general multiperiod dynamic games. This is largely because of immense technical and computational difficulties. We avoid many of these difficulties by looking mostly at simple two-period examples.

This section can be seen as a stepping stone for further analysis. In this first subsection, we present a simple model in which the government can tax labor and capital. Sections 6.2 and 6.3 compare equilibrium tax policy with and without policy commitments, both from a positive point of view and from a normative point of view. Section 6.4 then shows how the same setup, with minor modifications, can be used to analyze other forms of wealth taxation, such as seignorage and public debt repudiation. Some concluding comments are collected in Section 6.5.

In the next section we extend this preliminary analysis of wealth taxation. In particular, we investigate whether second-best equilibrium tax policies in the commitment regime can be sustained even in the absence of commitments. As before, we look at reputational mechanisms, as well as institutional reforms that change various aspects of the fiscal policy decision process.

6.1.1. A Model of Capital Taxation

The model we suggest is essentially the same two-period model as the one we presented in Section 1; the difference is that we have a slightly more general specification of private preferences. The private sector is atomistic; and the representative consumer has the utility function:

$$U(c_1) + c_2 - V(l), \qquad (6.1)$$

where U is increasing and concave and V is increasing and convex. As in Section 1, c_t denotes consumption in period t and l denotes labor time in period 2.

In period 1, the consumer receives an exogenous endowment e, which is split between consumption and investment, k. (For simplicity, we abstract from labor supply decisions in period 1.) Thus, his first period budget constraint is:

$$c_1 + k \le e. \qquad (6.2)$$

There is a natural nonnegativity constraint on capital. Furthermore, it simplifies the analysis to assume that the consumers are not allowed to borrow, so that total savings are always non-negative too: $k \ge 0$.[86] In period 2, the consumer chooses consumption and labor hours. His

---

[86] If borrowing were allowed, we would get the same results by assuming that investment is not deductible from capital income taxation. In this case, the second period budget constraint would have to be written differently depending on whether $k > 0$ or $k < 0$. Otherwise, we would have to endogenize the interest rate so as to have zero borrowing in equilibrium.

disposable income consists of the gross return to capital and of labor income, both net of taxes. Thus, his second period budget constraint is:

$$c_2 \leq R(1 - \theta)k + (1 - \tau)l, \qquad (6.3)$$

where $R > 1$ is the gross return on capital, θ and τ are the tax rates on capital and labor income, and the real wage has been set equal to unity by an appropriate scaling of the (linear) technology. The returns on investment are constant for any aggregate amount invested.

Thus, taxes are paid only in period 2, and there is no non-distortionary fiscal instrument. Even though the reason for this lack of fiscal instruments is not explicitly modeled, it must ultimately have to do with an informational constraint, namely that the government can not observe individual types. Strictly speaking, there can be no such constraints here, since every agent in the private sector is identical. Similar results would go through even with heterogeneous agents, however.[87] Finally, as in the previous sections, we continue to assume that the policy game is anonymous. Thus, only the *average* economic variables and policy are observable.[88]

The government sets tax rates, τ and θ, so as to maximize the consumer's welfare, subject to the government budget constraint:

$$g \leq \tau l + \theta Rk. \qquad (6.4)$$

In (6.4) g is the government's revenue requirement, which arises from a predetermined amount of (per capita) public expenditure in period 2. Since public expenditure is exogenous, it does not matter whether we include g in the consumer's utility function or not.

6.2. Commitment

Consider first a fiscal regime with commitments: In period 1, before any private economic decisions are made, the government announces

---

[87] Heterogeneity is introduced in our model of capital taxation in Section 7.

[88] The anonymity assumption, though very natural, is more problematic in this context. In writing down equations (6.2) and (6.3), we have implicitly assumed that the government can enforce the private budget constraints, and hence that it can enforce tax collection of labor and capital income. The nature of the enforcement technology has been left implicit; but presumably it must rely on the government being able to impose a penalty (at least probabilistically) to any consumer who violates its budget constraint. Hence, we have implicitly assumed that the government (or some of its agencies) can observe at least a sample of individual actions and endowments. We return to this issue in the concluding subsection.

and commits to a tax policy (τ, θ) for period 2. What is the equilibrium tax policy in this regime? This is, in fact, precisely the question posed in the literature on optimal taxation. By equilibrium we mean a Stackelberg equilibrium with the government as the dominant player, analogus to the equilibrium with commitment in Section 2. In this equilibrium: (i) The individual labor supply and saving functions are optimal for every consumer, for any tax policy announced by the government and given all the other equilibrium labor supply and savings functions. (ii) The tax policy is optimal for the government, given the equilibrium aggregate labor supply and savings functions.

The equilibrium is computed as in any optimal taxation problem. At a private sector optimum, the following first-order conditions (derived from (6.1)–(6.3)) must be satisfied:

$$U_c(e - k)/R \geq (1 - \theta), \ [k \geq 0] \tag{6.5}$$

$$V_l(l) = (1 - \tau). \tag{6.6}$$

The weak inequality and the square bracket in (6.5) reflect the non-negativity constraint on k: Strict inequality between marginal utility and the after-tax return implies $k = 0$. Throughout the section we assume that $U_c(e) < R$, so that the consumer invests a positive amount when the tax on capital is zero.

Equations (6.5) and (6.6) emphasize the distortionary effect of taxation. In (6.5), the tax on capital drives a wedge between the marginal rate of transformation between goods in periods 1 and 2, R, and the marginal rate of substitution of goods in periods 1 and 2, $U_c(\cdot)/1$. In (6.6), the tax on labor drives a wedge between the marginal rate of transformation between goods and labor, unity, and the marginal rate of substitution between goods and labor, $V_l(l)$. Equations (6.5) and (6.6) implicitly define equilibrium labor supply and savings as a function of the tax rates:

$$k = \text{Max}[0, K(\theta)], \text{ with } K(\theta) \equiv e - U_c^{-1}(R(1 - \theta)) \tag{6.5}'$$

$$l = L(\tau) \equiv V_l^{-1}(1 - \tau). \tag{6.6}'$$

Here, the partials K_θ and L_τ are both negative. Note that the separability and linearity in (6.1) make the supply of each tax base a function of the tax rate on that tax base only. These supply functions are constraints on the government's optimization problem. Higher tax rates lead to lower tax bases and hence to larger excess burdens. An equilibrium tax policy minimizes the overall excess burden, subject to the government budget constraint.

6.2.1. *Equilibrium Tax Policy*

More precisely, an equilibrium tax policy solves the following government optimization problem: Choose θ and τ to maximize consumer welfare, (6.1), subject to the private first-order conditions, (6.5) and (6.6), the government budget constraint, (6.4), and the aggregate resource constraints in period 1, (6.2), and in period 2,

$$c_2 + g \leq l + Rk. \tag{6.7}$$

The problem can be simplified, by stating it in terms of l and k. To do that, substitute (6.5) and (6.6) into (6.4) and rewrite the government budget constraint as:

$$g \leq (1 - V_l(l))l + (R - U_c(e - k))k. \tag{6.4'}$$

Next, substitute (6.7) and (6.2) into (6.1). The problem can then be written as:

$$\begin{array}{c} \text{Max}[U(e - k) + l + Rk - g - V(l)] \\ l,k \end{array} \tag{6.1'}$$

subject to (6.4)', with g predetermined. (Alternatively, we can substitute (6.5)' and (6.6)' into (6.1)' and maximize over θ and τ.)

The first-order conditions to the problem say:

$$\frac{1 - V_l(l)}{1 - V_l(l) - lV_{ll}(l)} = \frac{U_c(e - k) - R}{U_c(e - k) - R - kU_{cc}(e - k)}. \tag{6.8}$$

As is common in optimal taxation problems, we have no guarantee that the first-order conditions are sufficient. Although the policy objective (6.1)' is concave, the constraint (6.4)' need not be convex because of the non-linear terms in l and k. In the following, we simply assume that the second-order conditions are fulfilled.

Despite its complicated appearance, equation (6.8) has a very intuitive interpretation. The numerators measure the marginal tax distortions; that is, they measure the wedges between the marginal rate of transformation in production and the marginal rate of substitution in consumption. Referring to the discussion of equations (6.5) and (6.6), we see that the numerator on the left hand side is the marginal distortion of the tax on labor and the numerator on the right hand side is the marginal distortion of the tax on capital. It is easy to demonstrate that the denominators in (6.8) measure the increase in revenue of higher tax rates (on labor on the left hand side and on capital on the right hand side). Hence, equation (6.8) is an instance of the well-known Ramsey rule: Under an optimal tax structure, the distortion that the last dollar of revenue creates is equated across tax bases.

Making use of (6.5) and (6.6), the Ramsey rule in (6.8) can be expressed in perhaps more familiar terms as:

$$\frac{1-\tau}{\tau} \bigg/ \frac{1-\theta}{\theta} = \epsilon_l / \epsilon_k. \tag{6.8}'$$

In (6.8)' $\epsilon_l = V_l(l)/lV_{ll}(l)$ is the elasticity of the labor supply function and $\epsilon_k = -U_c(e-k)/kU_{cc}(e-k)$ is the elasticity of the savings supply function, both with respect to rates of return net of taxes. If the two elasticities happen to equal each other, the optimal tax rates θ and τ are also equal. Otherwise, the more inelastic tax base is taxed more heavily.

An important result follows immediately from (6.8)'. If ϵ_l and ϵ_k are both positive but finite, the equilibrium tax policy always calls for taxing *both* labor and capital, though less than at 100%. The intuition is simple: If any tax rate is zero, increasing it marginally brings about only a second-order distortion, but a first-order increase in tax revenue. But if a tax rate is positive, increasing it marginally always brings about a first-order distortion. If follows that—in a fiscal regime with commitments—no equilibrium tax policy can rely on only one of the two distortionary taxes.

Finally, note that the tax policy implied by (6.8)' leaves the economy at a second-best allocation: Since both taxes are distortionary, private welfare would be higher if the government had access to an additional non-distorting fiscal instrument to finance public consumption. It is precisely the lack of fiscal instruments that explains why this tax policy is not credible in a regime where commitments are ruled out.

6.3. Discretion

Suppose now, more realistically, that the government cannot enter into binding commitments regarding its fiscal policy, but instead reoptimizes at the beginning of each period. Thus, the timing of moves is as follows: In period 1, each consumer chooses how much to save, based on his expectations about future tax policy. At the beginning of period 2, the government selects a tax policy as a function of the aggregate amount saved. Finally, having observed government tax policy, each consumer chooses how much to work.

The equilibrium in this discretionary policy environment is defined by our usual sequentially rational Nash condition, that the strategy of every agent is an optimal response to the equilibrium strategies of all other agents at any possible information set that can be reached in the game. More precisely: (i) In period 1, the capital accumulated by every consumer is optimal, given the equilibrium policy rule for setting θ and τ and given the equilibrium capital accumulation of other consumers. And in period 2, the labor supply function is optimal for every consumer for any observed tax policy and given the equilibrium labor supply functions of other consumers. (ii) In period 2, the policy rule for setting τ and θ is optimal for the government, for any aggregate amount saved by consumers and given the equilibrium aggregate labor supply functions.

6.3.1. *The Credibility Constraint*
Private optimal behavior is still defined by the first-order conditions (6.5) and (6.6), except that the actual tax on capital, θ, is replaced by its expectation, θ^e.

However, the equilibrium tax policy in the previous section is not credible under discretion. From the vantage point of period 2, that tax policy is not *ex post* optimal for the government. Once the private sector has locked itself into a savings decision, a tax on capital is not distortionary, because consumers can no longer reduce investment in response to an increase in the tax rate. Formally, the government's *ex post* problem is still to maximize (6.1)′ subject to (6.4)′ with g predetermined. But *ex post* the aggregate capital stock is predetermined and not given by (6.5) as in the *ex ante* problem. In other words, even though the *ex ante* elasticity of savings with respect to the after-tax rate of return, $1 - \theta$, is positive, the *ex post* elasticity of savings is zero. It follows from (6.8)′ that the *ex post* optimal tax structure must rely on the capital tax to the largest possible extent. Thus, in equilibrium we must have:

$$\theta(k) = \text{Min} \, [1, g/Rk]. \tag{6.9}$$

The equilibrium labor tax, τ, is determined residually from the government budget constraint; in particular $\tau = 0$ if $\theta < 1$. Equation (6.9) is thus a further incentive constraint that any equilibrium tax policy has to satisfy. It is a credibility constraint similar to those that we studied earlier, in the context of monetary policy.

To close the model we now go back to period 1. We obtain the equilibrium tax policy by combining the private sector first-order condition, (6.5), with the credibility constraint (6.9). Note that because consumers are atomistic, they take the capital k entering in (6.9) as given, because (6.9) is conditional on *aggregate* (or average) capital, not on the investment decision of single consumers.

Figure 6.1 illustrates the equilibrium. The 'Laffer curve' in the leftmost diagram depicts the *ex ante* revenue function from capital taxation, when the government can commit to a tax structure as in the previous subsection.[89] Any equilibrium under discretion must also lie on this curve, because otherwise private sector expectations would not be fulfilled. The rightmost diagram depicts the *ex post* revenue function from capital taxation. *Ex post*, in period 2, aggregate capital is given. Hence, the revenue function is simply a straight line through the origin, with slope $RK(\theta^e)$.

6.3.2. *Full Expropriation*

Suppose that aggregate capital is zero, because no individual consumer saves anything. According to (6.9), then $\theta = 1$. It follows from the first-order condition in (6.5) that k = 0 is indeed optimal for each individual consumer. In terms of Figure 6.1, the *ex post* revenue function coincides with the horizontal axis of the rightmost diagram, and point C in the leftmost diagram is an equilibrium point, In this equilibrium, each consumer expects to be fully expropriated and does not save anything. A capital tax of 100% is indeed imposed. Nevertheless, the tax does not raise any revenue since aggregate capital is zero.

Notice that this equilibrium is the worst possible from a welfare point of view. This is because: (a) the government is forced to rely exclusively on labor taxes, so that the excess burden of taxation is very

---

[89] A sufficient condition for the *ex ante* revenue function to be globally concave as drawn in Figure 6.1 is that $U_{ccc}(\cdot) \geq 0$; this property is satisfied by any utility function with non-increasing absolute risk aversion. If $U_{ccc}(\cdot) < 0$, then the *ex ante* revenue function need not be concave everywhere. But it would still be downward sloping past some value of θ, and it would still go to zero as θ approaches unity. The results are not affected in any relevant way by whether the *ex ante* revenue function is concave everywhere or not.

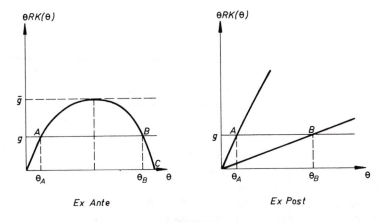

FIGURE 6.1

high; and (b) consumers forego potentially fruitful investment opportunities. (Recall that $U_c(e) < R$, so that the marginal product of investment is higher than the marginal utility of first period consumption when consumers save nothing).

Yet, despite its obvious suboptimality, the equilibrium is fully consistent with sequential rationality by each individual consumer. This is because the private sector is atomistic and because the savings decision is made simultaneously by all consumers. Since the policy rule (6.9) is contingent on aggregate capital, when everybody expects everyone else to anticipate $\theta = 1$, full expropriation becomes inevitable irrespective of the single consumer's investment decision. Hence, it is individually rational for each consumer not to accumulate any capital. In this respect, the equilibrium is very similar to a banking panic, where the fear of a bad outcome is made self-fulfilling when everyone makes a simultaneous decision about withdrawing his bank deposit.[90]

6.3.3. Partial Expropriation

Consider the leftmost diagram in Figure 6.1. Define $\bar{g}$ as the maximum possible revenue from the capital income tax: $\bar{g} = \underset{\theta}{\text{Max}} [\theta RK(\theta)]$. If public spending exceeds $\bar{g}$ only one equilibrium exists. If $g > \bar{g}$, a tax on

---

[90] Calvo [30] has drawn the analogy between banking panics and debt repudiation (which we show in the next subsection to be analogous to capital taxation) in an interesting recent paper.

capital alone is never sufficient to fully finance public spending. It follows from the credibility constraint (6.9) that $\theta = 1$ in any possible equilibrium. Thus the full expropriation equilibrium is the unique outcome when $g > \bar{g}$. Interestingly, the full expropriation equilibrium continues to exist even if $g \leq \bar{g}$. If all consumers expect $\theta = 1$, their optimal response is to save nothing irrespective of the value of g. But given that aggregate capital is small (or zero), it is indeed optimal for the government to set $\theta = 1$ (as long as $g > 0$). Given that other consumers fear full expropriation, it is optimal for every single consumer to save nothing. This way, the expectation of full expropriation becomes self-fulfilling.

However, when g is below $\bar{g}$, other equilibria with more desirable properties also exist. Consider again the leftmost diagram in Figure 6.1, and let public spending correspond to the horizontal line labelled g. Then point A is an equilibrium; and so is point B. At point A, every consumer expects $\theta^e = \theta_A$ and invests $K(\theta_A)$. Given the resulting level of aggregate capital, the government can exactly finance g by setting $\theta = \theta_A$. As shown in the rightmost diagram of Figure 6.1, the government then faces the *ex post* revenue function given by the dotted line and indeed finds it optimal to choose $\theta = \theta_A$. Hence, point A is an equilibrium. Similarly, at point B, every consumer expects $\theta^e = \theta_B$ and saves $K(\theta_B)$. And *ex post*, the government finds it optimal to fulfill these expectations by setting $\theta = \theta_B$.[91]

Clearly, welfare is higher at point A than at point B (since B is on the wrong side of the Laffer curve), and in both equilibria it is higher than in the equilibrium at point C. However, welfare is still lower at point A than in the equilibrium with commitments. Both at A and at B, $\theta < 1$, and therefore—recalling the previous discussion—$\tau = 0$ at both A and B. In both equilibria the equilibrium tax policy exploits the capital tax too heavily. If the government could credibly commit to a lower capital tax, it could reduce the excess burden of taxation by approaching the solution in Section 6.2

To summarize, capital is always excessively taxed in the equilibrium with discretion, while labor can be overtaxed (if $\theta = 1$) or undertaxed

---

[91] The equilibrium tax rates θ_A and θ_B corresponding to points A and B can be formally defined as the values of θ that solve the following equation (obtained combining (6.5) and (6.9)):

$$U_c(e - g/R\theta) - R(1 - \theta) = 0.$$

(if $\theta < 1$) compared to the second-best commitment equilibrium. Moreover, if spending is sufficiently low (or the first-period endowment is sufficiently large), then multiple discretionary equilibria exist. These equilibria can be Pareto ranked, the better ones corresponding to higher equilibrium levels of capital and lower capital tax rates. But there is no way the government can select one of these equilibria.

6.3.4. Comments

In previous sections we argued that multiplicity of equilibria indicated an incomplete theory. But here one may argue that the multiplicity reflects a more fundamental indeterminancy in the economy itself. In the absence of commitments, the government loses control of private expectations. This may result in an intrinsic 'fragility' of any discretionary equilibrium. Equilibrium policy is conditional on a variable (aggregate capital) determined by average market expectations in the previous period. Hence, private expectations are not nailed down by any economic fundamentals, but can change widely depending on private conjectures of what these average expectations are.

We did not encounter this multiplicity of discretionary equilibria in the one-shot version of our monetary policy model. This was because we assumed a well-behaved problem with a concave government objective function and a linear constraint describing private behavior. With a less stylized model of the private sector—and maybe with better correspondence between government and private objectives—a multiplicity of discretionary equilibria could well occur also in the monetary policy model.

The above discussion points in two interesting directions. First, the value of policy commitments may be understated by a comparison of the second-best and third-best outcomes. Commitments can also reduce strategic uncertainty about which equilibrium will prevail; in other words, they can remove an important indeterminacy. For example, if the same government revenue is generated either by a low tax rate and a high tax base or by a high tax rate and a low tax base, then the government would simply commit to the lower tax rate. And conversely, the lack of commitments may result in outcomes that are far worse than the third best (the equilibrium with full expropriation in our model above was far worse than the equilibria with partial expropriation). Second, if commitments are impossible, the government could benefit greatly if it could exert some limited influence on market expectations, through reputation or through other policy instruments. This second implication is explored in the next section. In the remainder of this section, we briefly illustrate how the same problem that we have studied in the previous pages can arise under different forms of wealth taxation.

6.4. Other forms of wealth taxation

The results in the previous subsections all derive from our assumptions about timing. Without commitments, consumers have to make an investment decision before the government selects tax policy. Therefore, the tax base of the capital tax is predetermined once the tax rate is chosen. This timing is common to all taxation of wealth. In this subsection we show that our previous results apply almost identically to other kinds of wealth taxes besides capital taxation.

6.4.1. Surprise Inflation

Consider again the model in Section 6.1, and suppose that only the government has access to the investment technology. For simplicity, we fix the returns to investment at unity. That is, we set $R = 1$. In order to save, consumers must sell their first-period endowment to the government against fiat money. The stored endowment can then be repurchased tomorrow at the going market price. Thus, fiat money is the only form in which the private sector can accumulate wealth. The nominal quantity of money in circulation in every period is determined by the government.

Under these assumptions, the representative consumer's constraints for periods 1 and 2 can be written as:

$$c_1 + m_1 \leq e \tag{6.10}$$

$$c_2 + m_2 \leq l(1 - \tau) + m_1(1 - \pi). \tag{6.11}$$

Here, m_t is the real money balances at the end of period t, and π is the inflation rate between periods 1 and 2, divided by the gross inflation rate. That is, π is defined by: $\pi \equiv (p_2 - p_1)/p_2$. The remaining variables are defined as in Section 6.1.

In order to have a well defined demand for money in the last period, we assume that real money balances in period 2 enter the consumer's utility function. This assumption is justified if money balances provide liquidity services and can be derived from more primitive hypotheses about the transactions technology.[92] We then formulate the representative consumer's utility function as:

$$U(c_1) + c_2 - V(l) + H(m_2). \tag{6.12}$$

The specification in (6.12) makes the demand for real money balances in the second period constant, by the first-order condition: $H_m(m_2) = 1$. The demand for real money balances in period 1, on the other hand, is determined exactly like the savings function of the previous subsections. Specifically, the first-order conditions—when we maximize (6.12) with respect to m_1 subject to (6.10) and (6.11)—yield:

$$U_c(e - m_1) \geq 1 - \pi^e, \quad [m_1 \geq 0]. \tag{6.13}$$

In (6.13), π^e denotes the period 1 expectation of π, and the weak inequality plus the bracket reflect a non-negativity constraint on m_1: If the inequality is strict, then $m_1 = 0$. According to (6.13), a higher expected inflation rate reduces the expected return to real money balances, and hence reduces m_1 (if $m_1 > 0$).[93]

The government can now collect revenue by two means: by taxing labor, and by printing money. Consolidating its single-period budget constraints and retaining the assumption that public spending only occurs in period 2, government decisions have to satisfy:

$$g \leq \tau l + m_2 + \pi m_1. \tag{6.14}$$

Equation (6.14) shows that—for given m_1—inflation provides revenues for the government. Essentially, inflation is a tax on nominal wealth: In period 2 inflation reduces the purchasing power of the money that was printed in period 1 in exchange for the goods that the government invested. Hence, inflation reduces the real value of the nominal claims issued by the government in the previous period, and thus redistributes wealth from the private to the public sector.

It should be clear by now that the formal structure of this model is identical to that of the previous sections. If we relabel, m_1 as k and π as θR, it is easy to verify that the model is almost identical to that of Section 6.1. The main difference is that π is not under the direct control

---

[92] By this formulation we ignore the problem of who ends up holding the money at the end of our finite horizon model.

[93] Adding m_1 to the utility function and assuming that the consumer has access to the investment technology — as we do in the next section — would not change the nature of the results.

of the government, but is a market price. The government only controls the nominal quantity of money in period 2, M_2. But this difference plays no significant role, since there is a one-to-one relationship between π and M_2 through the money market equilibrium condition.[94] The results derived in Sections 6.2 and 6.3 therefore extend identically to this reformulated model, as the reader can easily verify by repeating the steps in our previous argument.

If the government can commit its money growth for the next period, then its equilibrium policy collects some revenue through the inflation tax and some through the labor tax, according to the optimal proportions in (6.8)'. But if commitments are impossible, the second-best inflation tax is not credible. The government has an *ex post* incentive to surprise, since by creating unexpected inflation it can collect revenue without reducing the demand for real money balances, and thus without distorting the savings decision.[95] In a discretionary equilibrium the private sector anticipates the government incentives. And hence the government ends up overinflating relative to the second-best equilibrium, but there are no surprises. As the previous section showed, there could be multiple Pareto ranked equilibria under discretion. The worst equilibrium, which always exists, has $\pi = 1$ and $m_1 = 0$. As in the previous subsection, the government fully expropriates any existing nominal wealth, by driving the price level of period 2 to infinity. The private sector, anticipating this outcome, does not hold any nominal wealth.[96]

6.4.2. *Debt Repudiation*

In order to analyze the government borrowing and debt repayment decisions, consider yet another version of the previous model, where

---

[94] Specifically, from the money market equilibrium condition $p_2 m_2 = M_2$, the definition of π, and the private sector first-order condition for m_2, it is easy to verify that:

$$d\pi/dM_2 = (1 - \pi)/M_2.$$

[95] In a more general model with other assets, where the demand for m_1 reflects the liquidity services of money, the inflation tax distorts the provision of liquidity services, rather than the savings decision. (See Section 7.1 in the next section).

[96] This argument abstracts from the cost of operating the printing press. The model, as stated, implies that second period money growth and prices both go to infinity in a way that maintains the condition $m_2 = H_m^{-1}(1)$. At such extreme rates of money expansion, one may argue that the marginal seigniorage may not be worth the cost of printing infinite amounts of money.

public debt, b, is the only store of value. There is no money and all variables denote real magnitudes. To avoid some problems with corner solutions and to introduce the concept of tax smoothing across time, which will appear in subsequent sections, we now assume that the representative consumer works and can be taxed in both periods. His preferences are now given by:

$$c_1 - V(l_1) + c_2 - V(l_2). \tag{6.15}$$

To simplify the exposition, we thus make the utility function linear in consumption in both periods, but the qualitative argument does not hinge on this assumption. The notation and the $V(\cdot)$ function are the same as above. Letting $1/R$ be the market price of public debt when issued, the consumer's two-period budget constraint can be written as:

$$c_1 + b/R \leq l_1(1 - \tau_1)$$
$$c_2 \leq l_2(1 - \tau_2) + b(1 - \theta), \tag{6.16}$$

where τ_t is the tax rate on labor income in period t and θ is the tax rate on the debt outstanding in period 2 (equivalently, θ can be thought of as the fraction of debt repudiated by the government).

The first-order conditions to this problem are:

$$V_l(l_t) = (1 - \tau_t), t = 1, 2 \tag{6.17}$$
$$b = 0 \text{ if } R(1 - \theta^e) < 1$$

$$b = Rl_1(1 - \tau_1) \text{ if } R(1 - \theta^e) > 1 \tag{6.18}$$
$$b\epsilon [0, Rl_1(1 - \tau_1)] \text{ if } R(1 - \theta^e) = 1.$$

Equation (6.17) is identical to (6.5) in Section 2, and defines the labor supply function in each period. Since utility is linear in consumption in both periods, there is no income effect on labor supply: In each period, labor supply only depends on the labor tax rate in that period.

Equation (6.18) is equivalent to (1.8) in Section 1, and defines savings as a function of the expected real interest rate net of taxes. In deriving (6.18), we used the assumption that the consumer cannot borrow (that is: $b \geq 0$). Since consumption in one period is a perfect substitute for consumption in the other, the consumer only cares about the net return on government debt. If the return is negative he saves nothing, if it is positive he saves as much as he can, otherwise he is indifferent.

Now, suppose that there is exogenous government spending only in period 1, rather than in period 2. Then, the government budget constraints for periods 1 and 2 are:

$$g \geq b/R + \tau_1 l_1 \qquad (6.19)$$
$$b(1 - \theta) \leq \tau_2 l_2.$$

Consider a policy environment where the government can commit to honoring its future debt obligations; thus, $\theta = 0$. The choice of a tax policy now involves choosing τ_1, and τ_2, or, equivalently, τ_1 and b (since once b has been issued, τ_2 is uniquely determined from the government budget constraint in period 2). Once the government has committed to $\theta = 0$ (or to any other value of θ), there is no other commitment issue in this model, since g is predetermined. It is easy to show that the equilibrium tax policy in this regime must have $\tau_1 = \tau_2$. Intuitively, the Ramsey principle now calls for equating the tax distortion that the last dollar of revenue creates across (the same tax base in) different periods. The symmetry of the model makes the elasticity of labor supply the same in each period if $\tau_1 = \tau_2$. Hence, the Ramsey rule requires tax rates to be equal across periods, given that $R(1 - \theta^e) = 1$.

In order to implement this tax policy, the government must issue public debt in period 1. Thus, public debt allows the government to reduce the overall excess burden of taxation, by smoothing the tax distortions over time. In order to induce consumers to lend to the government, the government has to issue public debt at a price $1/R = 1$.[97] In period 1, the government then sets τ_1, so as to satisfy:

$$\tau_1 L(\tau_1) = g/2. \qquad (6.20)$$

The remainder of public consumption is financed by issuing public debt amounting to $g/2$. The debt is repaid in period 2 with the proceeds of the period 2 tax on labor. Despite the tax smoothing, the government only achieves a second-best allocation, since taxes are distortionary.

But what if the government cannot commit to honoring its future debt obligations? Then, clearly, the policy we have described is not credible. In period 2, with b predetermined, the government would always find it optimal to repudiate all the outstanding debt to eliminate the excess burden of taxation. Anticipating this outcome, individual

---

[97] If the government had precommitted to a positive (but less than unity) value of θ, then the market price of debt would have to satisfy $R(1 - \theta) = 1$.

consumers would not buy the debt in period 1 at any positive price, however. Under discretion there is therefore only one equilibrium, in which $\theta = 1$, $b = 0$, and all public spending is financed by period 1 taxes alone.[98] Clearly, this raises the excess burden of taxation compared to the commitment equilibrium.

6.5. Discussion

All the results in this section stem from the same logic. Once an investment decision has been made, the tax base corresponding to the investment becomes predetermined. And it becomes *ex post* optimal to tax it as much as needed (or as much as possible).

Even though this logic is inescapable within our simple model, the model's predictions run counter to factual observations. In the real world 100% (or very high) taxation of wealth is almost never observed. There are several explanations which do not resort to the assumption that governments have commitment capacity. First, and perhaps most obvious, is that the government may care about its reputation. We saw in Sections 3 and 4 how a link between current monetary policy and future expected policy provided a check on the government's temptation to engage in surprise inflation. In the same way, a link between current fiscal policy and future expected policy may provide a check on the government's temptation to engage in surprise taxation of wealth. But even neglecting the force of reputation, the government may care about the adverse redistributional consequences of wealth expropriation. Or it may face transaction costs in changing the existing tax legislation. Moreover, the assumption that an investment decision makes the tax base corresponding to that investment predetermined is probably a gross exaggeration. Very high tax rates induce tax evasion. In the case of wealth taxes, an expropriating tax rate may lead to capital flight or to other forms of tax avoidance.

This section has drawn a close analogy between different forms of wealth taxation. However, it is important to point to clear differences between capital taxation and the inflation tax on money balances.

---

[98] Calvo (1988) shows that multiple equilibria would reappear if the discretionary equilibrium involved only partial (rather than full) debt repudiation; he obtains this by postulating that the government faces an exogenous cost whenever it repudiates, and that the cost is proportional to the amount repudiated.

The possibility for tax evasion or tax avoidance may be very different for different assets, depending on the physical character of the asset. But different institutions in the procedure for making tax policy decisions are also important, because it is the time elapsed between the announcement of a tax change and the actual collection of the tax that gives room for tax avoidance. One may argue that money is different from capital in both respects. The nature of money makes it harder to avoid surprise inflation. And monetary policy can be changed on very short notice by an administrative decision while taxation of capital (or debt repudiation) may require a parliamentary decision and debate before it can be enacted.

All the above reasons may explain why governments may find it optimal even *ex post* to keep relatively low taxes on wealth. Some of them are investigated in the next section.

Let us end this section on a methodological note. What we have dealt with in this section is really dynamic games, although in a very simple form. The literature on dynamic games has largely been developed as an extension of control theory. This theory has developed its own terminology, which does not always correspond to that of standard game theory. In that terminology, the equilibria in fiscal regimes with commitments would be described as 'open-loop equilibria'. The equilibria in the fiscal regimes with discretion would instead be classified as 'closed-loop equilibria'. What separates open-loop and closed-loop equilibria are the information sets you allow to be mapped into the strategies of different players: An open-loop strategy is based only on the information set at the beginning of the game, while a closed-loop strategy takes later information sets into account and is therefore based on the development of economic state variables over time. This terminology thus offers a natural language for discussing general multiperiod policy problems with genuine economic dynamics.

Although conceptually appealing, such dynamic policy problems very soon become very complicated. Complications arise particularly if one wants to characterize the closed-loop equilibria that naturally apply to a fiscal regime with discretionary policymaking. What becomes so complicated is basically the interaction between the state variables and the strategic incentives of the players. Even with the popular 'feedback' restriction—the actions at date t are allowed to depend only on the state variables at t—it is very hard to analytically characterize closed-loop equilibria. The exception is when you have problems where the objectives are quadratic and the constraints are linear in the state variables. But unfortunately, that structure fits the typical fiscal policy problem poorly. The reason is that any taxation problem, almost by definition, revolves around a nonlinear term in the government budget constraint: To arrive at government revenue we have to multiply tax bases by tax rates and both the tax bases and the tax rates will be functions of the stable variables.

Rather than tackling these different problems in the following, we shall deal mostly with simple two-period examples where the difficulties can be handled in a relatively simple way.

6.6. Notes on the literature

The 'capital levy problem' studied in this section has a long history in economics. Eichengreen [50] provides a historically oriented account of the capital levy problem. More recently, the credibility problem in capital taxation was formulated in an illustrative two-period model by Fischer [55]. An early treatment of the surprise-inflation problem is Auernheimer [15], but the classic here is definitely Calvo [29]. Calvo [30] deals with repudiation of domestic debt.

One of the first papers to apply the theory of dynamic games to economic policy was Kydland [84]. A general treatment of dynamic games from a control-theoretic point of view is the book by Basar and Olsder [24], while several applications to macroeconomic policy can be found in Buiter and Marston [27]. Levine and Holly [87] stress the control-theoretic approach in their survey of the literature on time consistency of economic policy. Cohen and Michel [39] show how to compute the equilibrium of a discretionary policy regime in a dynamic game with a linear-quadratic structure. Finally, Fudenberg and Tirole [61] to some extent bridge the gap between standard game theory and the theory of dynamic games.

7. SOCIAL INSTITUTIONS AND CREDIBLE TAX POLICY

7.1. Introduction

The previous section found that discretionary wealth taxation may impose binding credibility constraints on policymakers that lead to welfare losses for society. However, these results are just an initial step on the route towards understanding equilibrium fiscal policy. Wealth taxation is quite moderate in most countries and a positive theory of fiscal policy should be able to explain why. The theory should thus explain how the credibility constraints can be relaxed so that desirable tax policies become credible. Understanding how the credibility constraints can be relaxed is also important from a normative point of view.

The basic insight we want to push in this section is that institutions might have developed, or can be developed, to relax the credibility constraints. Institutions can relax credibility constraints by imposing social costs of surprise taxation of wealth. These costs may create a mechanism strong enough to support second-best tax policies even though the policymaker acts under discretion. We enrich the basic model of wealth taxation from Section 6 in several dimensions to illustrate how such mechanisms may be introduced.

Section 7.2 highlights the incentive effects of different government 'capital structures'. In particular, we show how careful government debt management may eliminate the incentives for surprise inflation and help enforce a second-best outcome, otherwise achievable only under commitment. This idea can be seen as a normative prescription.

Section 7.3 considers heterogeneous consumers and redistributive effects of tax policy. Such redistributive effects limit the temptation to tax wealth *ex post* and thus contribute to a better positive theory of policy. Normative results also follow, since assigning specific distributional goals to the policymaker may give full credibility to second-best tax policies. Like in monetary policy, appointing a policymaker whose preferences do not fully reflect society's true preferences may be welfare improving when there is a credibility problem.

Section 7.4 turns to 'reputation' in fiscal policy. The mechanism that supports second-best policies is quite different from the ones we studied in monetary policy. Again, consumer heterogeneity plays an important role. But heterogeneity is based on an overlapping generations structure and matters because tax policies can be regarded as social contracts which one generation 'sells' to the next one. The reputational incentives can be strong enough to bring the economy from a third-best to a second-best tax policy even if a tax reform is costly.

The approach in this section is to discuss the economic policy problem as an institutional design problem. This line of research is still in its infancy, and much remains to be done. Section 7.5 discusses the approach and gives suggestions for future research.

7.2. Government debt structure

We now build further on the two-period models of wealth taxation in Section 6. In this subsection we combine the two setups in Section 6.4 and formulate a model with money as well as government bonds.[99] When bonds are present (and pay a positive nominal rate of return), consumers need some additional incentive to hold money balances (which pay a zero nominal rate of return). We assume that real money balances yield liquidity services and that these services are appropriately captured by entering money in the utility function. The representative consumer's preferences are

$$c_1 - V(l_1) + H(m_1) + c_2 - V(l_2) + H(m_2), \tag{7.1}$$

with the same notation as before.

The budget constraints for period 1 and 2 in this extended model can be written

$$c_1 + b/R + m_1 \le l_1(1 - \tau_1) \tag{7.2}$$

$$c_2 + m_2 \le l_2(1 - \tau_2) + m_1(1 - \pi) + b. \tag{7.3}$$

Here, b is real—indexed to the second period price level—government debt, τ_t is the tax rate on labor in period t and π, defined by $\pi \equiv (p_2 - p_1)/p_2$, is the per unit depreciation in the real value of money. (There are non-negativity constraints on m_1 and m_2.) Compared to Section 6, the formulation is different in that there is no debt repudiation nor taxation of debt interest. This is *not* just for simplification. On the contrary, assuming that the government can commit not to tax debt above a certain level will be crucial in the analysis. But it is the *limit* in debt taxation which is crucial. That we choose to set the limit to zero is less important.

The utility function (7.1) is linear in c_1 and c_2. Therefore, consumers will choose a corner solution for b unless they are indifferent between c_1 and c_2, which (as in Section 6.4.2) requires R = 1. Because we will deal

[99] The two-period model in this section illustrates an idea that is developed in a general infinite horizon model in Persson, Persson and Svensson [101].

with equilibria with an interior solution for b, we already now impose the equilibrium condition $R = 1$. It is then easy to derive the labor supply and money demand functions:

$$l_t = L(\tau_t) \equiv V_l^{-1}(1 - \tau_t), t = 1, 2 \qquad (7.4)$$

$$m_1 = M(\pi^e) \equiv H_m^{-1}(\pi^e) \text{ and } m_2 = H_m^{-1}(1). \qquad (7.5)$$

As in Section 6.4.1, period 2 demand for real balances is constant. But the equilibrium supply of each of the other tax bases depends on the corresponding tax rate, or the expected tax rate in the case of the inflation tax. These supply functions act as constraints on the government taxation problem, as do the resource constraints

$$c_1 + g = l_1 \qquad (7.6)$$

$$c_2 = l_2, \qquad (7.7)$$

and the government budget constraints

$$g = \tau_1 l_1 + m_1 + b \qquad (7.8)$$

$$b + m_1 = \tau_2 l_2 + \pi m_1 + m_2. \qquad (7.9)$$

Thus, there is exogenous government spending only in period 1. Since m_2 is like a lump sum tax, we have to assume $g > m_2$ for the problem to be interesting.

7.2.1. Commitment Versus Discretion

Suppose first that commitments are feasible. That is, the government chooses a vector of tax rates (τ_1, τ_2, π) once and for all in period 1. To solve the optimal tax problem, we substitute the labor supply and money demand functions (7.4) and (7.5) and the resource constraints (7.6) and (7.7) into the utility function (7.1) and the government budget constraint (7.8)–(7.9). The first-order conditions for the three tax rates imply the Ramsey rule:

$$(\tau_1/(1 - \tau_1))\epsilon_l = (\tau_2/(1 - \tau_2))\epsilon_l = \epsilon_m. \qquad (7.10)$$

Equation (7.10) is the now familiar relation between tax rates and elasticities of tax bases. We see that the equilibrium policy under commitment exploits all three tax rates to finance government spending in period 1. Furthermore, the symmetry in preferences make the equilibrium tax rates on labor equal across time periods.

When there is no commitment, and the government acts under

discretion, the policy defined by (7.10) runs into a binding credibility constraint. The reason for this was discussed repeatedly in Section 6: Once consumers have accumulated their first period money balances, the government can tax them by surprise inflation in the second period. And the revenue from surprise inflation can then be used to lower the distortionary tax on labor income. Formally, the government in period 2 has the *ex post* budget constraint

$$b + m_1 - m_2 = \tau_2 L(\tau_2) + \pi m_1, \qquad (7.11)$$

where π appears as a lump sum tax because m_1 has zero *ex post* elasticity. It follows that any credible (*ex post* optimal) tax structure must exploit the inflation tax to the largest possible extent. As long as τ_2 is above zero, there is a temptation to drive the second period price level towards infinity; that is, to drive π towards 1. A discretionary equilibrium will thus most likely overtax money balances and period 1 labor, and undertax period 2 labor, relative to the commitment solution.

We shall leave the discretionary equilibria and multiplicity issue aside for now. Instead, we shall show how a richer menu of government debt instruments makes it possible to sustain the commitment solution as an equilibrium policy under discretion.

7.2.2. *Nominal Debt as an Incentive Device*

So far we have assumed that the government can issue real debt only. Suppose instead that there is both nominal and indexed debt. The quantity of nominal debt is denoted by B. Nominal debt promises one unit of account in period 2 and is not indexed to the period 2 price level. Let $\tilde{b}$ be the real value of the nominal debt in terms of period 1 goods, $\tilde{b} = B/p_1$, and let the period 1 price of nominal debt (also in terms of period 1 goods) be $1/\tilde{R}$. In period 2 the nominal debt has real value of $B/p_2 = \tilde{b}p_1/p_2 = (1 - \pi)\tilde{b}$. The quantity of indexed debt is denoted by b. As before, it has a period 1 price of $1/R$ and a period 2 value of b.

With these modifications, we can write the consumer's budget constraints as

$$c_1 + m_1 + b/R + \tilde{b}/\tilde{R} = l_1(1 - \tau_1) \qquad (7.2')$$

$$c_2 + m_2 = l_2(1 - \tau_2) + m_1(1 - \pi) + b + \tilde{b}(1 - \pi). \qquad (7.3')$$

It is obvious that if the consumer holds both types of debt, the parity condition $\tilde{R} = R/(1 - \pi)$ must hold. The condition is, of course, nothing but the well-known Fisher relation, expressing the gross nominal interest rate as the product of the gross real interest rate and the gross inflation rate. $(1/(1 - \pi)$ equals the gross inflation rate p_2/p_1.) The Fisher relation makes the two types of debt perfect substitutes from the viewpoint of consumers. As above, we set $R = 1$ in the following to avoid a corner solution for total government debt.

The modification of the model changes nothing in the fiscal regime with commitment. The inflation rate is chosen once and for all in period 1, and therefore nominal and indexed debt are perfect substitutes for the government, too. The commitment equilibrium determines the total amount of government borrowing, but allows an arbitrary split between nominal and indexed debt.

In the discretionary regime, things are different: Equilibrium inflation needs to be consistent with *ex post* optimality. In period 2 there is also a crucial difference between indexed and nominal debt: While the value of indexed debt is immune to surprise inflation, the value of nominal debt falls with surprise inflation.[100] To illustrate this we write out the *ex post* government budget constraint that parallels (7.11)

$$\bar{b} + b + m_1 - m_2 = \tau_2 L(\tau_2) + \pi(m_1 + \bar{b}). \qquad (7.12)$$

Surprise inflation in period 2 now acts like a lump sum tax on *total* private nominal claims on the government: nominal money plus nominal debt. But this suggests a mechanism that could eliminate the incentives for surprise inflation in period 2. Suppose the government enters period 2 with a net nominal position of zero towards the consumers. Then a surprise inflation does not raise any revenue, which obviously eliminates the incentive to use it. Furthermore, this situation is perfectly achievable. Let the government choose the following debt structure in period 1

$$\bar{b} = - m_1 \text{ and } b = \bar{b} + (1 - \pi)m_1, \qquad (7.13)$$

where $\bar{b} = g - \tau_1 l_1 - m_1$ is total real borrowing and m_1 is real money balances in the commitment solution. What (7.13) suggests is that the government should sell money to the consumers in period 1 and use all the proceeds to *buy* nominal bonds from the consumers. This indeed

---

[100] Recall that we have ruled out surprise taxation and surprise outright repudiation by assumption.

makes the government hold a zero nominal position. Any borrowing it needs to do should be done with indexed debt. If this 'capital structure' is adopted, the second-best tax policy is sustainable under discretion. Note that the debt structure which leads to such incentive compatibility is unique![101,102]

It may be useful to state the result in more general terms. The government in the model has access to a state variable—nominal debt—that enters in its future decision problem in a non-trivial way. By setting this state variable appropriately, the government can affect future incentives in such a way as to 'bind its own hands' to follow the desirable policy. Put differently, in this way the government can relax the credibility constraint, which results from the temptation to surprise inflation as the elasticity of money demand goes from negative to zero. This strategic use of state variables to affect future incentives will reappear in Sections 8 and 9.

A caveat is also in order. The result we have derived hinges crucially on the assumption that government debt is always honored, or put differently, that there is commitment in the (direct) taxation of capital income. At the present level of abstraction there is really no significant difference between debt repudiation and surprise inflation. But we do believe that there are differences between these two ways of raising revenue in the real world. The differences will depend on the exact institutional setup of the economy and on constitutional as well as legal aspects of the policymaking process. Naturally, one would like to model these institutional treats explicitly rather than assume them,

---

[101] The argument that a nominal net position of zero eliminates the incentives for surprise inflation appears in Persson, Persson and Svensson [101]. But as pointed out in the comment by Calvo and Obstfeld [32], the argument does not really hold in the multi-period model of Persson, Persson and Svensson [101] because the second-order conditions for an optimum policy are not fulfilled. Persson, Persson and Svensson [102] show that in a multi-period model, where the second-order conditions are fulfilled, the argument should be modified: The private net nominal position towards the government should be slightly above zero. The problem of second-order conditions does not arise in our simple two-period-model.

[102] That the second-best tax policy is exactly sustainable by the right debt structure depends on the assumption of perfect foresight. If there was uncertain government spending in period 2, having some non-zero nominal debt vis-à-vis the private sector would provide useful flexibility in financing particularly high government spending. Then the choice of government debt structure would be subject to the same tradeoff between credibility and flexibility that we encountered in Section 2. See Calvo and Guidotti [31] on this point.

particularly when the whole argument hinges on debt repudiation being qualitatively different from surprise inflation. Explaining this difference is an interesting task for further work.

7.3. Wealth distribution

Consider now the following extension of the two-period model of capital taxation in Sections 6.1–6.3: The economy is inhabited by two groups of atomistic consumers.[103] Consumers belonging to the first group are called 'capitalists'. Capitalists are born in period 1, live for two periods, and have access to a linear investment technology. Their only source of life-time income is an exogenous non-taxable endowment that they receive in the first period. In period 1, the representative capitalist allocates his endowment between consumption, c_1, and investment, k. In period 2, the proceeds from investment, net of any capital tax, are consumed. The representative capitalist maximizes the utility function

$$\tilde{U}(c_1, c_2) \equiv c_1 + U(c_2) \qquad (7.14)$$

subject to the budget constraints:

$$\begin{aligned} c_1 + k &\leq e \\ c_2 &\leq (1 - \theta)Rk. \end{aligned} \qquad (7.15)$$

The notation in (7.14) and (7.15) is like in Section 6 and the utility function $U(\cdot)$ is concave and satisfies the Inada condition: $\lim_{c \to 0} U_c(c) \to \infty$. Note that the utility function is supposed to be concave in c_2 and linear in c_1, whereas in the previous section we assumed the reverse (and in Section 7.2 utility was linear in both c_1 and c_2.). As we will see below, this specification makes the equilibrium capital tax an interior solution—rather than a corner solution—to the government optimization problem. This specification is the most convenient for our purposes, but can be changed without affecting the qualitative nature of the results.

Consumers belonging to the second group, which is equal in size to the first group, are called 'workers'. All workers are born in period 2,

---

[103] Rogers [111], discusses how distributional motives affect the government's incentives for capital taxation *ex post*. She derives results similar to those in Sections 7.3.1 and 7.3.2 in a more general model. The ideas in Section 7.3.3 are new.

live only one period, and have income only from labor. The representative worker maximizes the utility function

$$\tilde{V}(x, l) \equiv x - V(l) \tag{7.16}$$

subject to the budget constraint:

$$x \leq l(1 - \tau), \tag{7.17}$$

where x denotes consumption, l labor time and τ the tax rate on labor.

The government has to collect enough revenue from capitalists and workers to finance a predetermined amount of public spending in period 2

$$g \leq \tau l + R \theta k. \tag{7.18}$$

The government goal is to maximize the Pigovian welfare function

$$\varphi \tilde{U}(c_1, c_2) + \tilde{V}(x, l) \tag{7.19}$$

where φ is the relative weight assigned to the capitalists.

Here, the tax structure not only affects the excess burden of taxation. It also determines the distribution of welfare between the two groups of consumers. When considering policy surprises, the government therefore trades distribution consequences against efficiency consequences. As we shall see below, this trade-off may give credibility to otherwise incredible tax structures.

7.3.1. Commitments

Consider first the commitment regime, where the government sets θ and τ before any investment decision is undertaken by the capitalists. The private first-order conditions are the analogs of (6.5) and (6.6), namely

$$1/U_c(c_2)R = (1 - \theta) \tag{7.20}$$

for the capitalists and

$$V_l(l) = (1 - \tau) \tag{7.21}$$

for the workers. The government maximizes (7.19) subject to (7.18), (7.20), (7.21), and the private budget constraints.

Again, the optimal taxation problem is simplified by using the private sector first-order conditions to substitute away θ and τ from the government budget constraint. This yields the constraint:

$$g \le Rc_2 U_c(c_2) - c_2 + (1 - V_l(l))l. \qquad (7.22)$$

The optimal tax structure is found by maximizing (7.19) with respect to c_2, l and x, subject to (7.22) and to the private sector budget constraints. Tracing the steps of Section 6.2.1, we get the following necessary condition for an optimum:

$$\frac{\varphi U_c(c_2)}{1} = \frac{1 - \tau}{1 - \tau(1 + \epsilon_l)} \bigg/ \frac{1 - \theta}{1 - \theta(1 + \epsilon_k)}, \qquad (7.23)$$

where ϵ_l and ϵ_k are the elasticity of labor supply and savings with respect to their net (of taxes) rates of return.[104]

The left-hand side of (7.23) is the ratio between the marginal utility of wealth of capitalists in period 2 weighted by the distributional weight of capitalists (φ), and the marginal utility of wealth of workers (unity by the specification in (7.18)) weighted by the distributional weight of workers (unity by construction). Equation (7.23) reflects the trade-off between economic efficiency and wealth distribution that the government faces. To see this, consider the special case in which $\epsilon_l = \epsilon_k = 0$, so that neither form of taxation is distortionary. Then, according to (7.23), the equilibrium tax policy only reflects distributional considerations, and in equilibrium the two representative consumers have the same (weighted) marginal utility of wealth: $\varphi U_c(c_2) = 1$. Any departure from this policy must be due to differences in the marginal distortions of the two forms of taxation, as captured by the right-hand side of (7.23).

7.3.2. Discretion

Let us turn to the discretionary regime. As shown in the previous section, the equilibrium tax policy must be optimal for the government *ex post*, once the capitalists have committed to an investment decision. But *ex post*, the elasticity of savings with respect to θ is zero. Hence, the equilibrium tax policy under discretion must satisfy the following condition (obtained from (7.23) with $\epsilon_k = 0$):

$$\frac{\varphi U_c(c_2)}{1} = \frac{1 - \tau}{1 - \tau(1 + \epsilon_l)}. \qquad (7.24)$$

---

[104] Here, because of the different specification of the utility function

$$\epsilon_k = - [U_c(c_2)/c_2 U_{cc}(c_2)] - 1.$$

At the values of τ and θ that constitute the equilibrium under commitment, the right-hand side of (7.24) clearly exceeds the right-hand side of (7.23). Going to an equilibrium under discretion therefore requires decreasing τ (which decreases the right-hand side) and increasing θ (which increases the left-hand side). That is, capitalists are taxed more heavily in the discretionary regime. This result is very intuitive and can be explained along the lines of Section 6: The tax policy in (7.23) is not credible without commitment, since *ex post* a tax on capital is non-distortionary from an efficiency point of view.

However, unlike in the previous section, capitalists are never fully expropriated as long as $\varphi > 0$: Taxing capital here has a redistributive effect, which partly relaxes the credibility constraint because the government does not want to tax capital beyond a certain limit.

7.3.3. *Distorting Government Preferences*

Equations (7.23) and (7.24) suggest a way to make the second-best tax policy credible under discretion. Society ought to delegate the tax policy decisions to a policymaker who cares about the welfare of capitalists more than society itself does. Specifically, suppose society's true relative weight in the social welfare function (7.19) is φ. For the optimal tax structure in (7.23) to be credible, the policymaker must assign a weight

$$\tilde{\varphi} = \varphi \frac{(1 - \theta)}{1 - \theta(1 + \epsilon_k)} > \varphi \tag{7.25}$$

to capitalists. The larger is the *ex ante* elasticity of savings ϵ_k in the commitment solution, the larger is the required bias in favor of capitalists. Intuitively, a larger elasticity of savings reduces the *ex ante* optimal capital tax, which increases the capital stock and hence creates a larger incentive to surprise *ex post*. To counteract this larger incentive, a larger welfare weight has to be given to capitalists.

The result is analogous to the result in Section 2, that it may be desirable to have an independent and conservative central banker. Requiring credibility adds an incentive constraint to the government optimization problem. Appointing a policymaker with distorted preferences reduces the incentive to surprise, and hence relaxes the incentive constraint. It may therefore be welfare improving to distort the policymaker's preferences.

Unlike in the monetary policy model, distorted preferences are now a full substitute for commitments: a policymaker with preferences defined in (7.25) enables society to enforce the second-best tax structure under discretion. But this is only because there are no random shocks in the present model. In a more general stochastic model, a policymaker biased in favor of capitalists would bring about a suboptimal distribution of wealth in response to unexpected shocks. Hence, distorting the government preferences is not a perfect substitute for commitments; although it would be welfare improving under discretion, it would still leave society worse off than with full commitments. Also, distorted preferences do not eliminate the multiplicity of discretionary equilibria. Formally, equation (7.26) can be satisfied for more than one value of c_2 (or k) and l. Intuitively, if a capitalist expects other capitalists to save a little, he anticipates a high tax on capital; hence he also saves little. But given that aggregate savings, and hence the revenue from the capital tax, is small, the government is forced to rely heavily on labor taxes. Since these taxes are distortionary *ex post*, the government finds it optimal to tax capital at a relatively high rate, despite its distributional preferences. Hence, expectations of high capital taxes are self-fulfilling, and multiple Pareto ranked equilibria can exist.

The findings of this subsection lead naturally to the question of how society chooses the objective for its tax policy. This question will be taken up in Section 9 below, when we look at political economy foundations of models of fiscal policy. For now we limit ourself to the following remark: Lack of credibility may be a bigger problem for 'left-wing' than for 'right-wing' governments. Right-wing candidates thus may enjoy an advantage over their left-wing opponents in the eyes of the electorate. This advantage is enhanced if, as plausible, labor and capital are complementary in the production process. In this case, even workers might be better off with a government biased in favor of capitalists. Because a right-wing government gives higher investment, it may possibly also give higher real wages after tax, than would a left-wing government—even if the tax rate on labor is higher with a right-wing government.[105]

We think that this intuition can be formalized as follows. Suppose there were a continuum of agents with different factor endowments.

---

[105] Lars Svensson has suggested to us that this could be turned into an argument for right-wing dictatorship.

And suppose there were 'representative democracy' in the following sense: Individuals would vote in period 1 to elect a candidate that would implement the policy optimal for him or her in period 2. Our conjecture is that the individual with the median endowment would not win the election, even though individual preferences were single peaked. Instead a 'right-wing candidate'—that is, someone with a larger share of capital than the median—would win the elections.[106]

7.4. Social contracts

In this subsection we explore a different mechanism whereby a socially desirable tax policy may be sustained in a discretionary fiscal regime with capital taxation. The mechanism can be described as a reputational equilibrium, but we prefer to think about it as an implicit social contract between different generations in society. The social contract prescribes a second-best tax policy. But it also prescribes a transfer from young to old generations. This transfer can be thought of as a pay-as-you-go social security system or as the young adopting the debt of the old. The social contract is therefore like an 'asset', which is effectively sold from each old generation to the subsequent young generation. However, the asset has value only as long as the second-best tax policy is followed. That is, if the currently old cheat by overtaxing capital, they forfeit the transfer from the currently young. If the prospective capital loss on the social contract is large enough, it can balance the temptation to impose *ex post* capital levies and thus relax the credibility constraint.[107]

7.4.1. *Capital Taxation and Overlapping Generations*
To illustrate the idea, we extend our model of capital taxation from Section 6. Essentially, we embed that model in a conventional overlapping-generations structure. Our analysis aims at highlighting the efficiency issues in capital taxation. We shall therefore rule out all possibilities for intergenerational redistribution, except the transfer

---

[106] This conjecture came up in a conversation with Alberto Alesina. In Persson and Tabellini [108] we show that the conjecture is indeed true. That paper shows that the second-best tax policy under commitment can in fact be sustained as a political equilibrium under discretion.

[107] This social contracts idea comes from Kotlikoff, Persson and Svensson [79].

prescribed by the social contract.[108] To that end, each generation is assumed to have a purely representative body, labelled the 'council'. The council provides a public good when the generation is old and finances it with distortionary taxes. The council can only tax the members of its own generation when they are old and not the members of the coexisting young generation. Because only the old are factor owners in each time period, the generations do not interact in factor markets either. Thus, each generation is effectively self-governing.

Consider equilibria in a discretionary regime, where generations do not interact in any way. The council of each generation has the same problem as the government in the model of Section 6.3. To simplify matters, let us assume that public spending, g, exceeds the maximum revenue from capital taxation, $\bar{g}$. As we discussed in Section 6, the third-best equilibrium tax policy then has full expropriation of capital and no saving, so that all revenue has to be raised from labor taxes. Denote variables in that equilibrium with a caret (ˆ). The equilibrium tax rates fulfill

$$\hat{\theta} = 1 \text{ and } \hat{\tau}L(\hat{\tau}) = g, \qquad (7.26)$$

where $L(\cdot)$ is the labor supply function defined in $(6.6)'$.[109] Third-best utility is

$$\hat{u} = U(e) + L(\hat{\tau}) - g - V(L(\hat{\tau})). \qquad (7.27)$$

7.4.2. Social Contracts

We shall now discuss how interaction between the generations may help enforce a tax policy very close to the equilibrium tax policy under commitment, even though each council chooses the tax structure under complete discretion. In the equilibrium we shall establish, it will appear as if there is a self-enforcing 'social contract' between the generations. That social contract can be written as follows:

(C1) The capital tax rate should be below $\bar{\theta}$, $\bar{\theta} < 1$.

(C2) The council of the young pays a transfer Q to the council of the old.

If the councils of the successive generations in society indeed stick to

---

[108] Strategic aspects of intergenerational redistribution are taken up in Section 9.

[109] The equation $\hat{\tau}L(\hat{\tau}) = g$ may have more than one solution. If so, we assume that the council chooses the solution with the lowest τ.

the two clauses of the contract (C1-2), each young generation effectively 'purchases' the contract from the coexisting old generation.

It is necessary to be precise about the sequential structure of the intergenerational game. In each time period, the council of the old first decides on tax policy. Thereafter the young decide whether or not to pay a transfer to the old. Having observed these two 'public policy' decisions, the young individuals decide how much to save out of their fixed endowment. We could think of the size of the transfer as being determined by a bargaining process between the councils of the two generations, but we do not study the details of the bargaining process. Below, we will give the potential equilibrium range for the transfer, Q. Since we deal with a stationary environment, it seems reasonable to treat Q as a constant.

Index time periods by t, and index generations by the time period when they are born. Assume now that (the council of) each individual generation t follows an identical strategy, namely

Pay Q_t if $\theta_t \leq \bar{\theta}$ and Q_{t-1} was paid (7.28a)

Pay Q_t if $\theta_t \leq \bar{\theta}$ and Q_{t-1} was not paid, but $\theta_{t-1} > \bar{\theta}$
or Q_{t-2} was not paid. (7.28b)

Do not pay Q_t otherwise (7.28c)

and

Set $\theta_{t+1} = \bar{\theta}$ if Q_t was paid (7.29a)

Set $\theta_{t+1} = \bar{\theta}$ if Q_t was not paid, but $\theta_t > \bar{\theta}$
or Q_{t-1} was not paid (7.29b)

Set $\theta_{t+1} = 1$ otherwise. (7.29c)

Here, $\bar{\theta}$ is a tax on capital—associated with a tax $\bar{\tau}$ on labor—to be defined below. The substrategy in (7.28) requires a *young* generation to pay a transfer to the coexisting old generation if that generation: (a) obeyed the social contract, or (b) punished the previous generation for breaking the social contract. If (c) the old generation did not obey the social contract, it is punished by not receiving the transfer. The substrategy in (7.29) requires an *old* generation not to overtax capital, if as young: (a) it rewarded the coexisting old for obeying the social contract, or (b) punished the coexisting old for breaking the social contract. If (c) the old themselves broke the social contract when young, they instead choose the discretionary capital tax: $\hat{\theta} = 1$.

If the strategy (7.28)–(7.29) is followed we have an equilibrium with the following properties: Starting from a society without a social contract, a social contract is set up by an initial generation. And once set up, the contract is obeyed by all subsequent generations. We shall now demonstrate that (7.28)–(7.29) form a Subgame perfect equilibrium in the sequential intergenerational game. Strategies in a Subgame perfect equilibrium satisfy the Nash conditions as well as the conditions for sequential rationality that we discussed in Section 3.[110] In doing so we consider the incentives to deviate from (7.28)–(7.29) first for a typical young generation, then for a typical old generation.

Consider a young generation when the coexisting old generation has either obeyed the social contract or punished a previous generation for breaking it.[111] If the generation purchases the social contract (pays the transfer Q) when young, as (7.28) requires, and is able to resell it (receives a transfer Q) when old, the council faces the following budget constraints

$$Q = b \qquad (7.30a)$$

$$g + Rb - Q = \theta RK(\theta) + \tau L(\tau), \qquad (7.30b)$$

where b denotes the council's borrowing from its generation. $K(\theta)$ is now total saving of the young, that is private holdings of capital plus the council's bonds. Together, (7.30) implies

$$g + (R - 1)Q = \theta RK(\theta) + \tau L(\tau). \qquad (7.31)$$

What (7.31) says is that the council effectively rents the social contract for $(R - 1)Q$: Since the contract is sold when old for the same sum as it was purchased when young, there is an interest loss of $(R - 1)$ times the price of the contract. The optimal tax rates on capital and labor are those that fulfill (7.31) and the Ramsey rule (6.8). Denote these tax rates by $\bar{\theta}$ and $\bar{\tau}$. The council's budget constraint (7.31) together with the consumers' utility function and budget constraints (6.1)–(6.3), allow us to express the resulting utility level as

---

[110] We refer the reader to the definition of Subgame perfect equilibria in Section 3.2.

[111] Notice that a deviating generation is not punished by a generation that is damaged by the deviation. As we discuss further in Section 7.4.4, this is different from the situation in Section 3.

$$\bar{u} = U(e - K(\bar{\theta})) + RK(\bar{\theta}) + L(\bar{\tau}) - g - (R - 1)Q - V(L(\bar{\tau})). \quad (7.32)$$

It is easy to see that $\bar{u}$ is equal to the utility under commitment when $R = 1$ or $Q = 0$. But when $R > 1$ and $Q > 0$ utility is lower, because the rent for the social contract adds to the revenue requirement which makes taxes higher than in the commitment equilibrium.

Purchasing the social contract has to be compared to the best possible alternative. The best possible alternative for the youngs' council is to follow the third-best policy: If the council does not pay Q to the old who have obeyed the contract, it will receive no transfer when the generation is old according to (7.28). Hence, the council will find it optimal to set $\theta_t = 1$ (as explained below). Anticipating this outcome, young individuals do not save. So a refusal to pay Q leaves the generation in the third best, where utility is $\hat{u}$. For purchasing the contract to dominate, obviously we must have $\bar{u} - \hat{u} > 0$. We can use (7.27) and (7.32) to express the condition as

$$\bar{u} - \hat{u} = RK(\bar{\theta}) - [U(e) - U(e - K(\bar{\theta}))] +$$
$$L(\bar{\tau}) - L(\hat{\tau}) - [V(L(\hat{\tau})) - V(L(\bar{\tau}))] - \quad (7.33)$$
$$(R - 1)Q > 0.$$

The expression on the right-hand side of (7.33) has an intuitive interpretation. The terms on the first and second row are deadweight losses in first-period consumption (saving) and second-period labor supply. These deadweight losses are avoided by going from the third-best discretionary equilibrium in the direction of the commitment equilibrium; an illustration is given in Figure 7.1. The condition in (7.33) is thus that the saving of deadweight loss dominates the rent of the social contract. This clearly puts an upper bound on the price of the contract Q.

Consider next the incentives for the young if the coexisting old either have followed the third-best policy, so that no social contract exists, or have broken the social contract by overtaxing capital or by not paying the transfer to the old. Then (7.28) requires the council of the young not to pay the transfer Q. This is clearly optimal, for by not paying Q the young stand the chance of getting Q when old (and will indeed get Q provided capital is not overtaxed), while according to (7.28) they forfeit the transfer when old if they pay the transfer.

What about the incentives for an old generation? According to (7.29)

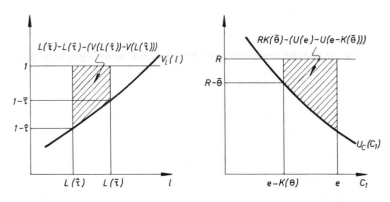

FIGURE 7.1

the old should tax capital at the rate $\bar{\theta}$ if they either rewarded the previously old for obeying the social contract or punished them for breaking it. If the council of the old sticks to the tax rates $\bar{\theta}$ and $\bar{\tau}$, it receives the transfer Q. Second-period utility for the representative old is then

$$\bar{u}^2 = L(\bar{\tau}) + RK(\bar{\theta}) - g - (R - 1)Q - V(L(\bar{\tau})). \tag{7.34}$$

The best alternative is to forego the transfer Q by imposing a capital levy on savings. Since the maximum possible revenue from the capital tax falls short of g and the council's expenditure when old is $g + RQ$, it is then *ex post* optimal to set $\theta = 1$. Denote the resulting tax rate on labor supply by $\tilde{\tau}$, with $\tilde{\tau}L(\tilde{\tau}) = g + RQ - RK(\bar{\theta})$. Imposing the capital levy, the council thus eliminates part of the tax distortion in labor supply, but it also forgoes the transfer from the currently young. Second-period utility if deviating from the social contract is thus

$$\tilde{u}^2 = L(\tilde{\tau}) + RK(\bar{\theta}) - g - RQ - V(L(\tilde{\tau})). \tag{7.35}$$

For sticking to the social contract to be optimal, we need $\bar{u}^2 > \tilde{u}^2$, or

$$\bar{u}^2 - \tilde{u}^2 = - \{ L(\tilde{\tau}) - L(\bar{\tau}) - [V(L(\tilde{\tau})) - V(L(\bar{\tau}))] \} + Q > 0. \tag{7.36}$$

The first term on the right-hand side of (7.36) is the deadweight loss in labor supply that the capital levy eliminates; see Figure 7.2. The loss in revenue from not being able to sell the social contract Q, must be large enough to balance this gain in efficiency. Clearly the condition (7.36) puts a lower bound on Q.

Finally, (7.29) requires the old to set $\theta + 1$ if they have broken the

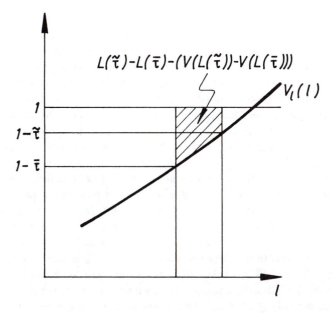

FIGURE 7.2

social contract or failed to punish the previous generation for breaking it. Since the old, by (7.28), will not get a transfer from the young in this situation whichever way they behave, they are in the same situation as in the purely discretionary regime. Therefore, it is indeed optimal to 'accept the punishment' and set $\theta = 1$.

In summary, we have found that it is not optimal to deviate from the strategy in (7.28)–(7.29) if the conditions (7.33) and (7.36) are satisfied. Because these conditions apply equally to all generations, we have a Subgame perfect equilibrium in the intergenerational game if they are fulfilled. In that equilibrium the social contract $C(1 - 2)$ is instituted once and then 'sold' from generation to generation. The price of the social contract has to obey the following inequality, obtained from (7.33) and (7.36)

$$L(\tilde{\tau}) - L(\bar{\tau}) - [V(L(\tilde{\tau})) - V(L(\bar{\tau}))]$$
$$< Q < \tag{7.37}$$
$$\{RK(\bar{\theta}) - [U(e) - U(e - K(\bar{\theta}))] + L(\hat{\tau}) - L(\hat{\tau})$$
$$- [V(L(\hat{\tau})) - V(L(\bar{\tau}))]\}/(R - 1).$$

A sufficient condition (if $1 < R < 2$) for the equilibrium to exist is that the welfare gain in going from the third-best to the second-best equilibrium is at least as large as the welfare gain from cheating in the second-best equilibrium. If this condition is satisfied, the council in charge of tax policy can be 'bribed' to resist the temptation to cheat. Essentially, the bribe transfers some of the future welfare gains of remaining at the second best (rather than falling to the third best) from the current young to the current old who are in charge of tax policy.

From the discussion below (7.32), it may appear as if Q should be expected to lie close to the lower bound in (7.37), since the utility level when the social contract is in place is closer to the utility level under commitment the lower is Q. But the first generation to propose the social contract—as well as any generation required to punish a deviating previous generation—clearly wants Q as high as possible, since that generation receives Q when old without having paid Q while young. Therefore it is an open question where Q is likely to lie in the interval identified by (7.37). Presumably Q could be pinned down by studying the bargaining process between young and old in each period. But as already mentioned, that is outside the scope of our present treatment.

7.4.3. Social Contracts and Costs of Tax Reform

The social gains from introducing a social contract may be substantial since the contract enables society to escape the welfare losses in the third-best discretionary equilibrium. Furthermore, in the equilibrium of the previous subsection, the incentives to establish the social contract are very strong: The generation to introduce a contract captures a large share of the surplus (by receiving Q without paying anything). This suggests that the switch from an inefficient third-best tax structure to a more efficient one may take place even though there are transitional costs in carrying out such a 'tax reform'.

To illustrate the argument, assume that the council that changes the third-best tax structure ($\theta = 1$, $\tau = \hat{\tau}$) in the direction of the second-best structure incurs a lump sum cost T when old. Let the strategies (7.28)–(7.29) remain as our candidate for equilibrium. It should be intuitively clear that we still have a social-contracts equilibrium provided that T is not too high. It is straightforward to show that an initial young generation will carry out tax reform—that is, institute the social contract—if the following condition is met

$$RK(\bar{\theta}) - [U(e) - U(e - K(\bar{\theta}))] +$$
$$L(\bar{\tau}) - L(\hat{\tau}) - [V(L(\hat{\tau})) - V(L(\bar{\tau}))] + \qquad (7.38)$$
$$+ Q > T.$$

In (7.38) the labor tax rate $\bar{\tau}$ fulfills $\bar{\tau}L(\bar{\tau}) + \bar{\theta}RK(\bar{\theta}) = g - (T - Q)$. Thus, $\bar{\tau} > \hat{\tau}$ if $T > Q$. Clearly (7.38) is not binding if the cost of tax reform T is below the lower bound on Q in (7.37). A higher T may raise the lower bound, however. The need to compensate the initial generation for the cost of tax reform can therefore limit the welfare gains of subsequent generations; their utility is decreasing in Q since they have to rent the contract. Finally, if T is large enough—above the upper bound for Q in (7.37) less the first two terms in (7.38)—it may prevent tax reform and the social contract from being established.

Of course, one may argue that some costs may be incurred in the 'tax reform' when a capital levy is imposed. Such costs would only strengthen the enforcement of second-best policies. But if there are costs associated with a capital levy, a capital levy is really not like a lump sum tax. Any such costs will limit the temptation to surprise the private sector and therefore help relax the credibility constraint.

7.4.4. Discussion

At this point it may be instructive to compare the equilibria in this subsection with the reputational equilibria we encountered in Section 3. There are clear similarities. First, an infinite horizon of the game is a necessary condition in both cases. (If there would be a finite horizon in the present context the backward induction argument would start from the 'last' generation refusing to purchase the social contract.) In that sense, both types of equilibria are an application of the Folk theorem. Second, the reputational equilibria in Section 3 all relied on trigger strategies. Clearly, there is a trigger strategy element also in (7.28)–(7.29).

But there are also important differences. First, in Section 3 the disincentive to deviate for an *infinite*-horizon policymaker came from a threat of low payoffs in *future* play, possibly forever. Here, the disincentive to deviate for a *finite*-horizon policymaker instead comes from a threat of an *immediate* capital loss on the social contract. Second, in Section 3 the threat that supported the good equilibrium was a reversion to the bad one-shot equilibrium in the future. Here, a deviating generation is not punished by succeeding generations reverting to the one-shot equilibrium, which here is the third-best tax structure. Instead, it is punished by the next generation refusing to pay the transfer and instead reinstating the social contract on its own. We believe this aspect makes the equilibrium more plausible than the standard trigger-strategy equilibrium.

There remains, however, one similarity of the social contracts equilibrium to equilibria in standard reputation models and that is the incentive constraint for the young (equation (7.33)). Suppose that the currently old have set $\theta_t = \bar{\theta}$ according to the contract. The punishment that prevents the young from deviating and setting $Q_t = 0$ is the fear of falling to the third-best equilibrium. This fear is dictated by their expectation that $\theta_{t+1} = 0$ if $Q_t = 0$ and $\theta_t = \bar{\theta}$, irrespective of whether $\theta_{t+1} = \bar{\theta}$ or not. It is this expectation that resembles the trigger-strategy feature of the reputation equilibria examined in Section 3.[112]

The transfer from the young to the old in our model looks as a contribution of the young to the financing of public goods consumption by the old. Of course, payments across generations may take many different forms, such as contributions to pay-as-you-go social security systems or by the young adopting debts of the old. Even though we have spoken figuratively about the social contract as an asset, it is important to realize that there is no need for an explicit contract or certificate. What is needed is simply an implicit contract: An understanding that the *quid pro quo* for the old to maintain the institution of moderate capital taxation is that the young do indeed contribute an appropriate sum towards the old's public goods consumption.

7.5. Discussion

We believe that the models in Sections 7.3 and 7.4 give some insight into how societies create institutions that help escape disastrous equilibria due to credibility problems. Thus we think there is hope for

---

[112] The currently young could presumably set $Q_t = 0$ and then $\theta_{t+1} = \bar{\theta}$, hoping to 'renegotiate' with the young generation in period $t + 1$ (when the old generation at t is dead). And both the generations could gain from jointly deviating from the specified strategy in period $t + 1$. This possibility is not explored when we checked for a Subgame perfect equilibrium, because equilibrium concept only requires that *individual* deviations, as opposed to *joint* deviations, do not pay. A strong equilibrium selection criterion such as renegotiation proofness (see Section 3), might therefore reject the suggested social-contracts equilibrium.

developing a positive theory of fiscal policy with testable predictions. A successful positive theory should not only be able to explain a low average level of wealth taxation, and differences in the average level across countries. It should also be able to explain the single episodes of very high taxation of wealth, in connection with wars and other peaks in government spending: How do policymakers get away with such temporary levies on wealth without triggering expectations about future wealth taxation and low savings?[113]

To study those additional issues, one should extend the analysis to include uncertainty. In particular, one should introduce shocks either to the government's revenue requirement or to tax bases other than wealth. In the context of the model in Section 7.3, where distributional concerns prevent *ex post* taxation of wealth, one could presumably extend the argument along the lines of Section 2.4. A trade-off between credibility and flexibility, similar to that in monetary policy, would call for appointing a policymaker with 'right-wing' views, but not extremely right-wing views. In an explicitly political model, distributional concerns may prevent the political majority from overtaxing capital in normal times. But efficiency concerns may become so important that the majority would allow overtaxing capital in abnormal (bad) times.

In the context of the social-contracts model in Section 7.4, one could presumably extend the argument along the lines of Section 3.4. Specifically, the social contract could prescribe a rule for tax policy with an 'escape clause'. That is to say, the tax on capital would be low in normal times, but would be high in abnormal times; abnormal times would be defined by conditions on the government's revenue requirement and the tax base for other taxes such as the labor tax.[114]

A positive theory of wealth taxation could potentially also contribute to an explanation for the observed different levels of savings and capital accumulation, across countries and across stages of development. For example, different distributions of abilities and human capital would lead different economies to different equilibrium

---

[113] For a documentation of historical episodes in Europe with such temporary wealth taxation—either by outright repudiation of government debt or by inflation—see Alesina [6].

[114] Bohn [26] shows that nominal government debt may fulfill a similar function: Nominal bonds may allow the government capital gains (through inflation) when they have particularly high revenue requirements.

tax policies and different levels of capital formation. Exactly how different 'structural characteristics' would translate into different tax policy would depend on political institutions (which, of course, themselves ultimately would depend on the structural characteristics). Clearly, the models discussed in this section have abstracted a great deal from political institutions. More detailed modeling of the political institutions may be crucial for a successful positive theory of tax policy. This is one of our motivations for studying political equilibrium models of fiscal policy in Section 9.

7.6. Notes on the literature

The idea about using nominal government assets to balance the outstanding money stock and diminish the incentive for surprise inflation is taken from Persson, Persson and Svensson [101].

Rogers [111] discusses how distributional concerns may limit the government's *ex post* temptation to tax capital, as do Hillier and Malcolmson [76]. Rotemberg [119] outlines a distributional argument for why government debt will be honored and not repudiated. Alesina and Tabellini [12] consider distributional incentives in a paper about equilibrium tax policy, external debt and capital flight.

Kotlikoff, Persson and Svensson [79] develop the social contracts idea in the context of capital taxation. The idea is applied to other policy problems by Engineer and Bernhardt [51], who study transfer institutions between generations, and by Alesina and Spear [8], who study decisions within political parties. The general idea about cooperation in ongoing organizations with overlapping generations of decision makers is analyzed by Kreps [81] and Crémer [41].

8. CREDIBILITY AND PUBLIC DEBT MANAGEMENT

8.1. Introduction

Sections 6 and 7 dealt with credibility problems in wealth taxation and some possible solutions to these problems. The tax base in those sections was an asset (or income from that asset), such as capital, debt or money. *Ex ante*—before the asset had been accumulated—the supply of the tax base was elastic with respect to the tax rate. But *ex post*—after the asset had been accumulated—the supply of the tax base became *completely* inelastic. It was this drastic change in elasticity that caused the credibility problems by creating incentives for policy surprises in the form of capital levies.

It seems to be a widespread belief that 'capital-levy problems' are necessary for fiscal policy to lack credibility. In this section we show that credibility problems appear under much more general circumstances. Indeed, we argue that credibility problems are generic in dynamic taxation whenever the government lacks a commitment technology. Section 8.2 illustrates this argument in a two-period example of labor taxation. The example resembles the models we have studied in the two previous sections with the exception that there is no money, and debt or capital cannot be taxed by assumption. Nevertheless, the second-best policy, which is optimal under commitment, still lacks credibility under discretion. The basic reason is again that the *ex ante* and *ex post* elasticities of the government tax base—labor supply in this case—are different.

Section 8.3 shows that the resulting credibility constraints may potentially be relaxed. As in Section 7.2, the mechanism relies on the government choosing a particular 'capital structure' of the public debt. But here it is the composition of the public debt into different maturities that matters, rather than the composition into indexed and non-indexed debt. We illustrate the mechanism in a three-period example of labor taxation. In the example there is a unique debt structure of 'short-term' and 'long-term' securities that supports the optimal second-best policy, even when the government has discretion over time in its choice of tax rates.

8.2. Credibility problems in labor taxation

8.2.1. *Labor Taxation* Ex Ante
Consider a two-period setup with our usual linear technology. There are unitary input-output coefficients both for labor and capital:

$$f(k_t, l_t) = k_t + l_t, t = 1,2, \qquad (8.1)$$

so the real wage and the gross return to capital are both unity. (Alternatively, we could think of an open economy facing a given world interest rate of zero; then k_t would correspond to the economy's foreign assets). Capital depreciates completely after one period. The initial endowment k_1 is equal to zero, while k_2 depends on period-1 investment.

There is a representative consumer with preferences over private consumption, c_t, and labor supply, l_t, in both periods and government consumption in period 2, g (there is no government consumption in period 1). His utility function is:

$$u^1 = F(c_1, l_1, c_2, l_2; g). \tag{8.2}$$

For simplicity g enters $F(\cdot)$ in an additively separable way: that is, all the cross-partials F_{gx} are equal to zero. The consumer can save in the form of capital and government bonds which both pay the same (zero) return. His consolidated intertemporal budget constraint is

$$c_1 + c_2 - (1 - \tau_1)l_1 - (1 - \tau_2)l_2 = W_1 = 1, \tag{8.3}$$

where τ_t is the labor tax in period t and W_1 is initial wealth.

Optimal consumption decisions result in the *ex ante*—denoted with superscript 1—indirect utility function

$$J^1 (1 - \tau_1, 1 - \tau_2, W_1; g). \tag{8.4}$$

Maximized utility depends (positively) on the after-tax wage rates, initial wealth and government consumption. The associated *ex ante* labor supply functions depend on the same arguments, except g (due to the separability assumption):

$$l_t^1 = L_t^1(1 - \tau_1, 1 - \tau_2, W_1), \ t = 1, 2. \tag{8.5}$$

The policymaker is strictly Pigovian and strives at choosing government consumption and the intertemporal profile of taxation so as to maximize private welfare. Hence we depart from our previous models of taxation in that government consumption is now endogenous. Apart from being interesting in its own right, this extension is necessary for credibility problems to arise: Since there is only one tax base available in period 2, there is no trade-off in period 2 unless government consumption is variable.

Suppose initially that the government can commit to taxes and government consumption once and for all at the beginning of period 1. It faces the intertemporal budget constraint

$$\tau_1 l_1 + \tau_2 l_2 = g. \tag{8.6}$$

An optimal fiscal policy under commitment maximizes indirect utility (8.4) subject to the private incentive conditions (8.5) and the government budget constraint (8.6).[115] Simplifying the notation somewhat by suppressing constant arguments from (8.4) and (8.5), we can write the Lagrangean of the policy problem as

$$\mathscr{L} = J^1(\tau_1, \tau_2, W_1; g) + \lambda^1[\tau_1 L_1^1(\tau_1, \tau_2) + \tau_2 L_2^1(\tau_1, \tau_2) - g]. \quad (8.7)$$

The multiplier on the government budget constraint, λ^1, will have an intuitive interpretation as the *ex ante* 'marginal cost of public funds'.

The first-order conditions of the problem are

$$\mathscr{L}_g = J_g^1 - \lambda^1 = 0 \qquad (8.8a)$$

$$\mathscr{L}_{\tau_1} = J_{\tau_1}^1 + \lambda^1[l_1 + \tau_1 L_{1\tau_1}^1 + \tau_2 L_{2\tau_1}^1] = 0 \qquad (8.8b)$$

$$\mathscr{L}_{\tau_2} = J_{\tau_2}^1 + \lambda^1[l_2 + \tau_1 L_{1\tau_2}^1 + \tau_2 L_{2\tau_2}^1] = 0. \qquad (8.8c)$$

The first condition sets the marginal utility of public consumption equal to the marginal cost of public funds. The next two are the familiar Ramsey conditions that equate the distortion on the last dollar raised across the two sources of revenue. For future reference it is useful to rewrite (8.8c) in terms of *ex ante* elasticities of labor supply (with respect to the after-tax rates of return). To do that we use Roy's identity (which here says $J_{\tau_2}^1 = -J_w^1 l_2$) and the definition of the elasticities ($\epsilon L_1^1/\epsilon\tau_2 \equiv (1 - \tau_2) L_{1\tau_2}^1/l_1$ and $\epsilon L_2^1/\epsilon\tau_2 \equiv (1 - \tau_2) L_{2\tau_2}^1/l_2$). After some straightforward algebraic manipulations, we obtain

$$J_w^1/\lambda^1 = [1 + (\tau_1 l_1/\tau_2 l_2)\epsilon L_1^1/\epsilon\tau_2 + \epsilon L_2^1/\epsilon\tau_2]. \qquad (8.9)$$

Condition (8.9) determines the ratio between the private marginal utility of income and the marginal cost of public funds, a ratio which will be below unity at an optimum. The negative 'own elasticity' $\epsilon L_2^1/\epsilon\tau_2$ is larger in absolute value than the positive 'cross elasticity' $\epsilon L_1^1/\epsilon\tau_2$ (weighted by period-1 revenue relative to period-2 revenue). Finally, we can combine (8.9) with (8.8a) to get the optimal ratio between the marginal utilities of private and government consumption:

$$J_w^1/J_g^1 = [1 + (\tau_1 l_1/\tau_2 l_2)\epsilon L_1^1/\epsilon\tau_2 + \epsilon L_2^1/\epsilon\tau_2]. \qquad (8.10)$$

---

[115] There is no need to separately impose the resource constraints $l_1 = c_1 + k_2$ and $k_2 + l_2 = c_2 + g$, because by Walras' law, they follow from the government budget constraint (8.5) and the private budget constraint (8.3) which is implicitly imposed by (8.4).

8.2.2. Ex Post *Incentive Compatibility*

If there were indeed a commitment technology, as we assumed above, government incentives in period 2 would not matter. But if the government acts under discretion, we have to consider its *ex post* incentives. As before, we shall find that the second-best policy under commitment is not *ex post* optimal under discretion and therefore not credible. The discussion leads up to a 'no-cheating condition', which needs to hold for the policy to be credible.

What are private and government incentives in period 2 when period-1 private labor supply and consumption decisions, as well as period-1 government tax decisions, are already bygone? The consumer maximizes (8.2)—with c_1 and l_1 predetermined—subject to the budget constraint

$$c_2 - (1 - \tau_2)l_2 = (1 - \tau_1)l_1 - c_1 \equiv W_2, \tag{8.11}$$

where W_2 denotes savings from period 1 in the form of capital and government bonds. Optimal choices result in the *ex post*—denoted by the superscript 2—indirect utility function

$$J^2(1 - \tau_2, W_2; g). \tag{8.12}$$

And there is an associated *ex post* labor supply function

$$l_2 = L_2^2(1 - \tau_2, W_2). \tag{8.13}$$

The government faces an *ex post* budget constraint

$$g + (W_2 - k_2) = \tau_2 l_2, \tag{8.14}$$

where the second term on the left-hand side is government debt at the beginning of period 2.

For *ex post* optimality, fiscal policy decisions in period 2 must maximize (8.12) subject to (8.13) and (8.14). The first-order conditions with respect to g and τ_2 are

$$J_g^2 - \lambda^2 = 0 \tag{8.15a}$$

$$J_{\tau_2}^2 - \lambda^2[l_2 + \tau_2 L_{\tau_2}^2] = 0, \tag{8.15b}$$

where λ^2, the multiplier on (8.14), is the *ex post* marginal cost of public funds. Similar manipulations as in the previous section allow us to rewrite (8.15b) in elasticity terms and to combine the resulting expression with (8.15a), to get

$$J_w^2/J_g^2 = [1 + \epsilon L_2^2/\epsilon\tau_2]. \qquad (8.16)$$

Condition (8.16) must hold for *ex post* optimality.

We are almost ready to formulate our incentive-compatibility, or 'no-cheating condition'. As a last preliminary step, notice that $J_w^1 = J_w^2$ and $J_g^1 = J_g^2$ when the derivatives are evaluated at the same point. Therefore, the left-hand sides of (8.10) and (8.16) are equal if evaluated at the allocation prescribed by the second-best policy under commitment. If the right-hand sides are also equal then the second-best policy is *ex post* optimal under discretion. But if the right-hand sides are not equal there is an incentive to cheat *ex post* and the policy is not credible. The incentive-compatibility condition can thus be formulated as follows:

$$(\tau_1 l_1/\tau_2 l_2)\epsilon L_1^1/\epsilon\tau_2 + \epsilon L_2^1/\epsilon\tau_2 = \epsilon L_2^2/\epsilon\tau_2. \qquad (8.17)$$

If (8.17) does not hold, when evaluated at the second-best tax rates, the equilibrium policy under commitment cannot be a rational expectations equilibrium under discretion.

An alternative way to describe the incentive-compatibility condition is to argue in terms of the marginal cost of public funds. It is only when the *ex ante* and *ex post* marginal costs of public funds, λ^1 and λ^2, are equal that the second-best policy is credible. For if the *ex post* marginal cost is, say, lower, there is an incentive to increase government consumption when in period 2. Once this incentive to policy surprise is recognized, the second-best fiscal policy is not credible under discretion.

Clearly, there is no reason to expect condition (8.17) to hold for all possible specifications of preferences. The left-hand side involves a weighted sum of elasticities of *ex ante* labor supplies. This is because a change in τ_2 announced in period 1, changes labor supply—and therefore government revenue—in both periods, since the consumer substitutes intertemporally. The right hand side is the elasticity of *ex post* labor supply. Because intertemporal substitution is no longer possible, a change in τ_2 changes government revenue only by changing labor supply in period 2. For the same reason, we should expect $\epsilon L_2^2/\epsilon\tau_2$ to be smaller (in absolute value) than $\epsilon L_2^1/\epsilon\tau_2$.

Unfortunately, it is very hard to find any general conditions for the commitment policy to be credible under discretion. But one can find both examples and counter examples. Suppose that private preferences in (8.2) have the following form (similar to what we used in previous sections).

$$F(c_1, l_1 . c_2, l_2; g) = U(c_1) - V(l_1) + c_2 - V(l_2) + H(g). \qquad (8.18)$$

With these preferences, we know that labor supply in period t depends only on the after-tax wage in t. Thus the cross elasticity in (8.17) is zero and the *ex ante* and *ex post* own elasticities are equal: $\epsilon L_2^1 / \epsilon \tau_2 = \epsilon L_2^2 / \epsilon \tau_2$. Thus, (8.17) is indeed fulfilled at the commitment optimum in this case. But, however convenient, the preferences in (8.18) are very special.

Suppose, on the other hand, that preferences are like in (8.18) except that the linearity is in c_1 and not in c_2:

$$F(c_1, l_1 . c_2, l_2; g) = c_1 - V(l_1) + U(c_2) - V(l_2) + H(g). \qquad (8.19)$$

Then condition (8.17) is violated. The reason is that the *ex ante* and *ex post* elasticities of period 2 labor supply, $\epsilon L_2^1 / \epsilon \tau_2$ and $\epsilon L_2^2 / \epsilon \tau_2$, are different: While $\epsilon L_2^1 / \epsilon \tau_2$ does not incorporate any income effect, $\epsilon L_2^2 / \epsilon \tau_2$ does.[116]

It should maybe be stressed that the differences between *ex ante* and *ex post* elasticities do not derive solely from the stark assymmetry between the first and the second period in our two-period example. Differences between *ex ante* and *ex post* elasticities remain even in more general multiperiod models.

Given these examples, we believe that *ex post* optimality of the second-best policy is the exception rather than the rule. As a qualitative matter, credibility problems arise in dynamic fiscal policy because *ex ante* and *ex post* elasticities of tax bases are not the same. In wealth taxation the *ex post* elasticity of the tax base is zero, but that is just a special case of a more general principle. As a quantitative matter, it may be that the credibility problems tied to capital levies are more 'serious', but that must remain a conjecture awaiting further research.

If the second-best fiscal policy is not credible under discretion, what

---

[116] Results can also be found for more general preference structures. Rogers [112] and Razin, Persson and Svensson [110] have studied whether (8.17) holds for more general preference structures. They have shown (numerically) that for a CES-function, equation (8.17) holds at the commitment equilibrium only if there is complete symmetry in all periods, so that labor supply and consumption are exactly equal in each period. As soon as the symmetry is removed, for instance because the time discount factor differs from the rate of interest, (8.17) is violated.

does a credible fiscal policy look like? In principle, it is clear how we would determine that. As before, we would solve the government's fiscal policy problem with the added credibility constraint that the policy was *ex post* optimal. That is, we would impose condition (8.16) as an additional constraint on the period-1 problem. But it turns out to be very hard to characterize the solution to that problem. Even for very simple examples, it is difficult to verify analytically how the added incentive constraint affects the equilibrium level of government consumption and the equilibrium time profile of taxes. It is possible to characterize the solution by means of numerical simulations, but we shall not pursue the matter here.

8.3. Debt structure as an incentive device

In Section 7 we learned how the government could use the composition of the public debt into indexed and non-indexed debt to eliminate the *ex post* incentives for surprise inflation. We will now illustrate how a similar mechanism can be used to relax credibility problems in labor taxation and support second-best policies in a discretionary regime. Again the composition of the public debt is crucial, but what matters now is the maturity structure of the public debt.

8.3.1. *A Three-Period Model of Labor Taxation*
We have to modify the model of Section 8.2 for our present purposes. The time horizon is now three periods (denoted 1, 2, and 3); without at least three periods, we cannot make any meaningful distinction between debt of different maturities. With three periods there is an interesting choice to be made in period 2—in a discretionary regime— namely the choice between taxes in periods 2 and 3. We shall concentrate the analysis around this choice, so to simplify we again make government consumption exogenous. Finally, the government's ability to change interest rates by its policies plays an important role in the argument. We therefore look at a closed economy without capital.

In period 1 there is no endogenous production, so private consumption and government consumption are constrained by an exogenous endowment:

$$c_1 + g_1 = e \qquad (8.21a)$$

In periods 2 and 3, on the other hand, production is equal to (endogenous) labor supply, but there is no government consumption:

$$c_t = l_t, t = 2,3. \qquad (8.21b)$$

Thus the government has to finance its period-1 expenditure with borrowing, which is subsequently repaid by raising taxes in periods 2 and 3.

Private utility is given by

$$u^1 = c_1 + U(c_2) - V(l_2) + U(c_3) - V(l_3). \qquad (8.22)$$

Let b denote 'short-term' debt issued by the government in period 1— that is, debt which matures in period 2—and let r_1 be the corresponding (gross) short-term interest rate. Correspondingly, let B be the the 'long-term' debt issued in period 1—the debt which matures in period 3. Denote the interest rate between periods 2 and 3 by R_2. For both types of debt to be bought in period 1, the long-term interest rate between periods 1 and 3 must be equal to $r_1 R_2$. We can then write the consumer overall intertemporal budget constraint as:

$$c_1 + c_2/r_1 + c_3/r_1 R_2 = e + (1 - \tau_2)l_2/r_1 + (1 - \tau_3)l_3/r_1 R_2. \quad (8.23)$$

The consumer maximizes (8.22) subject to (8.23). The first-order conditions to this problem can be rewritten as

$$r_1 = 1/U_c(c_2) \qquad (8.24a)$$

$$R_2 = U_c(c_2)/U_c(c_3) \qquad (8.24b)$$

$$\tau_t = 1 - V_l(l_t)/U_c(c_t), t = 1,2. \qquad (8.24c)$$

The government budget constraint in present value form at the beginning of period 1 is:

$$g_1 = \tau_2 l_2/r_1 + \tau_3 l_3/r_1 R_2. \qquad (8.25)$$

8.3.2. Ex Ante *Incentives*

As usual we start by assuming that the government can commit to a tax policy in period 1. The government problem then is to maximize the consumer welfare (8.22) subject to the incentive conditions (8.24), the resource constraints (8.21) and the government budget constraint (8.25). After some straightforward substitutions, we can write the Lagrangean of this problem as follows:

$$\mathscr{L}^1 = (e - g_1) + U(l_2) - (l_2) + U(l_3) - V(l_3) + \qquad (8.26)$$
$$\lambda^1[(U_c(l_2) - V_l(l_2))l_2 + (U_c(l_3) - V_l(l_3))l_3 - g_1]$$

We thus have a problem in two variables alone, l_2 and l_3, which correspond to the two tax rates τ_2 and τ_3. The optimal allocation must satisfy the two first-order conditions

$$(1 + \lambda^1)(U_c(l_2) - V_l(l_2) + \lambda^1(U_{cc}(l_2) - V_{ll}(l_2))l_2 = 0 \qquad (8.27a)$$

$$(1 + \lambda^1)(U_c(l_3) - V_l(l_3) + \lambda^1(U_{cc}(l_3) - V_{ll}(l_3))l_3 = 0. \qquad (8.27b)$$

It is easy to rewrite the conditions in (8.27) on elasticity form as we have been doing before, but here we stop short of doing so. The only information we want to draw from (8.27) is that an optimal tax policy under commitment has equal labor supplies in periods 2 and 3. Put differently, there is complete tax smoothing to smooth out the tax distortions across the two periods. This should hardly be surprising, given the symmetry we have imposed in this simple example.

8.3.3. Ex Post *Incentives*

We now look at the government's incentives in period 2 in a discretionary regime. Is the optimal policy calculated in period 1 under commitment *ex post* optimal under discretion from the viewpoint of the government in period 2? The government's problem is still to maximize private welfare in (8.22), only now c_1 is given. It still faces the private incentive constraints in (8.24), but (8.24a) is no longer relevant. Similarly, the government still faces the resource constraints in (8.21), but (8.21a) is no longer relevant. Finally, the government budget constraint, from the viewpoint of period 2 is now:

$$b + B/R_2 = \tau_2 l_2 + \tau_3 l_3 / R_2. \qquad (8.28)$$

We can write the Lagrangean of the government's period-2 problem as

$$\mathscr{L}^2 = U(l_2) - V(l_2) + U(l_3) - V(l_3) + \qquad (8.29)$$
$$\lambda^2[(U_c(l_2) - V_l(l_2))l_2 + (U_c(l_3) - V_l(l_3))l_3 - bU_c(l_2) - BU_c(l_3)].$$

In (8.29) we have multiplied the government budget constraint by $U_c(l_2)$ to scale the problem in a way that makes it comparable to the period-1 problem in (8.26). The two first-order conditions to this problem are

$$(1 + \lambda^2)(U_c(l_2) - V_l(l_2)) + \lambda^2(U_{cc}(l_2) - V_{ll}(l_2))l_2 - \lambda^2 U_{cc}(l_2)b = 0 \quad (8.30a)$$
$$(1 + \lambda^2)(U_c(l_3) - V_l(l_3)) + \lambda^2(U_{cc}(l_3) - V_{ll}(l_3))l_3 - \lambda^2 U_{cc}(l_3)B = 0 \quad (8.30b)$$

The question is whether the values of l_2 and l_3 that solve the period 1 first-order conditions in (8.27) also solve the period 2 first-order conditions in (8.30). Two things distinguish the conditions in (8.30) from those of the period 1 problem in (8.27). First, the multiplier λ^2 can differ from λ^1; that is, the marginal cost of public funds can differ *ex ante* and *ex post*. We already learned in Section 8.2 that this difference—due to differences in *ex ante* and *ex post* labor supply elasticities—could entail an *ex post* incentive for policy surprise. In the present model, this incentive is not present, however, because the model is perfectly symmetric and government spending is predetermined.[117]

The second difference between the *ex ante* and *ex post* first-order conditions is that the debt carried over from period 1 appears in (8.30) but not in (8.27). The reason the debt appears in (8.30) is that changing the distribution of taxes between periods 2 and 3 changes the interest rate between these periods which changes the value of the government's outstanding debt obligations. In other words, an unexpected change in the short-term interest rate may act as a capital levy on the outstanding government debt. This possibility may also give rise to an *ex post* incentive for policy surprise. Whether or not this incentive is present depends on the maturity structure of the outstanding debt.

Suppose that the outstanding debt is unbalanced towards short maturities, in the sense that the *ex ante* optimal tax policy involves rolling over some short-term debt in period 2. If $b > B$, the government has to sell some new debt in period 2, since $\tau_2 l_2 = \tau_3 l_3$ and hence $b - \tau_2 l_2 > 0$. The period-2 government then has an incentive to unexpectedly reduce R_2,—the interest rate between period 2 and period 3—so that it can sell the new debt at a higher price. If, on the other hand, the debt is unbalanced towards long maturities, the incentive goes in the opposite direction. In this case, some long-term debt has to be retired in period 2. By unexpectedly raising R_2, the government can then reduce the market value of the outstanding long-term debt. Hence, the debt can be bought back at a lower price and a capital loss can be inflicted on debt holders.

To confirm this intuition, consider the extreme case in which all

---

[117] To see this, note that if this were a small open economy facing a given real interest rate, the last term on the left hand sides of (8.30), $\lambda^2 U_{cc} b$ and $\lambda^2 U_{cc} B$, would drop out; in which case the only solution to (8.30) would involve $l_2 = l_3$, as in (8.22). See also Footnote 116 above.

outstanding debt is short-term, so that $B = 0$. In this situation, the *ex post* first-order conditions in (8.30) can be rewritten as:

$$H(l_2, \lambda^2) - \lambda^2 U_{cc}(l_2)b = 0 \qquad (8.31a)$$

$$H(l_3, \lambda^2) = 0, \qquad (8.31b)$$

where $H(\cdot)$ is a decreasing function.[118] Since b is positive, the second term in (8.31a) is negative. This means that *ex post* l_2 should be set higher than l_3. To do that, the period-2 government should drive up τ_2 and drive down τ_3. This implies setting the gross interest rate R_2 below unity—recall that $R_2 = U_c(c_2)/U_c(c_3) = U_c(l_2)/U_c(l_3)$—rather than at unity as the second-best policy prescribes.

Only a balanced maturity structure—so that the maturing debt in each period is exactly equal to the *ex ante* optimal tax revenue (net of government spending, if any)—can eliminate the incentive to surprise. In this example, the *ex ante* optimal tax policy is to collect equal amounts of revenue in each period. A perfectly balanced maturity structure means having equal amounts of short and long term debt outstanding: $b = B$. This follows immediately from equation (8.30): l_2 and l_3 can be equal in (8.30a) and (8.30b) only if b and B are equal to each other. Hence, there is a unique maturity composition of the public debt which makes the *ex ante* optimal tax policy incentive compatible under discretion: namely, a perfectly balanced composition.

If the model specification is reformulated to eliminate the perfect symmetry—for instance allowing for unequal amounts of exogenous government spending in periods 2 and 3—there would be two incentives to surprise instead of one: The period-2 government would still retain the incentive to impose capital levies on the outstanding debt through changes in the interest rate. And the difference between the *ex ante* and *ex post* marginal cost of funds would create a second incentive to surprise. However, it turns out that if the maturity structure of debt issued in period 1 is chosen in the right way, these two incentives can always be matched against each other, so that the net incentive for policy surprise is zero!

To see how the incentives can be matched, consider a situation where the *ex ante* and *ex post* marginal cost of funds are indeed different,

---

[118] $H(\cdot) \equiv (1 + \lambda^2)(U_c - V_l) + \lambda^2(U_{cc} - V_{ll})l_2$ is decreasing in l_2 under the reasonable condition that one term of ambiguous sign, which involves third derivatives of $U(\cdot)$ and V $(\cdot)$, does not dominate several negative terms involving first and second derivatives.

because the *ex ante* and *ex post* labor supply elasticities are different. Suppose this difference creates an *ex post* incentive to shift the tax burden from period 3 to period 2, relative to the second-best policy. However, as we explained above, a predominantly short-term debt creates the opposite incentive: to shift the tax burden from period 2 to period 3. To maintain the incentives to follow the second-best policy, the government should therefore have a composition of debt unbalanced towards the short run. More generally, a unique maturity composition of debt can always be found so that the two incentives to surprise exactly offset each other.[119]

To sum up: While the maturity structure of the public debt is of no importance in a commitment regime, it is of crucial importance in a discretionary regime. It is of crucial importance because changes in fiscal policy affect interest rates and this in turn devalues or revalues outstanding debt of different maturities. Therefore, future government policy is influenced by debt inherited from the past. Put differently, the debt structure is an important state variable that allows the government to relax the credibility constraints, and in our simple example relax them completely. Note that for this incentive mechanism to work, it is important that (real) interest rates are affected by fiscal policy. If interest rates were not affected—because the technology was linear in capital or because we were dealing with a small economy facing given world interest rates—the two incentives to surprise could not be matched against each other and the credibility problem described in Section 8.2 could not be overcome.

8.4. Discussion

The conclusion that a particular choice of the maturity structure of the public debt can support second-best fiscal policies under discretion can be extended in several directions. It holds true in an infinite-horizon model of labor taxation, provided the government can issue debt of all maturities. It holds true even if the model is extended to uncertainty, provided the government can also issue debt of all contingencies.

Nevertheless, the conclusion is quite fragile. In particular, to support the second-best policy each government needs as many debt instruments as there are choice variables in next period's policy problem. In

---

[119] The proof closely follows the proof (for a more general case) in Persson, Persson and Svensson [101] and is not included here.

our example above the government in period 1 had two debt instruments—long-term and short-term debt—and the government in period 2 had two choice variables—the tax rates in period 2 and 3. It is easy to think of situations when there are fewer debt instruments than choice variables. With endogenous government consumption in periods 2 and 3, for example, no debt structuring scheme would have been able to support the second-best policy. Intuitively, the government could then use government spending, in addition to the tax rates, so as to influence the interest rate and induce capital gains and losses on public debt. And this would make it impossible to match one incentive to surprise against the other. However, even with fewer debt instruments than choice variables, the third-best equilibrium under discretion should be closer to the second-best equilibrium the more debt instruments there are available to control future incentives.[120] We should also remind the reader that the analysis in this section has relied on the public debt being honored and not repudiated (or taxed directly by surprise). As in Section 7.2, this has been an assumption, not a result of the analysis.

The general ideas we wish the reader to extract from this section are two: (1) Credibility problems are inherent in almost all dynamic taxation problems; (2) If the current government controls some state variables that enter into future policy problems, it can influence future policy. We have used (2) in Sections 7.2 and 8.3 to show how the government can sometimes 'tie its own hands' at a future date to escape credibility problems. But a moment's reflection reveals that a similar mechanism could be used when current and future governments do not share the same preferences. The ability to affect future policy incentives could then help the current government to impose its preferred policy on a future government with different preferences. In the next section we do turn to an analysis of political equilibria in which governments can use state variables such as the public debt to influence future governments with different preferences.

8.5. Notes on the literature

A discussion of the credibility problems that arise even in the absence of capital levies can be found in Rogers [112] and Persson and

---

[120] Rogers [114] studies a three-period problem of labor taxation with endogenous government consumption and obtains precisely this result.

Svensson [106]. The idea that a particular maturity structure of government debt may enforce second-best tax policy was first suggested in the seminal paper by Lucas and Stokey [92]. The results are interpreted in Persson and Svensson [104] and extended to a monetary economy by Persson, Persson and Svensson [101]. Rogers [113] suggests that the implied maturity structure is consistent with private investors following a particular portfolio strategy. Finally, Rogers [114] discusses how well a government can control its own future policy when it has access to fewer debt instruments than there are future policy variables.

9. THE POLITICAL ECONOMY OF GOVERNMENT DEBT

9.1. Introduction

A striking stylized fact is the different public debt policies in different countries, and in the same country in different periods of time. This section presents some recent attempts to explain such differences in debt policies, which have one thing in common: They relate debt policy to the political environment. Throughout the section, fiscal policy is chosen directly by the voters under majority rule. But the political majority is not stable over time. The precise nature of the political instability shapes equilibrium debt policy.

Sections 9.2 and 9.3 rely on an idea which we introduced in Sections 7 and 8, namely that debt issue changes the incentives of future policymakers. When governments that represent different political majorities alternate in office, this simple idea has some striking implications. In Section 9.2 different majorities differ in their desired level of government consumption. When the current majority issues public debt, it can give the future majority incentives to bring public consumption in the direction the current majority prefers. Equilibrium public debt policy depends on the nature of conflict between the alternating majorities. In Section 9.3 various majorities differ in their desired composition of government consumption. If the current political majority can be replaced in the future by a different majority, the current majority favors budget deficits. Thus, political instability can induce 'collective myopia', even though each voter is rational and forward looking. This analysis leads naturally to normative suggestions for institutional reforms.

In Sections 9.2 and 9.3, the economic role of the public debt is to shift tax distortions over time. But issuing public debt also has a second economic role: It redistributes revenue across generations. Section 9.4 analyzes this aspect of debt policy, in a setup where voters choose the desired amount of intergenerational redistribution. The model has two features: First, voters choose to what extent to honor the debt obligations inherited from previous governments. Thus, future generations are not bound by the debt policy of previous generations. Second, there is heterogeneity within each generation. Debt policy can therefore redistribute income both within and across generations. These two features interact in determining equilibrium debt policy. Section 9.5 concludes with some general remarks.

9.2. Fiscal deficits and the size of government

Consider a two-period small open economy.[121] The economy is inhabited by a continuum of individuals indexed by i. The preferences of the ith individual are:

$$F(c_1, c_2, l_1, l_2) + \alpha^i H(g) = U(c_1) + c_2 - V(l_1) - V(l_2) + \alpha^i H(g). \quad (9.1)$$

The notation is similar to that in previous sections. Because utility is linear in c_2 the *ex ante* and *ex post* elasticities of labor supply coincide, so that the credibility problem discussed in Section 8.2 does not arise. All individuals are alike in their preferences over private consumption and labor supply. But they differ in their evaluation of government consumption: Different consumers have different α^i's and $H(\cdot)$ is a well-behaved concave utility function. There is public consumption only in period 2.

We have a political equilibrium when: (i) All economic agents behave optimally given actual and expected policies, and their choices satisfy the budget constraints and the resource constraints; (ii) In each period, a majority of the voters prefer the policy in that period to any other policy; (iii) Individual expectations are fulfilled, when individuals act as voters, as well as consumers.

Consider first individuals *qua* consumers, where they all act alike. As in previous sections, a linear technology transforms one unit of labor

---

[121] This subsection draws on Persson and Svensson [107], but extends the analysis in that paper to an explicit political equilibrium.

into one unit of output. International capital markets are perfect, and the world real interest rate is zero. Only labor income can be taxed, at a rate τ_t in period t. All this leads to the consumers' first order conditions:

$$U_c(c_1) = 1 \qquad (9.2a)$$

$$V_l(l_t) = 1 - \tau_t, t = 1, 2. \qquad (9.2b)$$

Consider next individuals *qua* voters. If b denotes (real) public debt, the government budget constrains in periods 1 and 2 are:

$$\tau_1 l_1 + b \geq 0$$
$$\tau_2 l_2 \geq b + g. \qquad (9.3)$$

Any government tax revenue in period 1 is lent out (that is, $b < 0$) at the international capital market, since there is no public spending in period 1. Policy is chosen by majority rule at the beginning of each period. The winning majority is committed to honor the debt obligations inherited from the past, but is otherwise free to reoptimize. The winning majority in period 1 chooses τ_1 and b; the majority in period 2 chooses τ_2 and g, taking b as given. Because of the budget constraints in (9.3), we can think of the first majority as choosing b and the second majority as choosing g.

Voters are rational and forward-looking; they vote for the policy that maximizes their utility. With the preferences in (9.1), policy preferences in each period are single peaked. Therefore, there is only one policy that cannot be defeated under majority rule; the policy preferred by the median voter. Let α_t^m be the weight that the median voter in period t, t = 1, 2, attaches to the utility of public consumption. The value of α_2^m is supposed to be known in period 1. Then the equilibrium policy in period t is the policy that maximizes

$$F(c_1, c_2, l_1, l_2) + \alpha_t^m H(g), \qquad (9.4)$$

subject to the relevant constraints. If $\alpha_1^m \neq \alpha_2^m$, the identity of the winning majority changes over time and different majorities have different preferences over the level of public consumption. This can occur because the composition of the electorate changes or because voter participation changes. We call a majority with a higher α^m 'more liberal'. Our goal is to illustrate how political conflict between the two successive majorities shapes equilibrium debt policy in period 1.

9.2.1. *Preliminary Results*

We can combine equations (9.1)–(9.3) to obtain each consumer's private indirect utility as a function of government debt and public spending, J(b, g). That is, $J(\cdot)$ denotes the consumers' utility from private consumption and leisure in an economic equilibrium, as a function of the two policy instruments, b and g.[122] Our specification of private preferences makes labor supply functions in periods 1 and 2 identical. Then, as explained in Section 6, a policy that sets $\tau_1 = \tau_2$ minimizes the tax distortions, and maximizes private indirect utility J(b, g). In other words, to minimize the tax distortions the government should run a surplus in period 1, setting b = − g/2. Assuming that the second order conditions are satisfied, this means that the indirect utility function $J(\cdot)$ has the property,

$$J_b(b, g) \lesseqgtr 0 \text{ as } b \gtreqless - g/2, \tag{9.5}$$

for any given g ≥ 0. If b is above − g/2, too little taxes are raised in period 1 meaning that higher debt increases $J(\cdot)$, while the opposite is true for b < − g/2.

9.2.2. *The Last Period*

In the last period, the winning majority sets taxes and spending to maximize (9.4) subject to (9.3), (9.2), and the private budget constraint. The first-order condition of the median voter optimum can be written as:

$$J_g(b, g) + \alpha_2^m H_g(g) = 0. \tag{9.6}$$

Recalling that $J(\cdot)$ is private indirect utility, the partial derivative $J_g(\cdot)$ denotes (the negative of) the *ex post* marginal cost of public spending. This marginal cost has two components: the resources subtracted from the private sector that would otherwise be available for private consumption; and the excess burden of distortionary taxation. In equilibrium, this marginal cost must be equal to the marginal utility of public spending for the median voter in period 2.

Equation (9.6) defines equilibrium government spending as a function of b and α_2^m: $g^* = G(b, \alpha_2^m)$. Applying the implicit function

---

[122] Consumption and labor supply in the two periods are functions of the two tax rates (and of exogenous parameters). The tax rates, in turn, are functions of b and g.

theorem to (9.6), we obtain the intuitive results that $G_b(\cdot) < 0$, $G_\alpha(\cdot) > 0$:[123] Inheriting more debt from the past forces the majority to cut public spending, and a more liberal majority spends more.

9.2.3. Equilibrium Debt Policy

Consider now how a median voter with weight $\alpha_1^m \neq \alpha_2^m$ chooses public debt in period 1. Since the median voter is forward looking, he or she realizes that public spending will be set according to the function $G(b, \alpha_2^m)$. The $G(\cdot)$ function thus becomes an incentive constraint on the problem of the period-1 median voter. Subject to this incentive constraint, the period-1 majority chooses b so as to maximize:

$$J(b, G(b, \alpha_2^m)) + \alpha_1^m H(G(b, \alpha_2^m)). \tag{9.7}$$

Making use of (9.6), we can write the first-order condition for an interior optimum to this problem as:

$$J_b + (\alpha_1^m - \alpha_2^m) H_g G_b = 0. \tag{9.8}$$

Since $G_b < 0$ and $H_g > 0$, equation (9.8) reveals that the sign of J_b must equal the sign of $(\alpha_1^m - \alpha_2^m)$. Specifically, it follows from (9.5) that

$$b \gtreqqless \times g/2 \text{ as } \alpha_1^m \gtreqqless \alpha_2^m. \tag{9.9}$$

In words, if the median voters in the two periods are identical ($\alpha_1^m = \alpha_2^m$), public debt is chosen to minimize the excess burden of taxation ($b = -g/2$). But if the future majority is more liberal than the current majority ($\alpha_1^m < \alpha_2^m$), too much government debt is issued in equilibrium ($b > -g/2$); or more precisely, the equilibrium surplus is too small to minimize tax distortions. And finally, if the current majority is more liberal than its successor ($\alpha_1^m > \alpha_2^m$), too little debt is issued in equilibrium.

How does equilibrium public debt depend on the conflict between the current and future majorities? To answer this question, fix α_2^m and consider b as a function of α_1^m. Applying the implicit function theorem

---

[123] These results can be proved as follows. Since the consumer indirect utility function is time separable, and given the government budget constraint in (9.3), $J_{gb} = J_{gg}$. The private sector second-order conditions imply that $J_{gg} < 0$. The rest follows by applying the implicit function theorem to (9.6) and recalling that $H_{gg} < 0$.

to (9.8), and appealing to the second-order conditions, one can show that equilibrium debt is decreasing in α_1^m. That is, a more liberal majority runs a smaller deficit (surplus), whereas a more conservative majority runs a larger deficit (smaller surplus).

These results have a very intuitive explanation. In the model, public debt serves two purposes: It smooths tax distortions, and it influences future public spending decisions. The majority in office in period 1 trades off a suboptimal distribution of tax distortions (and therefore of private utility) over time against a more favorable level of public spending. If the period-1 majority perceives the period-2 majority as too liberal, the period-1 majority is prepared to accept a larger debt than would be necessary to minimize tax distortions. This policy, though economically inefficient, raises the *ex post* marginal cost of public funds for the liberal majority. In this way, public debt is used strategically to force a spending cut on the succeeding majority.[124]

9.2.4. *Final Remarks*

We have shown how different political majorities at different points in time may affect equilibrium public debt policy. While our results were derived under perfect foresight about the identity of the future median voter, it is reasonable to treat that identity as uncertain. But we conjecture that similar results would still hold under uncertainty: A government with preferences to the right of the *expected* future median voter would run larger deficits than a government with preferences to the left.

Our model misses out on one aspect of public debt policy, however. We argued that one of the reasons why the median voter's preferences might change over time is because the composition of the electorate may change. But such a change would largely be associated with the entry of new generations of voters consisting of young domestic individuals or immigrating foreign individuals. Then, public debt policy also has redistributive effects across generations. We shall return to these redistributive effects in Section 9.4.

Finally, our findings have potentially testable implications for the

---

[124] Note that this strategic use of debt policy can only occur if public debt is non-neutral (here the non-neutrality is due to tax distortions). In a model with Ricardian equivalence and lump sum taxes, the time path of debt is irrelevant, and debt cannot be used strategically.

time-series properties of fiscal deficits in any given country: *Ceteris paribus*, right-wing governments would run larger deficits than left-wing governments, the more so the larger the disagreement over the size of public spending between the current and prospective future government.

9.3. Political instability as a cause of fiscal deficits

Can society find a way to eliminate political distortions like those in the previous subsection? We attempt to answer this question, by studying a slightly different two-period model. In this model voters disagree over the *composition* of public spending. To simplify the analysis, we focus on the spending decision, treating the revenue side as predetermined.[125] Once again, if the political majority changes over time, the economically efficient debt policy cannot be an equilibrium under majority rule. In particular, under an appropriate condition on the voters' preferences, a majority always favors running a budget deficit. The model in this subsection can be used to discuss whether a constitutional balanced budget amendment is desirable and enforceable.

9.3.1. *The Model*
Consider an economy with heterogeneous individuals, each living for two periods. Individuals decide by majority rule on the consumption of two public goods, g and f. The economy can borrow or lend at a zero real interest rate at the world credit market. It is endowed with one unit of output in each period. The two resource constraints are:

$$g_1 + f_1 \leq 1 + b \equiv R_1, \qquad (9.10a)$$

$$g_2 + f_2 \leq 1 - b \equiv R_2, \qquad (9.10b)$$

where b is borrowing (in period 1) and R_t is total resources spent in period t.

At the beginning of each period all individuals vote on how much to consume of each public good in that period. The majority in period 1 cannot commit to choosing a particular quantity of g_2 and f_2 for the following period. However, as in the previous subsection,

---

[125] This section draws on Tabellini and Alesina [131]. In a related paper, Alesina and Tabellini [10] consider a model in which the government also chooses tax policy.

the current majority can commit future majorities to honor their debt obligations.

The ith individual has the following utility function:

$$U^i(g_1, f_1) + U^i(g_2, f_2) \equiv \sum_{t=1}^{2} [\alpha^i H(g_t) + (1 - \alpha^i)H(f_t)] \qquad (9.11)$$

where $H(\cdot)$ is a concave twice continuously differentiable function. Thus, $\alpha^i \epsilon [0, 1]$ parametrizes the composition of public spending desired by different individuals.

Characterizing the political equilibrium is now a little more difficult than in the previous subsection. There the vote in each period was over a one-dimensional policy space, while here the policy space (in period 1) is two-dimensional. However, the utility function in (9.11) has a very useful property: The distribution of preferences is fully summarized by the distribution of α^i.[126] Since α^i is a scalar, the median-voter result once again applies and the majority-rule equilibrium coincides with the policy preferred by the individual with the median value of α.

If we denote the median voter preferences in period t by α_t^m, we can compute the equilibrium composition of public spending in period t for *given* R_t as follows: Maximize $U^i(g_t, f_t)$ subject to the relevant part of (9.10), with $\alpha_i = \alpha_t^m$ in (9.11). The following condition then determines the equilibrium of public spending:

$$\alpha_t^m H_g(g_t) - (1 - \alpha_t^m)H_f(f_t) = 0. \qquad (9.12)$$

This first-order condition together with the constraint (9.10) define the reaction functions $g_t^* = G(R_t, \alpha_t^m)$ and $f_t^* = F(R_t, \alpha_t^m)$. These in turn define the indirect utility function

$$J(\alpha^i; R_t, \alpha_t^m) = \alpha^i H(G(R_t, \alpha_t^m)) + (1 - \alpha^i)H(F(R_t, \alpha_t^m)). \qquad (9.13)$$

Thus the $J(\cdot)$ function evaluates the political equilibrium in period t from the ith voter's perspective.

If the median voter is the same in each period, it is straightforward to solve for equilibrium policy. The composition of public spending is constant over time, and defined by (9.12). Furthermore, equilibrium debt is zero, because the median voter wants to smooth consumption over time. Formally, the relevant median voter α^m chooses debt to

---

[126] See Grandmont [65] and Tabellini and Alesina [131] for a detailed discussion.

satisfy the following condition—obtained by substituting (9.10) and
(9.13) into (9.11) and maximizing with respect to b.

$$J_R(\alpha^m; 1 + b, \alpha^m) - J_R(\alpha^m; 1 - b, \alpha^m) = 0. \qquad (9.14)$$

Symmetry between the periods ensures that (9.14) is fulfilled at $b = 0$.

We now turn to an equilibrium where the median voters in the two
periods are different.

9.3.2. Equilibrium Debt Policy

Suppose that individual preferences remain stable, but that the median
voter is a different individual in the two periods (and hence that
$\alpha_1^m \neq \alpha_2^m$). In period 2, the two reaction functions $g_2^* = G(1 - b, \alpha_2^m)$
and $f_2^* = F(1 - b, \alpha_2^m)$ determine the composition of public spending.
As in the previous subsection, the period-1 majority uses these two
functions in assessing how debt issue affects next period's expenditure
decisions. Thus, once again, debt in period 1 is chosen strategically,
subject to an incentive constraint. In equilibrium, debt must maximize:

$$J(\alpha_1^m; 1 + b, \alpha_1^m) + J(\alpha_1^m; 1 - b, \alpha_2^m). \qquad (9.15)$$

Equilibrium debt must therefore satisfy the first-order condition:

$$J_R(\alpha_1^m; 1 + b, \alpha_1^m) - J_R(\alpha_1^m; 1 - b, \alpha_2^m) = 0. \qquad (9.16)$$

Equation (9.16) says that the marginal utility of higher public spending
in period 1 must equal the marginal disutility of lower public spending
in period 2, taking into account how the next period majority allocates
the spending cuts.

In order to characterize the solution to (9.16), we define the
'concavity index' of $H(\cdot)$ as: $\lambda(x) \equiv - H_{gg}(x)/(H_g(x))^2$. We also
assume that the concavity index is decreasing: $\lambda_x < 0$ for $1 > x > 0$.[127]
The meaning of this assumption is illustrated in Figure 9.1. In the
figure, the downward sloping line depicts the budget constraint for the
median voters in both periods if $b = 0$. A and B depict the points chosen
in periods 1 and 2 by median voters of type α_1^m and α_2^m, with
$\alpha_1^m > 1/2 > \alpha_2^m$. The indifference curves for the median voter of type
α_1^m in periods 1 and 2 are labelled I_1 and I_2. The upward-sloping EP_1
and EP_2 are the income-expansion paths of types α_1^m and α_2^m. With a

---

[127] The concavity index, so defined, was used in Debreu and Koopmans [45]. Any CES
function: $H(x) = x^\gamma/\gamma$, $\gamma > 0$, has a decreasing concavity index.

decreasing concavity index, the voters' indifference curves become flatter at higher levels of income; that is, the two public goods become closer substitutes. As a result, the divergence between the choices of the two median voters increases with income. Put differently, their income-expansion paths diverge.

If the concavity index is decreasing, one can show that if $\alpha_1^m \neq \alpha_2^m$, $J_R(\alpha_1^m; 1 + b, \alpha_1^m)$ exceeds $J_R(\alpha_1^m; 1 - b, \alpha_2^m)$ at the point $b = 0$. That is, the first term in (9.16) exceeds the second term. Appealing to the second-order conditions, the solution to (9.16) must then have positive debt. It can also be shown that the equilibrium level of debt is larger the greater is the difference between α_1^m and α_2^m. If the concavity index is increasing, the result is reversed: instability of the median voter's preferences results in a surplus, not a deficit.

Two opposite forces explain this ambiguity. By running a surplus (by setting $b < 0$), the median voter in period 1 moves A to the left along EP_1 and B to the right along EP_2; this reduces the distance between the indifference curves labeled J_1 and J_2. A surplus thus smooths out the utility over time for the median voter of period 1. This force makes a surplus today more desirable. By running a deficit (by setting $b > 0$), the median voter of period 1 moves B to the left along EP_2. A deficit thus moves the future composition of public spending closer to the point preferred by today's median voter. This force makes a deficit today more desirable. If the concavity index is decreasing, the second force dominates the first force.

This interpretation highlights the similarity between the results of this subsection and the previous subsection. There, debt was used strategically to influence the future size of government spending. Here, debt is used strategically to influence the future composition of government spending. In both cases the current majority trades an influence on future spending against a smooth utility over time.

It is easy to extend the results in this subsection to a stochastic framework, in which the identity of the future majority is a random variable. Then, equilibrium debt is larger, the greater the probability of α_2^m being very different from α_1^m. The results have testable implications that could explain the cross-country differences in debt policies. The governments of more politically unstable and polarized societies should have larger budget imbalances than those of more stable and homogeneous societies.

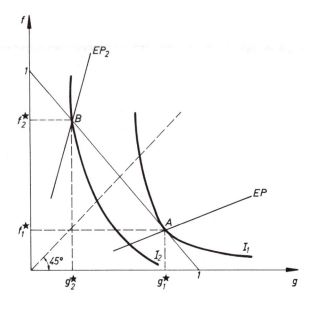

FIGURE 9.1

9.3.3. *Institutional Reform*

We have shown how political instability generates 'collective myopia', even though individual voters are rational and forward looking. This collective myopia can be understood as follows: Consider a rational individual who votes on how much to spend in the current period, and on which items. He thus votes on the intertemporal profile of spending, as well as on how to use the revenue acquired through debt issue (or lost through a surplus). But the future composition of public spending is likely to be different from the one he prefers because the future majority is likely to have preferences different from his own. Then a fundamental asymmetry arises: whereas the debt issuing majority chooses how to allocate the proceeds, it does not control how to allocate the burden of repaying the debt. This asymmetry prevents the current majority from fully internalizing the costs of budget deficits, the more so the greater is the difference between its preferences and those of the likely future majority.

Indeed, if the asymmetry is removed, the results change dramatically. Suppose that a vote on debt is taken under a 'veil of ignorance' about the composition of public spending in period 1. That is, when b is voted upon, the identity of the median voter in period 1 is still unknown, so that both α_1^m and α_2^m are random variables. Then it can be shown that all the voters are unanimous in choosing a balanced budget.[128]

This suggests that it may be desirable to set up institutions that enable society to separate its choices on how to allocate spending across time from its choices on how to allocate spending across different purposes at any given point in time. A constitutional balanced budget requirement would perform this role. However, a balanced budget requirement would not be durable under majority rule: As shown above, each current majority does not want to be bound by the requirement, even though it wants a binding requirement for all future majorities.

This durability problem can be overcome by requiring a qualified majority to abrogate the balanced budget requirement. But a qualified majority requirement may eliminate the flexibility to react to unexpected and exceptional events, such as wars or large recessions. Like in monetary policy, there seems to be an inescapable trade-off between rules and discretion.

9.4. Intergenerational redistribution

Issuing government debt shifts the tax burden onto future generations of taxpayers. Two key features distinguish this policy from other redistributive policies. First, issuing debt involves the promise of future transfers from yet unborn (or yet non-immigrated) generations. Second, the promise is made without the consent of the future generations who bear the burden of the redistribution. Two natural questions arise: Under what circumstances are these promises kept, and why? And why don't older generations take full advantage of future generations?

These questions were touched upon in Section 7. Here we take them up again, focusing explicitly on policies that constitute a political equilibrium. Our analysis combines two central features. First, we allow for altruism between parents and kids; this altruism moderates the conflict across generations. Second, we allow for intragenerational

---

[128] See Tabellini and Alesina [131].

heterogeneity; this heterogeneity makes debt policies redistribute both across and within generations. The political equilibrium reflects both features.[129]

9.4.1. *The Model*

Consider a two-period closed economy. In period 1 only one generation of agents—called 'parents'—is alive. In period 2 another generation—called 'kids'—is born. Parents live two periods and kids live one period. Both generations are altruistic. Thus, the ith parent maximizes

$$W^i \equiv \text{Max}[U(c_1^i) + c_2^i + \delta V(x^i)], \ 1 > \delta > 0, \qquad (9.17a)$$

where c_t^i denotes the parent's consumption in period t and x^i denotes the kid's consumption in period 2. And the ith kid maximizes:

$$J^i = [\gamma c_2^i + V(x^i)], \ 1 > \gamma > 0. \qquad (9.17b)$$

The functions $U(\cdot)$ and $V(\cdot)$ are well-behaved concave utility functions, and the coefficients δ and γ measure the altruism of parents and kids.

We consider the following government policy. In period 1, each parent receives a non-negative lump-sum transfer, g. The transfer is financed by issuing government debt, b. In period 2, the debt is repaid by a combination of taxes on the kids' income and on the parents' wealth. Clearly, if the kids pay a positive tax, this policy redistributes revenue in favor of the parents' generation. The question we address is why the kids would ever vote to sustain such a policy in period 2.

Different households have the same preferences but different endowments. At the beginning of his life, the ith parent receives $1 + e^i$ units of non-storable output. The individual-specific variable e^i can be either positive or negative, and is distributed in the population according to a known distribution $G(\cdot)$, with zero mean, non-positive median and bounded support inside the unit circle. Let s^i denote parent i's savings. Then we can write the ith parent's budget constraint for period 1 as:

$$c_1^i + s^i \leq 1 + e^i + g. \qquad (9.18)$$

Perfect capital markets enable the parents to borrow or lend at a gross-of-tax rate of interest R (this is also the rate of interest on government

---

[129] This subsection is based on Tabellini [129].

debt). Hence, $s^i \gtreqless 0$. But since output is non-storable, average savings must equal government debt in equilibrium:

$$\int_{-\alpha}^{\alpha} s^i \, dH(s^i) = b, \qquad (9.19)$$

where $H(\cdot)$ is the (endogenous) distribution of savings in the parents' population.

In period 2, all parents receive a second exogenous endowment, a, and repay their debts (if $s^i < 0$) or cash in on their savings (if $s^i > 0$). Savings are taxed at the rate $1 \geq \theta \geq 0$. If $s^i < 0$, then the ith parent receives a subsidy on his loan.[130] Kids receive one unit of output at the beginning of period 2, and pay a non-negative tax τ. Moreover, in period 2 parents can leave non-negative bequests to their kids and kids can give non-negative transfer (gifts) to their parents. Hence, the ith family's budget constraints for period 2 imply:

$$c_2^i + x^i \leq 1 + Rs^i(1 - \theta) + a - \tau \qquad (9.20a)$$

$$c_2^i \leq Rs^i(1 - \theta) + r^i + a \qquad (9.20b)$$

$$x^i \leq 1 - \tau + t^i, \qquad (9.20c)$$

where $r^i \geq 0$ and $t^i \geq 0$ denote gifts and bequests respectively. Thus, (9.20a) is the consolidated family budget constraint; (9.20b) and (9.20c) are implied by the non-negativity constraints on gifts and bequests.

There is no government consumption. If we denote average variables by omitting the i-superscript, the government budget constraint can therefore be written as

$$g \leq b$$
$$R(1 - \theta)b \geq \tau. \qquad (9.21)$$

Tax policy is chosen by majority rule, at the beginning of each period and before any private economic decision is made. In period 1 parents vote on how much debt to issue. And in period 2 both parents and kids vote on the tax rate on wealth, θ. The government budget constraints

---

[130] All the results generalize to the case in which s^i is constrained to be non-negative. See Tabellini [129].

determine the lump-sum transfer, g, and the lump-sum tax on kids, τ, residually. There is no uncertainty. Thus, the period 2 political equilibrium is fully anticipated in period 1, when the economic and voting decisions of the parents are made.

We look first at individuals as consumers. It is straightforward to verify that optimality for all consumers in period 2 implies:

$$1 \geq \delta V_x(x^i) \geq \delta\gamma, \text{ all i.} \qquad (9.22)$$

If the first inequality is strict parents are bequest constrained, and if the second inequality is strict, kids are gift constrained. Hence, because of the model specification, all families are in the same position with respect to the gift and bequest constraints: If one family is constrained, so are all the others. Since the function $- J(\cdot)$ and the parameters δ and γ are the same for all families, equation (9.22) implies that x^i too is the same for all families. From now on, therefore, we drop the i superscript from x. Throughout the section we also assume that $1 > \delta V_x(1) > \delta\gamma$. Thus, in the absence of policy intervention, no private transfer takes place between kids and parents.

Moreover, because parents' utility is linear in c_2^i, all parents consume the same amount in period 1. It follows from (9.18), (9.19) and the parents' first-order conditions that:

$$s^i = b + e^i, \qquad (9.23a)$$

$$c_1 = 1. \qquad (9.23b)$$

Therefore, the equilibrium interest rate is:

$$R = U_c(1)/(1 - \theta^e), \qquad (9.24)$$

where θ^e denotes the expected tax rate on savings.

9.4.2. The Equilibrium Wealth Tax

We now turn to a characterization of the political equilibrium. As always, we have to work backwards, starting from the last period. In period 2 both parents and kids vote. Our goal in this subsection is to discuss how the voters' preferences over the wealth tax in period 2 depend on the wealth distribution.

Consider the effect of changing θ on the ith parent's and kid's welfare: W_θ^i and J_θ^i. From the private and public budget constraints,

(9.20) and (9.21), these effects are:[131]

$$W_\theta^i = b \left[\delta V_x(x) - \frac{s^i}{b} \right]$$

$$J_\theta^i = b \left[V_x(x) - \gamma \frac{s^i}{b} \right] \tag{9.25}$$

These expressions have a simple interpretation. Consider W_θ^i first. Each additional dollar of revenue collected through the wealth tax has two opposite effects on the ith parent's welfare. On the one hand, it allows a rebate of his kid's tax, which increases the parent's welfare by δV_x. On the other hand, it forces the parent to pay a tax proportional to his relative wealth, s^i/b. An analogous interpretation holds for J_θ^i, that refers to the kids' evaluation of θ. Since δV_x is strictly decreasing in θ, (9.25) implicitly defines the tax rate preferred by the ith voter as a decreasing function of the ith parent's relative wealth, s^i/b. This function is different for a parent and for a kid, the parent always preferring a lower wealth tax than his own kid. Finally, it can be shown that individual preferences for θ are single peaked.

These findings are very intuitive. A tax on wealth combines elements of intergenerational and intragenerational redistribution: it redistributes from parents to kids; and it also redistributes from wealthy to poor. Hence, wealthier and older voters prefer lower tax rates on wealth.

These findings also enable us to rank voters by their relative wealth, and to conclude that the equilibrium tax policy is that preferred by the median voter of period 2. Specifically, let s^m/b be the relative wealth of the median voter parent in period 2. Inserting (9.20) and (9.21) in (9.25), we have that the equilibrium tax rate, θ^*, is defined by:

---

[131] To derive equation (9.25), proceed as follows. First, use the fact (proven in Tabellini [129]) that in any political equilibrium the non-negativity constraint on gifts and bequests is always binding. Then, insert (9.21) in (9.20) to substitute away g and τ. Let λ^i and μ^i be the Lagrange multipliers associated with (9.20a) and (9.20b). The envelope theorem implies that

$$W_\theta^i = -\lambda^i(s^i - b) - \mu^i s^i.$$

Equation (9.25) results because the parent's first-order conditions imply: $\mu^i = 1 - \delta V_x$, $\lambda^i = \delta V_x$. A similar procedure yields the second expression in (9.25).

$$\theta^* = 1, \text{ if } \frac{s^m}{b} < \delta V_x(1)$$

$$\theta^* = 0, \text{ if } \frac{s^m}{b} > \delta V_x(1 - Rb). \tag{9.26a}$$

Otherwise $1 > \theta^* > 0$ is defined by:

$$\frac{s^m}{b} - \delta V_x(1 - Rb(1 - \theta^*)) = 0 \tag{9.26b}$$

But under rational expectations and by (9.24), if $\theta^* < 1$ then $R = U_c(1)/(1 - \theta^*)$; whereas if $\theta^* = 1$ nobody is willing to buy any government debt. Hence, in a political and economic equilibrium, the period-1 majority can only issue debt in amounts that satisfy the condition:

$$\frac{s^m}{b} - \delta V_x(1 - U_c(1)b) \geq 0. \tag{9.27}$$

This condition thus defines an incentive constraint in the form of a *sustainable set*. Any amount of debt not in this set cannot be sold in equilibrium, whereas any amount of debt in this set is fully repaid in equilibrium. We now turn to a more careful investigation of condition (9.27).

9.4.3. *The Sustainable Set*

To characterize the sustainable set, we have to discuss how the relative wealth of the median-voter parent, s^m/b, is determined in equilibrium. That requires combining the two groups of voters, parents and kids, and using the equilibrium condition for individual savings, (9.23). After some computations, one obtains that s^m/b is a function of government debt, whose properties depend on the underlying distribution of initial endowments, $G(\cdot)$.[132]

---

[132] Specifically, using (9.23), $s^m/b = 1 + e_2^m/b$, where $e_2^m < 0$ is the initial endowment of the median voter parent. e_2^m is a decreasing function of b, defined implicitly by:

$$G(e_2^m) + G[(e_2^m + (1 - \delta\gamma)b)/\delta\gamma] = 1. \tag{*}$$

Equation (*) has been obtained using (9.25) to match each parent with a kid that votes exactly like him, and then combining the two groups of voters so that there are equal numbers on each side of the median. See Tabellini [129] for the details.

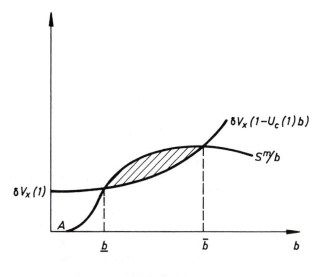

FIGURE 9.2

This function is depicted in Figure 9.2, which illustrates the sustainable set that corresponds to (9.27). The upward-sloping curve represents the second term in (9.27), δV_x. Since $V(\cdot)$ is concave, this term always has a positive slope. The median voter relative wealth, s^m/b, is drawn as a curve that first rises and then falls. In fact, the slope of s^m/b is positive only at point A in the diagram; elsewhere it is ambiguous. But when the distribution $G(\cdot)$ is uniform, s^m/b can be drawn as in the diagram. The sustainable set corresponding to (9.27) is represented by the interval $[\underline{b}, \bar{b}]$. This interval can be non-convex, or even empty, depending on the properties of s^m/b as a function of b. For a uniform distribution $G(\cdot)$, and an appropriate function $V(\cdot)$, the interval is non-empty, however.

The ambiguity in the slope of s^m/b reflects two opposite effects of issuing government debt. Since the proceeds of the debt issue are distributed as lump-sum transfers to parents, debt issue reduces the concentration of wealth. Less-concentrated wealth affects the political equilibrium in two opposite ways. On the one hand, it improves the relative wealth of whoever happens to be the median-voter parent (it can be shown that $s^m/b < 1$, so that a reduction in wealth concentration means that s^m/b rises). So the existing median wants a lower wealth tax. On the other hand, issuing government debt also changes the identity of the median voter parent. As debt rises, more kids are in favor of a higher wealth tax; this in turn makes the new median correspond to a poorer parent. This new median wants a higher wealth tax. These two offsetting effects are important, because they imply that issuing government debt can 'create facts' that affect future decisions, even if there is no commitment to repay the debt. So, debt can be used strategically to alter the future political equilibrium, just like in the previous two subsections.

We now turn to a brief discussion of the properties of the sustainable set. Figure 9.2 shows that the sustainable set is bounded both from above and from below. If debt is too large, most of the kids are in favor of repudiating it, and so are the poor parents. Hence, debt repayment is not politically viable. Boundedness from below is perhaps more surprising. If debt is too small, and it is held only by a minority of the parents, there is always a majority of the voters in favor of repudiating it. In other words, for debt repayment to be politically viable, the outstanding debt must be sufficiently widely held.

When is the sustainable set most likely to be non-empty? The answer is provided by Figure 9.2: when the relative wealth of the median voter is sufficiently large! The relative wealth of the median voter depends on the initial distribution of wealth within society (the function $G(\cdot)$). If initial wealth is highly concentrated, then s^m/b is low, and the sustainable set is more likely to be empty. The opposite is true if initial wealth is evenly distributed. In this case, debt is widely held, and issuing debt creates a large constituency in favor of repaying it.

We now turn to the question of how much debt is issued in equilibrium.

9.4.4. *Equilibrium Intergenerational Redistribution*

In period 1, only parents vote on debt issue. By assumption, the non-negativity constraint on bequests is binding when $b = 0$ (see above, p. 168). Hence, the political equilibrium in period 1 is very simple: with unanimity, all the parents vote to issue debt up to the upper bound of the sustainable set: $b = \bar{b}$.[133] If the set is non-empty, this policy redistributes revenue in favor of the parents and away from the kids.

---

[133] Recall that, as mentioned in Footnote 132, the bequest constraints are always binding for b belonging to the sustainable set.

Government debt thereby enables the parents to (partially) relax the non-negativity constraint on bequests.

It is striking that the absence of commitment does not preclude some intergenerational redistribution, particularly in light of the following. Suppose there were a vote taken in period 2 on a simple social security system that redistributes lump sums from the kids to the parents. Clearly, this system would be opposed by all kids, and could collect a strict majority of the voters only if the population were declining. No intergenerational redistribution from the kids to the parents would thus take place through the social security system. So why does government debt succeed where a simple social security system fails?

The answer is that government debt issue ties together the intergenerational and the intragenerational effects. Therefore, the parents gain support from a fraction of the kids for a policy that redistributes wealth in the parents' favor. This point is best seen with reference to an example. Suppose that a large enough stock of debt is issued, so that all parents save a positive amount. In this case, a vast majority of the parents is against wealth taxation. In addition, all the kids of the wealthy parents oppose wealth taxation. Their opposition is motivated exclusively by the adverse intragenerational redistributive effects of a wealth tax, and occurs even though their disposable income would increase by taxing wealth and even though in equilibrium the kids do not receive any bequest from their parents. A vote on the social security system, on the other hand, is exclusively a vote on intergenerational redistribution. Hence, no kid has any reason to support it.[134]

This difference between the political viability of debt and social security is reminiscent of the results in Sections 7 and 8. There we showed that without commitments, the composition and the maturity structure of government debt matter. Here too, the distinction between debt and social security is due to the incentive constraints on policymaking. If the parents could precommit future governments to honor their debts, then debt and social security would be equivalent instruments of intergenerational redistribution. But without commitments, this equivalence disappears. *Ex post*, taxing wealth (repudiating

---

[134] In the real world, the social security system too has some intragenerational redistributive effects. But since labor income inequality is much smaller than wealth inequality, these intragenerational effects are much less important than for debt taxation.

the debt) redistributes both across and within generations. Hence, the *ex post* incentives to honor the debt are different from the *ex post* incentives to honor the social security system. Even though *ex ante* debt and social security are equivalent, the *ex post* incentive constraints give rise to a crucial distinction between these two instruments of financial policy.

9.5. Discussion

In a dynamic environment, forward-looking voters and governments take into account how future policy decisions depend on state variables under the control of the current majority. We have applied this idea to explain why political majorities who anticipate being replaced by different political majorities may use public debt as a strategic variable. In Section 9.2 and 9.3, public debt altered the incentives of future policymakers by affecting the government budget constraint. A crucial assumption in these two sections was that future governments are committed to repaying the debt inherited from their predecessors. This assumption was relaxed in Section 9.4. There we found that public debt also changed the distribution of voters' preferences and hence the identity of the future median voter. Through this channel, issuing debt 'created facts' and could be used strategically, even without commitments to repay it. Similar strategic choices of state variables arise in other domains of public policy, such as privatization decisions, public spending in capital projects, or the formulation of tax reforms.

Like in Section 5, the models we have studied have testable empirical implications pointed out at the end of each subsection. The models also have normative suggestions for institutional reform. Future research on both of these aspects is likely to yield high payoffs.

9.6. Notes on the literature

The idea that public debt can be used strategically to influence the policies of future governments with politically different preferences was first independently studied by Persson and Svensson [107] (who analyzed the model of Section 9.2), and Alesina and Tabellini [10] (who analyzed the model of Section 9.3.). Tabellini and Alesina [131] extend the analysis to a political equilibrium in which voters (rather than governments) choose the policies. Alesina and Tabellini [12] and

Tabellini [130] consider debt policies in open economies.

The intergenerational model of Section 9.4 is based on Tabellini [129]. Cukierman and Meltzer [44] investigate a related model, in which the current generation can commit future generations by assumption. Related papers, with less explicit political mechanisms, are Hansson and Stuart [72] and Rotemberg [119]. Finally, the idea that issuing debt creates a constituency in favor of repaying the debt was also independently analyzed in Aghion and Bolton [2].

10. CONCLUSIONS

10.1. What have we learned?

The most important message we have tried to convey in the monograph is a way to think about economic policy. Policy is chosen by individuals or groups with well-specified objectives, who interact strategically with other economic or political agents. One can therefore analyze economic policy as the solution of a joint optimization problem, or, more precisely as the equilibrium outcome if a game. Naturally, it is a special kind of game, in which the policymaker typically is the only non-atomistic player.

This approach to the analysis of economic policy is quite recent and still not wide spread. Most economists instead take a short cut. They assume individual optimization when investigating the consequences of specific policy rules. And then they jump to normative conclusions about which policy rules are desirable. But this short cut must entail one of two implicit assumptions: Either governments do not optimize, unlike private agents. Or if they do optimize, they are only constrained by lack of knowledge about how the economy works, and not by incentive constraints.

The unifying theme of this monograph is that both assumptions are untenable. There is every reason to believe that policy makers have well-specified objectives for their actions, in the same way as consumers and firms have. And incentive constraints are generally inescapable, because the policy process is a collective decision process that takes the place sequentially over time. Binding political and credibility constraints are therefore the rule rather than the exception. It follows from this view that models of economic policy should recognize that the government responds to incentives, not to orders.

The early stage of the literature that we surveyed in this monograph focuses on some logical problems that had to be solved to model the incentive constraints: When is policy time consistent; how does time consistency relate to the standard concepts from game theory; how can one compute a time consistent policy in an explicitly dynamic environment, or in a model with an infinite horizon; and so on. With a few exceptions, the early literature was thus more concerned with the tools of the analysis than with substantive economic problems. This is particularly evident from the literature surveyed in Part I. Sections 3 and 4 essentially provide, what we hope to be, a pedagogical introduction to the methods of analysis. The economic content of these sections is perhaps less convincing. Partly this is because we still lack a good understanding of how monetary policy works; so in this case the 'knowledge constraint' may indeed be more binding than the incentive constraints.

The more recent contributions that we survey in Part II do not focus on methodology in the same way. Rather, they focus on developing positive as well as normative theories of policy. That is, the purpose is to explain the observed behavior of policymakers and to suggest ways to relax the incentive constraints in order to improve the policy outcomes. Examples of positive theories of policy that lead to testable predictions are the political business cycle models of Section 5 and the theories of government debt in Section 9. Examples of normative suggestions for institutional design are the formulation of rules with escape clauses in Section 2 and elsewhere, the delegation of policy decisions to independent agencies in Sections 2 and 7, and the constitutional balanced budget requirements in Section 9.

Trying to distinguish between positive theories of policy rules and normative theories of institution design creates an obvious tension: Where should we stop the positive analysis and where should we start the normative analysis? After all, institutions too are endogenous in a more general theory. Why can't we explain how they evolve over time in positive terms? But if we do, is there any remaining scope for a normative theory of policy?

These are difficult questions, which have no universal answers. However, it is possible to separate policy rules and institutions at a conceptual level, even though it may be hard to say exactly where to draw the line at a practical level. Policy rules typically result from the deliberate design of policymakers. But institutions are also shaped by history and custom and they evolve gradually over time. Their form and role at any specific moment in time are due to human design as well as to historical accident. If this is true, a historical approach may be needed to understand existing institutions. But there is also some scope for normative analysis to suggest gradual reform, so as to improve upon history.

10.2. What next?

We would like to close with some speculation on where the literature is headed. As we have already argued, the future research agenda ought to give high priority to modeling the details of political institutions. Adding institutional content is necessary to sharpen the empirical predictions of the theory, as exemplified in the political business cycle literature. It is also necessary to generate interesting normative prescriptions.

Maybe the most important single issue for future research is how political institutions enable society to commit its future course of action. In the language of this monograph, can political constraints help relax binding credibility constraints? One interesting idea appeared in Section 9. It was shown how current policy could affect future political equilibria by changing the distribution of wealth. In particular, it could change the incentives for future taxation of wealth. A second idea came up in Sections 2 and 7. There we argued that delegation of responsibility can act like a commitment technology and that such delegation might even arise endogenously in political equilibrium. This argument suggests an important distinction between direct and representative democracy, with the latter entailing more commitment capacity than the former. But much more remains to be done.

A second interesting line of research—completely neglected in this monograph but potentially very interesting—is the analysis of dynamic coalition formation. This line of research blends cooperative and non-cooperative game theory. It seems well suited to analyze how changing coalitions between existing political parties and exit and entry of parties affect current policy.

At a more applied level, many important problems remain to be investigated with the tools that we have outlined. A particularly exciting one is the study of tax reforms. Arguably, it takes time and resources to reform a tax system. In other words, a tax system can be thought of as a state variable just like capital or debt. Strategic considerations, similar to those in the analysis of government debt in Section 9, may therefore affect the tax reforms that are enacted in politico-economic equilibrium: Because current tax reform influences future policy formation, decisions about prospective tax reform may be subject to incentive constraints. In this way, 'inefficient' tax systems may persist for long periods of time.

More generally, we would relate the differences we observe in tax-transfer systems—across countries and across time—to differences in the economic and political environment. Such a positive theory of actual public-finance differences does not exist, but would be very interesting. For instance, how will drastic changes in the age structure of the population—like the changes most developed economies will experience in the coming decades—change equilibrium social security and other forms of public intergenerational transfers? And when the European integration in 1992 will require countries to bring their taxation of capital income and of consumption closer together, how will this alter taxation of other tax bases and public spending? These are questions that cannot be answered without a positive politico-economic theory of fiscal policy.

To explain how fiscal policies, tax systems and other economic institutions develop over time is not only important in its own right. It may also be necessary to understand why different countries—and different time periods in the same country—display so different rates of growth. Thus, coupling the recent theory of endogenous economic policy with the recent theory of endogenous economic growth can produce an interesting offspring. In particular, such an integrated theory may shed new light on old, but ill understood, questions about the role of income distribution in economic development.

The work we have surveyed and outlined is still far from a successful positive and normative theory of policy. On the way towards a successful theory, researchers face many difficult challenges. The challenges will be conceptual as well as methodological. The ride may be hard, but we believe it will be great fun.

Bibliography

[1] Abreu, D., D. Pearce and E. Stacchetti (1986). 'Toward a Theory of Discounted Repeated Games With Imperfect Monitoring.' Mimeo, Harvard University.

[2] Aghion, P. and P. Bolton (1990). 'Government Domestic Debt and the Risk of Default: A Political-Economic Model of the Strategic Role of Debt.' Mimeo, Massachusetts Institute of Technology.

[3] Alesina, A. (1978). 'Macroeconomic Policy in a Two-Party System as a Repeated Game.' *Quarterly Journal of Economics*, 102, 651–78.

[4] Alesina, A. (1988a). 'Credibility and Policy Convergence in a Two-Party System With Rational Voters.' *American Economic Review*, September, pp. 796–805.

[5] Alesina, A. (1988b). 'Macroeconomics and Politics.' In: *Macroeconomics Annual*, edited by S. Fischer. Cambridge: NBER.

[6] Alesina, A. (1988c) 'The End to Four Large Public Debts.' In: *High Public Debt: The Italian Experience*, edited by F. Giavazzi and L. Spaventa. Cambridge: Cambridge University Press.

[7] Alesina, A. (1989) 'Inflation, Unemployment and Politics in Industrial Democracies.' *Economic Policy*, (forthcoming).

[8] Alesina, A. and S. Spear (1989). 'An Overlapping Generations Model of Political Competition.' *Journal of Public Economics* (forthcoming).

[9] Alesina, A. and G. Tabellini (1987a). 'Rules and Discretion With Non Coordinated Monetary and Fiscal Policy.' *Economic Inquiry*, 25, 619–30.

[10] Alesina, A. and G. Tabellini (1987b). 'A Political Theory of Fiscal Deficits and Government Debt in a Democracy.' NBER Working Paper No. 2308.

[11] Alesina, A. and G. Tabellini (1988). 'Credibility and Politics.' *European Economic Review*, 32 542–50.

[12] Alesina, A. and G. Tabellini (1989). 'External Debt, Capital Flight and Political Risk.' *Journal of International Economics* (forthcoming).

[13] Atkeson, A. (1988). 'International Lending With Moral Hazard and Risk of Repudiation.' Mimeo, Stanford University.

[14] Atkinson, A. and J. Stiglitz (1980). *Lectures on Public Economics*, Maidenhead: McGraw-Hill.

[15] Auernheimer, L. (1974). 'The Honest Government Guide to the Revenue From the Creation of Money. *Journal of Political Economy*, 82, 598–606.

[16] Aumann, R. (1986). 'Agreeing to Disagree.' *Annals of Statistics*, 4:6, 1236–1339.

[17] Backus, D. and J. Driffill (1985a). 'Inflation and Reputation.' *American Economic Review*, 75, 530–38.

[18] Backus, D. and J. Driffill (1985b). 'Rational Expectations and Policy Credibility Following a Change in Regime.' *Review of Economic Studies*, 52, 211–21.

[19] Baldwin, R. (1987). 'Trade Policies in Developed Countries.' In: *Handbook of International Economics*, edited by Jones, R. and P. Kenen, Amsterdam: North-Holland Publishing House.

[20] Barro, R., (1983). 'Inflationary Finance under Discretion and Rules.' *Canadian Journal of Economics* 16, 1–25.

[21] Barro, R. (1986). 'Reputation in a Model of Monetary Policy With Incomplete Information.' *Journal of Monetary Economics*, 17, 1–20.

[22] Barro, R. and D. Gordon (1983a). 'Rules, Discretion and Reputation in a Model of Monetary Policy.' *Journal of Monetary Economics*, 12, 101–22.

[23] Barro, R. and D. Gordon (1983b). 'A Positive Theory of Monetary Policy in a Natural Rate Model.' *Journal of Political Economy*, 91, 589–610.

[24] Basar, T., and G. Olsder (1982). *Dynamic Non-Cooperative Game Theory*, London: Academic Press.

[25] Blackburn, K. and M. Christensen (1989).' Monetary Policy and Policy Credibility.' *Journal of Economic Literature*, **27:1**, 1–45.
[26] Bohn, H. (1988), 'Why Do We Have Nominal Government Debt?.' *Journal of Monetary Economics*, **21**, 127–140.
[27] Buiter, W. and R. Marston (1985). *International Economic Policy Coordination*, Cambridge: Cambridge University Press.
[28] Calvert, R. (1985). 'A Robustness of the Multidimensional Voting Model, Candidate Motivations, Uncertainty and Convergence.' *American Journal of Political Science*, **39**, 60–95.
[29] Calvo, G. (1978). 'On the Time Consistency of Optimal Policy in a Monetary Economy.' *Econometrica*, **46**, 1411–1428.
[30] Calvo, G. (1988). 'Servicing the Public Debt: The Role of Expectations.' *American Economic Review*, **78**, 647–661.
[31] Calvo, G. and P. Guidotti (1989). 'Indexation and Maturity of Government Bonds: A Simple Model.' Mimeo, International Monetary Fund.
[32] Calvo, G. and M. Obstfeld (1988). 'Time Consistency of Fiscal and Monetary Policy: A Comment.' *Econometrica* (forthcoming).
[33] Canzoneri, M. (1985). 'Monetary Policy Games and the Role of Private Information.' *American Economic Review*, **75**, 1056–1070.
[34] Canzoneri, M. and D. Henderson (1988). 'Is Sovereign Policymaking Bad?.' *Carnegie-Rochester Conference Series on Public Policy*.
[35] Carraro, C. (1987). 'A Folk Theorem of Monetary Policy.' Mimeo, University of Venice.
[36] Chari, V. and P. Kehoe (1989). 'Sustainable Plans.' Mimeo, University of Minnesota.
[37] Chari, V., P. Kehoe and E. Prescott. (1989) 'Time Consistency and Policy.' In: *Modern Business Cycle Theory*, edited by R. Barro, Cambridge: Harvard University Press.
[38] Cho, I. K. and D. Kreps (1987). 'Signaling Games and Stable Equilibria.' *Quarterly Journal of Economics*, **102**, 179–221.
[39] Cohen, D. and P. Michel (1988). 'How Should Control Theory be Used to Calculate a Time-Consistent Government Policy?' *Review of Economic Studies*, **55**, 263–274.
[40] Crawford, V. (1983). 'International Lending, Long-Term Credit Relationships, and Dynamic Contract Theory.' Mimeo, University of California at San Diego.
[41] Crémer, J. (1986). Cooperation in Ongoing Organizations. *Quarterly Journal of Economics*, **101**, 33–50.
[42] Cukierman, A. and A. Meltzer (1986a). 'A Theory of Ambiguity, Credibility and Inflation Under Discretion and Asymmetric Information.' *Econometrica*, **53**, 1099–1128.
[43] Cukierman, A. and A. Meltzer (1986b). 'A Positive Theory of Discretionary Policy, the Cost of a Democratic Government, and the Benefits of a Constitution.' *Economic Inquiry*, **24**, 367–388.
[44] Cukierman, A. and A. Meltzer (1990). 'A Political Theory of Government Debt and Deficits in a Neo-Ricardian Framework.' *American Economic Review* (forthcoming).
[45] Debreu, G. and T. Koopmans (1982). 'Additively Decomposed Quasi-Convex Functions.' *Mathematical Programming*, **24**, 1–38.
[46] de Kock, G. and V. Grilli (1989). 'Endogenous Exchange Rate Regime Switches.' Mimeo, Yale University.
[47] Driffill, J. (1987). 'Macroeconomic Policy Games With Incomplete Information: Some Extensions.' CEPR Discussion Paper No. 159.

[48] Driffill, J. (1988a). 'Macroeconomic Policy Games with Incomplete Information: A Survey.' *European Economic Review*, **32**, 533–541.

[49] Driffill, J. (1988b). 'Empirical Models of Credibility: A Survey.' Mimeo, Centre for Economic Policy Research.

[50] Eichengreen, B. (1989). 'The Capital Levy in Theory and Practice.' Mimeo University of California at Berkeley.

[51] Engineer, M. and D. Bernhardt (1988). 'Costly Institutional and Time Consistent Transfers Between Generations.' Mimeo, University of Guelph.

[52] Farrell, J. and E, Maskin (1987). 'Renegotiation in Repeated Games.' Mimeo, Harvard University.

[53] Ferejohn, J. (1986). 'Incumbent Performance and Electoral Control.' *Public Choice*, **50**, 5–26.

[54] Fischer, S. (1977). 'Long-Term Contracts, Rational Expectations and the Optimal Money Supply Rule.' *Journal of Political Economy*, **85**, 191–205.

[55] Fischer, S. (1980). 'Dynamic Inconsistency, Cooperation and the Benevolent Dissembling Government.' *Journal of Economic Dynamics and Control*, **2**, 93–107.

[56] Flood, R., and P. Isard (1988). 'Monetary Policy Strategies.' NBER Working Paper No. 2770.

[57] Friedman, J. (1986). *Game Theory With Applications to Economics*, New York: Oxford University Press.

[58] Fudenberg, D. and D. Levine (1988). 'Reputation and Equilibrium Selection in Games With a Patient Player.' Mimeo, University of California at Los Angeles.

[59] Fudenberg, D. and D. Levine (1989). 'Reputation and Equilibrium Selection in Games with a Patient Player.' *Econometrica*, **57**, 759–778.

[60] Fudenberg, D. and E. Maskin (1986). 'The Folk Theorem in Repeated Games With Discounting or With Incomplete Information.' *Econometrica*, **54**, 533–554.

[61] Fudenberg, D. and J, Tirole (1986). *Dynamic Models of Oligopoly*, monograph in this series, New York: Harwood Academic Publishers.

[62] Fudenberg, D. and J. Tirole (1990). 'Non-Cooperative Game Theory for Industrial Organization: An Introduction and Overview.' In: *Handbook of Industrial Organization*, edited by R. Schmalensee and R. Willig, Amsterdam: North Holland Publishing House (forthcoming).

[63] Giavazzi, F. and M. Pagano (1988). 'The Advantage of Tying One's Hand: EMS Discipline and Central Bank Credibility.' *European Economic Review*, **32**, 1055–1082.

[64] Glazer, A. (1987). 'Politics and the Choice of Durability.' Mimeo, University of California at Irvine.

[65] Grandmont, J. M. (1978). 'Intermediate Preferences and the Majority Rule.' *Econometrica*, **46**, 317–330.

[66] Green, E. (1980). 'Non-Cooperative Price Taking in Large Dynamic Markets.' *Journal of Economic Theory*, **22**, 155–182.

[67] Green, E. and M. Porter (1984). 'Non-Cooperative Collusion Under Imperfect Price Information.' *Econometrica*, **32**, 87–100.

[68] Grossman, H. (1988). 'Inflation and Reputation with Generic Policy Preferences.' Mimeo, Brown University.

[69] Grossman, H. and J. van Huyck (1986). 'Seignorage, Inflation and Reputation.' *Journal of Monetary Economics* **18**, 20–32.

[70] Gorssman, H. and J. van Huyck (1988). 'Sovereign Debt as a Contingent Claim: Excusable Default, Repudiation and Reputation.' *American Economic Review*, **78**. 1988–1997.

[71] Hamada, K. (1976). 'A Strategic Analysis of Monetary Independence.' *Journal of Political Economy*, **84**, 677–700.

[72] Hansson, I. and C. Stuart (1989). 'Social Security as Trade Among Living Generations.' *American Economic Review* (forthcoming).

[73] Harsanyi, J. (1967). 'Games With Incomplete Information Played by Bayesian Players.' *Management Science*, **14**, 159–182, 320–334, 486–502, 1967–1968.

[74] Harsanyi, J. and R. Selten (1988). *A General Theory of Equilibrium Selection in Games*, Cambridge: MIT Press.

[75] Hibbs, D. (1977). 'Political Parties and Macroeconomic Policy.' *American Political Science Review*, **71**, 1467–1487.

[76] Hillier, B. and J. Malcomson (1984). 'Dynamic Inconsistency, Rational Expectations and Optimal Government Policy.' *Econometrica*, **52**, 1437–1451.

[77] Horn, H. and T. Persson (1988). 'Exchange Rate Policy, Wage Formation and Credibility.' *European Economic Review*, **32**, 1621–1636.

[78] Hoshi, T. (1987). 'Monetary Policy Signalling: A Model of Government Reputation and Equilibrium Inflation.' Mimeo, Massachusetts Institute of Technology.

[79] Kotlikoff, L., T. Persson and L. Svensson (1988). 'Social Contracts as Assets: A Possible Solution to the Time-Consistency Problem.' *American Economic Review*, **78**, 662–677.

[80] Krasker, W. S. (1980). 'The "Peso Problem" in Testing the Efficiency of Forward Exchange Markets.' *Journal of Monetary Economics*, **6**, 269–276.

[81] Kreps, D. (1984). 'Corporate Cultures and Economic Theory.' Mimeo, Stanford University.

[82] Kreps, D. and R. Wilson (1982a). 'Sequential Equilibrium.' *Econometrica*, **50**, 863–894.

[83] Kreps, D. and R. Wilson (1982b). 'Reputation and Imperfect Information.' *Journal of Economic Theory*, **27**, 352–379.

[84] Kydland, F. (1975). 'Non-Cooperative and Dominant Player Solutions in Discrete Dynamic Games.' *International Economic Review*, **16**, 321–336.

[85] Kydland, F. and E. Prescott (1977). 'Rules Rather Than Discretion: The Inconsistency of Optimal Plans.' *Journal of Political Economy*, **85**, 473–490.

[86] Levine, P. (1988). 'Does Time Inconsistency Matter?' CEPR Working Paper No. 227.

[87] Levine, P. and S. Holly (1987). 'The Time Inconsistency Issue in Macroeconomics: A Survey.' Mimeo, The London Business School.

[88] Lindbeck, A. (1976). 'Stabilization Policy in Open Economics With Endogenous Politicians.' *American Economic Review Papers and Proceedings*, May, 1–19.

[89] Lizondo, S. (1989). 'Foreign Exchange Futures Prices under Fixed Exchange Rates.' *Journal of International Economics*, **14**, 69–84.

[90] Lohman, S. (1989). 'The Optimal Degree of Precommitment.' Mimeo, Carnegie–Mellon University.

[91] Lucas, R. (1976). 'Econometric Policy Evaluation: A Critique.' *Carnegie-Rochester Conference Series on Public Policy*, 19–46.

[92] Lucas, R. and N. Stokey (1983). 'Optimal Fiscal and Monetary Policy in an Economy Without Capital.' *Journal of Monetary Economics*, **12**, 55–94.

[93] Matsuyama, K. (1988). 'Credibility and Intertemporal Consistency: A Note on Strategic Monetary Policy Models.' Mimeo, Northwestern University.

[94] Milgrom, P. and J. Roberts (1982a). Limit Pricing and Entry Under Incomplete Information.' *Econometrica*, **50**, 443–460.

[95] Milgrom, P. and J. Roberts (1982b). 'Predation, Reputation and Entry Deterrence.' *Journal of Economic Theory*, **27**, 380–312.

[96] Milgrom, P. and J. Roberts (1986). 'Price and Advertising as Signals of Product Quality.' *Journal of Political Economy*, **94**, 796–821.
[97] Minford, P. (1988). 'A Political Model of Credibility.' CEPR Working Paper No. 255.
[98] Nordhaus, W. (1975). 'The Political Business Cycle.' *Review of Economic Studies*, **42**, 169–190.
[99] Obstfeld, M. (1987). 'Peso Problems, Bubbles and Risk in the Empirical Assessment of Exchange Rate Behavior.' NBER Working Paper No. 2203.
[100] Pearce, D. (1987). 'Renegotiation Proof Equilibria: Collective Rationality and Intertemporal Cooperation.' Mimeo, Yale University.
[101] Persson, M., T. Persson and L. Svensson (1987). 'Time Consistency of Fiscal and Monetary Policy.' *Econometrica*, **55**, 1419–1432.
[102] Persson, M., T. Persson and L. Svensson (1988). 'Time Consistency of Fiscal and Monetary Policy: A Reply.' Mimeo, Institute for International Economic Studies.
[103] Persson, T. (1988). 'Credibility of Macroeconomic Policy: A Broad Survey.' *European Economic Review*, **32**, 519–532.
[104] Persson, T. and L. Svensson (1984). 'Time Consistent Fiscal Policy and Government Cash Flow.' *Journal of Monetary Economics*, **14**, 365–374.
[105] Persson, T. and L. Svensson (1986). 'International Borrowing and Time-Consistent Fiscal Policy.' *Scandinavian Journal of Economics*, **88**, 273–295.
[106] Persson, T. and L. Svensson (1988). 'Checks and Balances on the Government Budget.' In: *Economic Effects of the Government Budget*, edited by Helpman. E., A. Razin and E. Sadka, Cambridge: MIT Press.
[107] Persson, T. and L. Svensson (1989). 'Why a Stubborn Conservative Would Run a Deficit: Policy With Time Inconsistent Preferences.' *Quarterly Journal of Economics* (forthcoming).
[108] Persson, T. and G. Tabellini (1989). 'Representative Democracy and Capital Taxation.' Mimeo, Institute for International Economic Studies.
[109] Persson, T. and S. van Wijnbergen (1988). 'Signalling, Wage Controls and Monetary Disinflation Policy.' Mimeo, Institute for International Economic Studies.
[110] Razin, A., T. Persson and L. Svensson (1988). 'Optimal Taxation Across Commodities and Across Time.' (Unpublished notes).
[111] Rogers, C. (1986). 'The Effects of Distributive Goals on the Time Inconsistency of Optimal Taxes.' *Journal of Monetary Economics*, **17**, 251–270.
[112] Rogers, C. (1987a). 'Expenditure Taxes, Income Taxes, and Time-Inconsistency.' *Journal of Public Economics*, **32**, 215–230.
[113] Rogers, C. (1987b). 'A Simple Rule for Managing the Maturity Structure of Government Debt.' Mimeo, Georgetown University.
[114] Rogers, C. (1988). 'Debt Restructuring With a Public Good.' Mimeo, Georgetown University.
[115] Rogoff, K. (1985). 'The Optimal Degree of Commitment to an Intermediate Monetary Target.' *Quarterly Journal of Economics*, **100**, 1169–1190.
[116] Rogoff, K. (1987). 'Reputational Constraints on Monetary Policy.' *Carnegie-Rochester Conference Series on Public Policy*, 24.
[117] Rogoff, K. (1990). 'Equilibrium Political Budget Cycles.' *American Economic Review* (forthcoming).
[118] Rogoff, K. and A. Sibert (1988). 'Elections and Macroeconomic Policy Cycles.' *Review of Economic Studies*, **55**, 1–16.
[119] Rotemberg, J. (1988). 'Constituencies With Finite Lives and the Valuation of Government Bonds.' Mimeo, MIT.
[120] Rotemberg, J. and G. Saloner (1986). 'A Supergame-Theoretic Model of Price

Wars During Booms.' *American Economic Review*, **76**, 390–407.

[121] Schelling, T. (1960) *The Strategy of Conflict*, Cambridge, Mass.: Harvard University Press.

[122] Shapiro, C. (1990). 'Theories of Oligopoly Behavior.' In: *Handbook of Industrial Organization*, edited by R. Schmalensee and R. Willig, Amsterdam: North–Holland Publishing House (forthcoming).

[123] Staiger, R. and G. Tabellini (1989). 'Rules and Discretion in Trade Policy.' *European Economic Review*, **32**, 1265–1278.

[124] Stein, J. (1989). 'Cheap Talk and the Fed: A Theory of Imprecise Policy Announcements.' *American Economic Review*, **79**, 32–42.

[125] Stella, P, (1983). PhD Dissertation, Stanford University.

[126] Tabellini, G. (1985). 'Accommodative Monetary Policy and Central Bank Reputation.' *Giornale degli Economisti e Annali oli Economia*, **44**, 389–425.

[127] Tabellini, G. (1987). 'Reputational Constraints on Monetary Policy: A Comment.' *Carnegie-Rochester Conference Series on Public Policy*.

[128] Tabellini, G. (1988). 'Centralized Wage Setting and Monetary Policy in a Reputational Equilibrium.' *Journal of Money, Credit, and Banking*, **20**, 102–118.

[129] Tabellini, G. (1989). 'Intergenerational Redistribution, Altruism and Politics.' Mimeo, University of California at Los Angeles.

[130] Tabellini, G. (1990). 'Domestic Politics and the International Coordination of Fiscal Policies. *Journal of International Economics* (forthcoming).

[131] Tabellini, G. and A. Alesina (1989).' Voting on the Budget Deficit.' *American Economic Review*, (forthcoming).

[132] Terrones, M. (1989). 'Macroeconomic Policy Cycles Under Alternative Electoral Structures.' Mimeo, University of Western Ontario.

[133] Tirole, J. (1989). *The Theory of Industrial Organization*. Cambridge, Mass.: MIT Press.

[134] van Damme, E. (1987). *Stability and Perfection of Nash Equilibria*, Berlin: Springer–Verlag.

[135] van Huyck, J., R. Battalio and R. Beil (1988). 'Strategic Uncertainty, Equilibrium Selection Principles and Coordination Failure in Average Opinion Games.' Mimeo, Texas A & M University.

[136] Vickers, J. (1986). 'Signalling in a Model of Monetary Policy With Incomplete Information.' *Oxford Economic Papers*, **38**, 443–455.

[137] Wittman, D. (1977). 'Candidates With Policy Preferences: A Dynamic Model.' *Journal of Economic Theory*, **14**, 180–189.

[138] Wittman, D. (1983). 'Candidate Motivation: A Synthesis of Alternatives.' *American Political Science Review*, **76**, 142–157.

[139] Wittman, D. (1988). 'Spatial Strategies When Candidates Have Policy Preferences.' Mimeo, University of California at Santa Cruz.

Index

185

FUNDAMENTALS OF PURE AND APPLIED ECONOMICS

SECTIONS AND EDITORS

BALANCE OF PAYMENTS AND INTERNATIONAL FINANCE
W. Branson, Princeton University

DISTRIBUTION
A. Atkinson, London School of Economics

ECONOMIC DEVELOPMENT STUDIES
S. Chakravarty, Delhi School of Economics

ECONOMIC HISTORY
P. David, Stanford University, and M. Lévy-Leboyer, Université Paris X

ECONOMIC SYSTEMS
J.M. Montias, Yale University

ECONOMICS OF HEALTH, EDUCATION, POVERTY AND CRIME
V. Fuchs, Stanford University

ECONOMICS OF THE HOUSEHOLD AND INDIVIDUAL BEHAVIOR
J. Muellbauer, University of Oxford

ECONOMICS OF TECHNOLOGICAL CHANGE
F. M. Scherer, Harvard University

EVOLUTION OF ECONOMIC STRUCTURES, LONG-TERM MODELS, PLANNING POLICY, INTERNATIONAL ECONOMIC STRUCTURES
W. Michalski, O.E.C.D., Paris

EXPERIMENTAL ECONOMICS
C. Plott, California Institute of Technology

GOVERNMENT OWNERSHIP AND REGULATION OF ECONOMIC ACTIVITY
E. Bailey, Carnegie-Mellon University, USA

INTERNATIONAL ECONOMIC ISSUES
B. Balassa, The World Bank

INTERNATIONAL TRADE
M. Kemp, University of New South Wales

LABOR AND ECONOMICS
F. Welch, University of California, Los Angeles, and J. Smith, The Rand Corporation

MACROECONOMIC THEORY
J. Grandmont, CEPREMAP, Paris

MARXIAN ECONOMICS
J. Roemer, University of California, Davis

NATURAL RESOURCES AND ENVIRONMENTAL ECONOMICS
C. Henry, Ecole Polytechnique, Paris

ORGANIZATION THEORY AND ALLOCATION PROCESSES
A. Postlewaite, University of Pennsylvania

POLITICAL SCIENCE AND ECONOMICS
J. Ferejohn, Stanford University

PROGRAMMING METHODS IN ECONOMICS
M. Balinski, Ecole Polytechnique, Paris

PUBLIC EXPENDITURES
P. Dasgupta, University of Cambridge

REGIONAL AND URBAN ECONOMICS
R. Arnott, Queen's University, Canada

SOCIAL CHOICE THEORY
A. Sen, Harvard University

STOCHASTIC METHODS IN ECONOMIC ANALYSIS
Editor to be announced

TAXES
R. Guesnerie, Ecole des Hautes Etudes en Sciences Sociales, Paris

THEORY OF THE FIRM AND INDUSTRIAL ORGANIZATION
A. Jacquemin, Université Catholique de Louvain

FUNDAMENTALS OF PURE AND APPLIED ECONOMICS

PUBLISHED TITLES